Moral Dilemmas in the Boardroom

Mijntje Lückerath-Rovers

Moral Dilemmas in the Boardroom

Striking the Balance in Ethical Decision Making

Mijntje Lückerath-Rovers
TIAS School for Business and Society
Tilburg University
Tilburg, The Netherlands

ISBN 978-3-031-65268-4   ISBN 978-3-031-65269-1   (eBook)
https://doi.org/10.1007/978-3-031-65269-1

The original submitted manuscript has been translated into English. The translation was done using artificial intelligence. A subsequent revision was performed by the author(s) to further refine the work and to ensure that the translation is appropriate concerning content and scientific correctness. It may, however, read stylistically different from a conventional translation.

Translation from the Dutch language edition: "Morele dilemma's in de boardroom" by Mijntje Lückerath-Rovers, © Mediawerf 2023. Published by Mediawerf. All Rights Reserved.

© The Editor(s) (if applicable) and The Author(s), under exclusive license to Springer Nature Switzerland AG 2024

This work is subject to copyright. All rights are solely and exclusively licensed by the Publisher, whether the whole or part of the material is concerned, specifically the rights of reprinting, reuse of illustrations, recitation, broadcasting, reproduction on microfilms or in any other physical way, and transmission or information storage and retrieval, electronic adaptation, computer software, or by similar or dissimilar methodology now known or hereafter developed.
The use of general descriptive names, registered names, trademarks, service marks, etc. in this publication does not imply, even in the absence of a specific statement, that such names are exempt from the relevant protective laws and regulations and therefore free for general use.
The publisher, the authors and the editors are safe to assume that the advice and information in this book are believed to be true and accurate at the date of publication. Neither the publisher nor the authors or the editors give a warranty, expressed or implied, with respect to the material contained herein or for any errors or omissions that may have been made. The publisher remains neutral with regard to jurisdictional claims in published maps and institutional affiliations.

Cover credit: "Image by Leremy".

This Palgrave Macmillan imprint is published by the registered company Springer Nature Switzerland AG
The registered company address is: Gewerbestrasse 11, 6330 Cham, Switzerland

If disposing of this product, please recycle the paper.

Contents

1 **Introduction**   1
   1.1 A Moral Compass or a Moral Scale?   1
   1.2 Careful Decision-Making May Be More Important than the Decision Itself   3
   1.3 Book Structure   5
       1.3.1 Terminology   6
   1.4 Disclaimers   6

Part I Foundations of Moral Judgement in the Boardroom

2 **Moral Identity**   11
   2.1 Social Identities   12
       2.1.1 Private and Public Parts of Moral Identity   13
       2.1.2 Identity Work   13
   2.2 Measuring Moral Identity   16

3 **Moral Judgement**   19
   3.1 Moral Development   20
   3.2 Utilitarian Versus Deontological Moral Judgement Formation   23
       3.2.1 Utilitarian Moral Judgement   24
       3.2.2 Deontological Moral Judgement   25
   3.3 Moral Dilemmas   26
   3.4 Measuring Utilitarian or Deontological Inclinations   29

		3.4.1	Traditional Score	29
		3.4.2	Process Dissociation Score	29
	3.5	Moral Identity and Moral Judgement		32
4	**Right-Right Dilemmas**			**39**
	4.1	Four Categories of Right-Right Dilemmas		40
		4.1.1	Truth Versus Loyalty	41
		4.1.2	Individual Versus Community	43
		4.1.3	Short Term Versus Long Term	44
		4.1.4	Justice Versus Mercy	46
	4.2	Dirty Hands		47
		4.2.1	Jean-Paul Sartre	48
		4.2.2	Dirty Hands for Right-Right Dilemmas?	49
		4.2.3	Moral Dilemmas Need Some Courage	49
5	**Stakeholderism**			**53**
	5.1	Maximising Which Utility		54
	5.2	The Pyramid of Corporate Social Responsibility		56
	5.3	The Purpose of a Corporation		58
		5.3.1	The US Business Roundtable	59
	5.4	Measuring Stakeholderism		61
		5.4.1	An Example	62
	5.5	Stakeholderism, Moral Judgement, and Moral Identity		62
6	**Gender Differences**			**67**
	6.1	Gender and Moral Identity		68
	6.2	Ethic of Care Versus Ethic of Justice		69
	6.3	Social Role Theory		71
	6.4	Gender Differences in Utilitarian or Deontological Choices		71
	6.5	Gender Differences in Stakeholderism		72
7	**Moral Values in the Boardroom**			**75**
	7.1	Corporate Mission and Core Values		76
		7.1.1	Mission	78
		7.1.2	Core Values	80
	7.2	Moral Values in the Boardroom		82
	7.3	Ethics in Corporate Governance Codes		86
		7.3.1	OECD Principles of Corporate Governance	87
		7.3.2	Sarbanes–Oxley Act	88
	7.4	Code of Ethics for Non-Executives		89
	7.5	UK Guidance on Board Effectiveness		91

8	**Decision-Making in the Boardroom**		**95**
	8.1	Different Outcomes in Decision-Making in the Boardroom	96
		8.1.1 Groupthink and Tunnel Vision	96
		8.1.2 Consensus	100
		8.1.3 Agree-to-Disagree	102
		8.1.4 Irreconcilable Differences of Opinions	103
	8.2	Upper Echelon Theory	104
	8.3	Biases	105
		8.3.1 Misplaced Loyalty	107
		8.3.2 Mores	107
		8.3.3 Four Perspectives of Moral Decision-Making	109
9	**The Interplay Between Legality, Morality, and Opinions**		**115**
	9.1	Legally Permissible? Or Morally Acceptable?	116
	9.2	Public Opinions	117
		9.2.1 The Risk of Ignoring Outside Perspectives	118
	9.3	CEO Activism	120
10	**A Five-Step Ethical Decision-Making Model**		**127**
	10.1	Ethical Decision-Making Models	128
	10.2	Defining the Dilemma (Frame)	130
		10.2.1 Socratic Questions	131
		10.2.2 Preventing Biases	132
	10.3	Exploring All Options (Shape)	132
	10.4	Evaluating the Best Options (Evaluate)	134
		10.4.1 Moral Consideration Matrix	134
	10.5	Refining the Choice (Refine)	137
	10.6	Implementing and Communicating the Decision (Act)	139
	Appendix		141

Part II Moresprudence: Ten Cases of Moral Judgement in the Boardroom

11	**The Case of Yahoo and the CEO Who Lied on His Resume**		**147**
	11.1	The Case	147
		11.1.1 The Activists' Letter	147
		11.1.2 Ethical Code	148
		11.1.3 The Process	148
		11.1.4 The Final Inevitable Step	150
	11.2	Considerations	151
	11.3	Epilogue	152

	11.3.1	Yahoo	152
	11.3.2	Thomson	153
11.4	Comparable Cases		153
	11.4.1	Bausch and Lomb: CEO Stayed but Bonus was Revoked	153

12 The Case of Maastricht University Paying Ransom After a Cyber Attack — 155

- 12.1 The Case — 155
  - 12.1.1 Paying Ransom to Hackers is Undesirable — 156
  - 12.1.2 Yet, Paying — 156
- 12.2 Considerations — 157
- 12.3 Epilogue — 158
  - 12.3.1 Recovered Ransom Proves Financially Beneficial — 158
  - 12.3.2 Considering a Ban on Ransom Payments — 159
- 12.4 Comparable Cases — 159
  - 12.4.1 Ferrari: Ransom Not Paid — 159
  - 12.4.2 Ashley Madison: Hackers' Demands Not Granted — 159
  - 12.4.3 MGM Resorts: Ransom Not Paid, Ceasars Entertainment: Ransom Paid — 161
  - 12.4.4 Royal Dutch Football Association: Ransom Paid — 162

13 The Case of the British Museum and Its Long-Time Partnership with BP — 165

- 13.1 The Case — 165
  - 13.1.1 Long-standing Relationship Reconfirmed in 2016 — 165
  - 13.1.2 Trustee Resigns — 166
  - 13.1.3 Open Letters — 166
  - 13.1.4 BP and the National Portrait Gallery — 167
  - 13.1.5 Rumours About the End of the Partnership — 167
- 13.2 Considerations — 168
- 13.3 Epilogue — 169
  - 13.3.1 December 2023 — 169
  - 13.3.2 Consensus, Agree to Disagree, Stepping Down — 170
  - 13.3.3 Support — 170

	13.4	Comparable Cases	171
		13.4.1 Tate Museum, National Portrait Gallery and Royal Shakespeare Company	171
		13.4.2 Van Gogh Museum and Shell	171
		13.4.3 Oxycontin and the Opioid Crisis	172
14		**The Case of Bud Light and the Partnership with a Transgender Influencer**	**175**
	14.1	The Case	175
		14.1.1 Bud Light	175
		14.1.2 Dylan Mulvaney	175
		14.1.3 Instagram Post	176
		14.1.4 Boycott	176
		14.1.5 Bud Light	177
		14.1.6 Donald Trump (1)	178
		14.1.7 Standing with the LGBTQ+ Community	178
		14.1.8 'Radical' Feminists' Perspective on Women's Rights and Safe Spaces	179
	14.2	Considerations	180
	14.3	Epilogue	182
		14.3.1 Mulvaney	182
		14.3.2 Bud Light	183
		14.3.3 Kid Rock	183
		14.3.4 Donald Trump (2)	184
	14.4	Comparable Cases	184
		14.4.1 Nike	184
		14.4.2 Target	185
15		**The Case of a Modern Art Museum and Conflict of Interests**	**189**
	15.1	The Case	189
		15.1.1 Beatrix Ruf	189
		15.1.2 Bonus	189
		15.1.3 Purchase/Donations from Board of Trustees	190
		15.1.4 Donation Not Free of Charge	190
		15.1.5 Cultural Governance Code 2014	190
	15.2	Considerations	191
	15.3	Epilogue	192
		15.3.1 Beatrix Ruf	194
		15.3.2 Cultural Governance Code 2019	194

	15.4	Comparable Cases	195
		15.4.1	Victoria and Albert Museum	195
		15.4.2	UK Code of Conduct for Board Members of Public Bodies 2019	195
		15.4.3	Response of the Museum	196
16	**The Case of G-Star and the Legal and Moral Obligations Towards a Vietnamese Supplier**			199
	16.1	The Case	199
		16.1.1	G-Star	199
		16.1.2	Vert Fashion	199
		16.1.3	The Framework Agreement	200
		16.1.4	Additional Agreement: Whistler Jackets	200
		16.1.5	Impact of COVID-19	200
		16.1.6	Termination of Both Contracts	201
	16.2	Considerations	202
	16.3	Epilogue	204
		16.3.1	Court Decisions	204
		16.3.2	Whistler Jackets	204
		16.3.3	Framework Agreement	205
		16.3.4	Final Judgment	205
		16.3.5	Acquired by WHP	206
	16.4	Comparable Cases	206
		16.4.1	Primark	207
17	**The Case of Heineken and Leaving Russia During the Ukrainian War**			209
	17.1	The Case	209
		17.1.1	Moral Calls to Leave Russia	209
		17.1.2	Gradual Withdrawal of Heineken from March 2022	210
		17.1.3	One Year Later, February 2023	211
		17.1.4	Follow the Money	211
		17.1.5	Heineken Statements	212
	17.2	Considerations	213
	17.3	Epilogue	215
	17.4	Comparable Cases	216
		17.4.1	Carlsberg	216
18	**The Case of ADIDAS and Kanye West (Ye)**			221
	18.1	The Case	221
		18.1.1	Kanye West, Ye	221

			Contents	xi

		18.1.2	Controversy	221
		18.1.3	The Limit is Reached	222
	18.2	Considerations		223
	18.3	Epilogue		225
		18.3.1	New CEO	225
		18.3.2	Financial Impact	225
		18.3.3	More Problems for Adidas Due to Kanye	225
	18.4	Comparable Cases		226
		18.4.1	Nike and Colin Kaepernick	226
19	**The Case of AJAX and the Inappropriate Behaviour of a Director**			**229**
	19.1	The Case		229
		19.1.1	AFC Ajax	229
		19.1.2	EGM	230
		19.1.3	Overmars' Resignation	230
		19.1.4	The Days In Between	231
		19.1.5	Media	231
		19.1.6	Van der Sar	232
	19.2	Considerations		232
		19.2.1	Reappointment at the EGM	233
		19.2.2	Resignation	234
	19.3	Epilogue		236
		19.3.1	Financial and Sporting Performances	236
		19.3.2	Overmars and Royal Antwerp	236
		19.3.3	Call for Overmars' Return	237
		19.3.4	The Internal Investigation	237
		19.3.5	The Disciplinary Investigation, Part 1	238
	19.4	Comparable Cases		239
		19.4.1	Just Eat Takeaway: Temporary Suspension of Director	239
		19.4.2	Luis Rubiales Kissing Jenni Hermoso at Football Worldcup	240
20	**The Case of ING and the Uproar over Executive Compensation**			**245**
	20.1	The Case		245
		20.1.1	ING	245
		20.1.2	Remuneration Policy	245
		20.1.3	Societal Outrage	247
		20.1.4	Stubborn?	248

		20.1.5	Money Laundering Affair	249
		20.1.6	Banker's Oath: Oath or Promise Regulation Financial Sector 2015	250
	20.2	Considerations		251
	20.3	Epilogue		252
		20.3.1	Non-Executives Responding in Public	252
		20.3.2	Verdict Banking Ethics Enforcement (August 2022)	253
		20.3.3	Appeal Banking Ethics Enforcement (April 2023)	254
		20.3.4	The CEO	254
21	**Conclusion**			257
	21.1	Moral Identity and Moral Judgment		257
		21.1.1	Right-Right Dilemmas and Stakeholderism	258
		21.1.2	Moral Consideration Matrix	258
	21.2	Lessons Learned by Moresprudence		259
	21.3	Practical Application for Directors		260
	21.4	Practical Application for Outsiders		260

About the Author

Prof. Dr. Mijntje Lückerath-Rovers is Professor of Corporate Governance at TIAS School for Business and Society/Tilburg University. She holds a Ph.D. in Financial Economics and a master's in Work and Organisational Psychology.

Her research focuses on the role of the Supervisory Board and the Executive Board in corporate governance, particularly in terms of long-term value creation and boardroom dynamics (including biases, independence, evaluation, transparency, and diversity). She is the author of the annual Dutch 'Female Board Index', co-author of the annual Dutch National Supervisory Board Survey, and the (chief) editor of the Corporate Governance Yearbook (Kluwer). Additionally, she is an experienced non-executive director and has served on the (supervisory) boards of international insurance company Achmea, the major Dutch newspaper NRC Media, Erasmus Medical Center, law firm Pels Rijcken, Rotterdam Zoo (Diergaarde Blijdorp), the Royal Dutch Guide Dogs Foundation, and the Investment Funds of the sustainable bank ASN. In April 2024, Mijntje was appointed as a crown member of the Social and Economic Council (SER), the most influential advisory council of the Dutch Government.

After obtaining her master's degree in Financial Economics in 1994 from Erasmus University Rotterdam, Mijntje held various financial positions at Rabobank International, lastly as Vice-President of Project Finance. From 2001, she worked at Erasmus University as Associate Professor of Financial Markets & Supervision. In 2007, she obtained her Ph.D., which focused on the usefulness of operational leases. In 2010, she became Professor of Corporate Governance at Nyenrode Business University.

Due to her interest in boardroom dynamics, and behaviour and culture in Corporate Governance, she started a bachelor's in Psychology at the Open University in 2019. In 2022, she obtained her master's degree in Work and Organizational Psychology with a thesis on moral judgement among supervisory board members. This led to her 2023 book (in Dutch), Moral Dilemmas in the Boardroom, which was nominated as Management Book of the Year (one of five nominations).

List of Figures

Fig. 3.1	Moral dilemmas and process dissociation (Derived from Conway & Gawronski, 2013, p. 220)	32
Fig. 4.1	Four right-versus-right dilemmas (Based on Kidder, 1995)	41
Fig. 5.1	Pyramid of corporate social responsibility. Adapted from Carroll (1991)	56
Fig. 7.1	Pyramid with mission, core values, strategy, and operational control. Adapted from Lückerath-Rovers (2020)	77
Fig. 8.1	Increasing intensity of discussion in boardroom decision-making	97
Fig. 8.2	Strategic choice under conditions of bounded rationality. Adapted from Hambrick and Mason (1984, p. 195)	105
Fig. 9.1	Legally permissible, morally acceptable, and public opinion	116
Fig. 10.1	The ethical triangle. Adapted from Jack Kem (2016)	129

List of Tables

Table 2.1	Internalisation and symbolisation of moral identity	13
Table 2.2	Four statuses of moral identity	15
Table 2.3	Nine attributes of a moral person	17
Table 3.1	Six stages of moral development	22
Table 3.2	Utilitarian versus deontological moral judgement	25
Table 3.3	Example of a moral dilemma: administering a drug with severe side effects	31
Table 5.1	Stakeholderism versus shareholderism	54
Table 6.1	Ethic of care and ethic of justice	70
Table 7.1	Code of ethics for non-executive directors	90
Table 7.2	Examples of questions for boards themselves, and for management	92
Table 8.1	Four perspectives ('lenses') in moral decision-making	110
Table 10.1	Three ethical questions	128
Table 10.2	Detecting and neutralising biases	133
Table 10.3	Moral consideration matrix	135
Table 10.4	Moral consideration matrix for ING's CEO salary Increase	137
Table 10.5	Final ethical tests	138
Table 10.6	Summary of ethical decision-making in the boardroom	141
Table 11.1	The moral consideration matrix for Yahoo's board	152
Table 12.1	The moral consideration matrix for Maastricht University's Board	158
Table 13.1	The moral consideration matrix for the British Museum Board of Trustees	169

List of Tables

Table 14.1	The moral consideration matrix for Bud Lights' Board of Directors	181
Table 15.1	The moral consideration matrix for the Stedelijk Museums' Board of Trustees	192
Table 16.1	The moral consideration matrix for G-Stars' Board of Directors	203
Table 17.1	The moral consideration matrix for Heinekens' Board of Directors	215
Table 18.1	The moral consideration matrix for Adidas' Board of Directors	224
Table 19.1	The moral consideration matrix for Ajax's Board of Directors	235
Table 20.1	The moral consideration matrix for INGs' Board of Directors	251

1

Introduction

1.1 A Moral Compass or a Moral Scale?

Executive and non-executive directors (hereafter: directors) bear significant responsibility. They must balance the interests of various stakeholders, including employees, customers, shareholders, and society at large. These considerations, often involving opposite interests of different stakeholders and conflicting moral values, lead to decisions in the boardroom that are not always understood, frequently criticised, and sometimes even deemed immoral or unethical.

For example, employees of Adidas sent an open letter to Rolling Stone criticising the board on how they handled controversies around statements of Kanye West, a celebrity with whom Adidas had a very successful partnership: 'The board members and the executive team turned their moral compass off by ignoring both Kanye's inflammatory public behaviour and the Yeezy team's complaints regarding troubling partner dynamics'.[1]

> The board members and the executive team turned their moral compass off
> —Adidas employees, open letter Rolling Stone, 2022

Another case highlights the divergent paths taken by the Boards of Trustees at the National Gallery, the Royal Shakespeare Company, and the British Museum regarding their sponsorship agreements with BP, an oil and gas corporation criticised for attempting to improve its public image through sponsorship. The National Gallery and the Royal Shakespeare Company terminated their partnerships, while the British Museum continued its relationship in 2023. The Royal Shakespeare Company called it 'a difficult decision' and 'there are many fine balances and complex issues involved and the decision has not been taken lightly or swiftly'.[2] These decisions resulted from careful deliberations, but nevertheless, the British Museum did experience the departure of two Trustees.

> There are many fine balances and complex issues involved
> —Royal Shakespeare Company in 2018

This book is all about these kinds of moral dilemmas in the boardroom. A dilemma implies a choice, otherwise it would not be a dilemma, and usually it involves multiple good or bad alternatives where various moral standards and interests are at play. Moral norms such as honesty, justice, loyalty, and good citizenship, along with short-term or long-term interests of employees or shareholders, individuals, or the company, may clash. Therefore, the assessments that directors must make in the boardroom are not always clear-cut, black or white, left or right. Therefore, it is too simplistic to claim that directors lack a moral compass when a decision seems unjustified from a single moral norm, perspective, or stakeholder. *The* moral compass, as if there is only one right direction, does not exist. Moral norms may conflict, and without a structured approach, there is a risk of overlooking aspects or stakeholders.

Perhaps a better metaphor would be a 'moral scale', where moral norms, consequences, and interests are weighed. This does not mean that everything carries equal weight or that the end justifies the means. However, what is morally appropriate can vary from person to person and is subjective. It refers to actions that align with an individual's sense of right and wrong, shaped by cultural, religious, and social norms, as well as personal beliefs and values. There is no objective standard for morality, and what is considered morally appropriate in one culture, society, or group may be deemed immoral in another.

This is equally relevant to moral judgements made by directors within the boardroom. Even there, differences may arise regarding what is considered ethically acceptable or which priorities should prevail. External observers, including the general public, also assess these ethical standards and interests, often holding divergent views on what constitutes moral correctness, leading to varying conclusions. This discrepancy partially explains why certain situations spark public outrage, with contrasts sometimes deliberately magnified by interest groups, politicians, and media.

For example, in 2015, the Starbucks 'Race Together' campaign abruptly ended less than a week after its launch. It aimed to encourage baristas to engage customers in discussions about race but quickly attracted significant backlash, with critics arguing that it unfairly burdened employees and that a coffee shop was not the right place for complex racial dialogues. Responding to the criticism, Schultz seemed to suggest that the backlash was anticipated to some degree and he 'didn't expect universal praise'.[3]

> We didn't expect universal praise
> —CEO Schultz of Starbucks in 2015

Other instances of public disapproval stem from the contrasting paces at which different corporations withdrew from Russia, reactions to overstepping behaviours and the #MeToo movement, and several corporate boycotts triggered by the involvement of controversial or non-conventional influencers. In such scenarios, directors are often faced with challenging decisions that might not appear justified from a singular viewpoint. In these cases, the clarity provided by detailing the decision-making process may be more crucial than justifying the outcome of the decision itself.

1.2 Careful Decision-Making May Be More Important than the Decision Itself

In situations of moral ambiguity, the decision-making process can be deemed more crucial than the decision itself. What constitutes 'careful decision-making' can vary widely among individuals, directors, boards, and institutions. For example, consider the controversy surrounding ING and its non-executive directors over a proposed 50% pay rise for the CEO. A disciplinary committee, vested with the legal authority to assess a formal complaint, initially found the complaint 'baseless'. Their ruling noted that although the public outcry against the remuneration proposal had 'undermined trust in the banking sector', the non-executive directors made a choice they believed favoured the bank's long-term well-being.[4] Thus, the well-informed committee determined the decision-making process was not 'careless' or 'lacking integrity'. However, upon appeal, the Appeals Committee diverged in opinion, suggesting that, although the integrity of the directors was still not doubted, their decision-making process was now considered 'reckless' for failing to give sufficient weight to all stakeholders.[5]

This divergence in opinions, even by two committees that were fully informed with all meeting minutes, highlights the complexity of decision-making. However, it also raises the question of how challenging it must be for those outside the situation, without all the information, to understand or evaluate such decisions.

Another case, at Uber in 2017, also underscores the necessity for boards to have a robust, ethical decision-making framework that balances all stakeholders' interests and guards against the risk of overlooking critical internal issues. In this case, the board of Uber neglected the perspective of different stakeholders when they initially supported the company's practices, even in the face of allegations pointing to a toxic work environment marked by sexual harassment, discrimination, and aggressive business strategies. The following public backlash highlighted the disconnect between the board's initial support and stakeholders' expectations. The incoming CEO, Dara Khosrowshahi, later stated that 'the moral compass of the company was not pointing in the right direction'.[6]

> The moral compass of the company was not pointing in the right direction
> —Uber CEO Dara Khosrowshahi in 2018

The rulings and investigations of these cases, and other cases discussed in part II of this book, underscore three key tenets for executive and non-executive directors. First, in evaluating directors' actions, the process by which decisions are made might hold greater significance than the outcomes of those decisions. Second, perceptions of what defines a diligent decision-making process can vary, making it even more challenging to ascertain if the resulting decision was made with due care. Lastly, without direct access to the internal deliberations, it becomes difficult for those on the outside to judge whether the decisions taken by directors were justifiable, considering the balance of the interests of all stakeholders.

The decision-making process often remains a black box to those outside the organisation, potentially leading to misunderstandings or misinterpretations of decisions as unethical or detrimental to stakeholders. In essence, gaining insight into the boardroom dynamics and how decisions are formulated is a complex task. Both executive and non-executive directors need to recognise this issue and strive towards a decision-making process that is both transparent and meticulous, ensuring it can be comprehended and justified to all stakeholders. Achieving such clarity is essential for maintaining, establishing, or rebuilding trust in the corporate sphere and among its leaders.

This book aims to navigate the complex terrain of moral decision-making, offering guidance through ten in-depth case studies followed by over twenty comparable yet briefer-described situations. These examples highlight the varied interests and ethical considerations that directors must juggle. The book intentionally refrains from passing judgement from the author, acknowledging that prioritising these interests and moral principles is a deeply personal and subjective task.

1.3 Book Structure

The subject matter of this book, moral dilemmas in the boardroom, is of paramount importance as it underscores the need to place a greater emphasis on behaviour and culture within the boardroom, with a particular focus on moral judgement. The early 2000s witnessed a series of business scandals that prompted the creation of numerous codes of good governance aimed at both executive and non-executive directors. Globally, these efforts have resulted in the establishment of almost 100 national governance codes[7] and even more sector codes (housing, care, education, etc.). Historically, these governance codes have prioritised defining directors' roles and responsibilities to safeguard their stakeholders' interests. Nevertheless, instances of flawed decision-making within the boardroom have led to a widespread agreement that corporate governance extends beyond mere structural and procedural aspects. It critically involves the conduct and decision-making processes of directors within those structures.

This book explores the moral dilemmas faced in boardrooms. It has two parts: Part I, which includes ten more theoretical and descriptive chapters and Part II, which is more practical and includes ten real-life cases in which companies and directors faced a moral dilemma.

Part I starts with insights into moral identity, moral judgement, moral dilemmas, and the principles of stakeholderism. Subsequently, this first part shifts towards moral judgement from the perspective of directors and corporate governance, addressing moral decision-making in the boardroom. Part I ends with a five-step decision-making model, including a Moral Consideration Matrix designed to organise moral judgements by systematically navigating through competing (moral) considerations. Secondly, Part II dives into the complexity and subjectivity of these moral evaluations by presenting ten real-life cases. It serves as a kind of moral jurisprudence: moresprudence. This part describes ten cases in detail, but over 20 shorter cases supplement these, each illustrating how similar dilemmas were approached differently or how these diverse considerations led to varied outcomes. Part II not only highlights the complexity of moral decision-making but also serves as a guide for directors in navigating their ethical landscapes, reinforcing the book's relevance in today's corporate governance discourse.

1.3.1 Terminology

In this book, 'directors' refers to board members, including executive and non-executive directors, and even trustees for public organisations. It's important to note that, for the purposes of discussion, the specific roles and decision-making capacities of these two types of directors are not our primary concern. We operate under the assumption that all directors, whether executive, non-executive, or trustees, share a collective responsibility for the decisions made within the boardroom. However, a clear distinction will be made in cases where decisions specifically differentiate between the responsibilities of the executive and non-executive directors, such as appointments and remuneration of the executives, which the non-executive directors explicitly make.

Furthermore, in corporate governance, it's essential to distinguish between a one-tier (unitary) and a two-tier (dual) board model. In the latter, we technically should refer to management and supervisory board members. However, for the sake of readability and simplicity, we also describe these as directors and, where necessary, supervisory board members as non-executive directors. This approach does not mean oversimplifying the complex governance structures but rather maintaining a consistent and accessible narrative throughout the text.

Lastly, it's worth mentioning that board members of non-profit organisations are typically referred to as trustees. This distinction underscores the different legal and fiduciary responsibilities associated with non-profit governance. Nonetheless, the overarching principles of board responsibility and oversight remain a common thread, regardless of the terminology or organisational structure.

1.4 Disclaimers

This book attempts to describe both the scientific and theoretical foundation and the practical applications of moral judgement in the boardroom and provide inspiration for anyone involved in corporate governance. However, it does not attempt to be a comprehensive work on ethics, morality, and moral judgement.

This book is also not intended as a guide for what constitutes good or bad decisions; on the contrary, it is not meant to be preachy or to judge previous decisions. Instead, this book aims to provide insight into the importance of this subject in the boardroom, its many aspects, and the complexity that executive and non-executive directors face.

Notes

1. Adidas launches probe into claims that Kanye West showed employees porn, Elisabeth Garber, *Rolling Stone*, November 24, 2022.
2. We are to conclude our partnership with BP, press release Royal Shakespeare Company, October 2, 2019.
3. Starbucks Ends Conversation Starters on Race, Ravi Somaiya, March 22, 2015, The New York Times.
4. Ruling of the Banking Sector Disciplinary Regulations, Report 3935, August 3, 2022.
5. Appeals Committee as referred to in the Disciplinary Regulations banking sector, Decision of April 13, 2023.
6. Moral compass' was off at Uber under co-founder Kalanick, says new CEO Dara Khosrowshahi, Matthew J. Belvedere, January 23, 2018, CNBC.
7. See for a complete list of national Corporate Governance Codes, www.ecgi.global/content/codes-0

Part I

Foundations of Moral Judgement in the Boardroom

Without a solid understanding of how ethical decisions are formed in the boardroom or a structured approach to this decision-making process, directors' choices may become short-sighted, biased, and ultimately flawed. Part I of this book is designed to equip the reader with the necessary theoretical knowledge and provide practical insights to avoid these pitfalls.

Understanding these basics is crucial because it will offer a robust foundation for navigating moral dilemmas. The eight foundational chapters, therefore, distinguish between the more general theoretical concepts of moral identity, moral judgement, and stakeholderism, and their practical applications for directors, their organisations, and their stakeholders.

First, Chapters 2 through 6 establish the theoretical underpinnings necessary for understanding directors' decision-making when facing a moral dilemma. They introduce core themes such as moral identity and moral judgement, which form the backbone of moral decision-making. In Chapter 2, moral identity is examined, highlighting how individuals define their moral selves in relation to their broader social contexts. Chapter 3 explores moral judgement, showing how people navigate ethical dilemmas by applying ethical frameworks like utilitarianism, which focuses on outcomes, and deontology, which focuses on moral principles. This chapter reveals how moral development and preferences towards these frameworks shape decisions and behaviour. It highlights the tensions in moral dilemmas, particularly in situations where there isn't a clear right answer. In Chapter 4, the focus shifts to these right-right dilemmas, understanding these helps readers recognise the multifaceted nature of moral dilemmas in business settings. Chapter 5 introduces the broader societal concepts of stakeholderism and emphasises the need for boards to balance the interests of diverse stakeholders. Chapter 6 describes possible gender differences in the previous themes.

Subsequently, Chapters 7 through 10 transition from the more general and theoretical aspects of moral judgement to the more specific and practical implications for directors and their boardrooms. They address how these moral principles directly impact decision-making in the boardroom. Chapter 7 dives into how moral values are embedded in the boardroom, influencing mission statements, core values, and corporate governance codes. Chapter 8 explores decision-making processes specific to the boardroom, identifying the challenges of groupthink, tunnel vision, and irreconcilable differences. It reveals how directors' limited visions shape outcomes. Chapter 9 examines the interplay between legality, morality, and public opinions, highlighting how legal frameworks intersect with moral obligations and societal perceptions, and also relates this to CEO activism. Finally, Chapter 10 introduces a five-step ethical decision-making model to guide directors through framing dilemmas, exploring options, and refining choices before implementing and communicating the decision. It presents a Moral Considerations Matrix, a practical tool in which the theoretical and ethical views on weighing consequences and sticking to principles are integrated.

2

Moral Identity

> The beginning of wisdom is that you know yourself.
> —Aristotle (384BC–322BC)

Imagine a boardroom with directors from diverse backgrounds. Each brings a unique compilation of personal experiences, cultural influences, and upbringing to the table. These experiences can change or strengthen one's perspective on certain norms and values and influence how one acts and makes decisions. So, when a moral dilemma arises, the boardroom may transform into a dynamic arena where varied moral identities are put to the test.

When facing a moral dilemma in the boardroom, directors must weigh multiple moral norms and values to which they, to a greater or lesser extent, want to adhere. These moral norms and values contribute to one's moral identity. Each director weighs a complex array of moral norms and values that shape their moral identity; these aren't just abstract concepts but personal commitments that guide their decisions.

For instance, consider whether to prioritise environmental sustainability over the organisation's financial stability. A director raised in a region where environmental conservation is paramount may advocate strongly for green initiatives, viewing this choice as not just strategic but ethically imperative. In contrast, another, whose upbringing emphasised economic stability and job creation, might argue that securing profits ensures employee welfare and community support, presenting a compelling counterpoint.

This interplay in the boardroom doesn't just shape corporate strategy; it reveals the rich, sometimes conflicting moral perspectives that influence decision-making at the highest levels. Such scenarios highlight why understanding and respecting diverse moral identities is crucial in navigating moral dilemmas.

2.1 Social Identities

Our self-image is based on multiple social identities: one's sense of who we are, based on social categories or group memberships, such as gender, race, religion, and school or work. A social identity reflects how we see ourselves and how others see us in relation to significant social categories.[1] For example, someone's cultural identity is determined by the language and traditions of the culture in which they grew up, political identity by beliefs, political parties, or ideologies, and religious identity by how someone identifies with a religion or spiritual belief. Generational identity is also one of our social identities, how someone identifies with their age group or generation, such as a baby boomer, millennial, or Generation Z.

These social identities can be activated in different contexts: people behave differently at work than at home, students behave differently with friends than with their parents, and executive directors and non-executive directors behave differently in the boardroom than at the tennis club. In general, one's social identity is the culmination of one's values, experiences, self-perceptions, and the meanings one assigns to oneself and their interaction with the environment.

Moral identity is one of these social identities and forms the basis for one's moral beliefs and values. These moral beliefs include both cognitive and affective components. The cognitive component relates to one's knowledge, beliefs, and attitudes about what is right and wrong. This includes understanding and accepting moral principles, norms, and values, as well as the rules and obligations that stem from them. The cognitive aspect of moral identity is more focused on making rational decisions based on the moral principles one has adopted. The affective component refers to the emotional and affective aspects of moral beliefs, including feelings of responsibility, empathy, guilt, and shame associated with moral decisions and actions. The affective aspect of moral identity is more focused on making intuitive decisions based on the moral principles one has adopted.

Table 2.1 Internalisation and symbolisation of moral identity

Internalisation	Symbolisation
Private part of moral identity	Public part of moral identity
Personality	Action
Autonomous	Visible to others
Inner world	Outer world
Emotions	Symbols, rituals, and objects
Feeling of norms and values	Communication of norms and values

Adapted from Erikson (1994) and Aquino and Reed (2002)

2.1.1 Private and Public Parts of Moral Identity

Like other forms of social identity, one's moral identity is rooted in the core of one's being and staying true to oneself in action. Therefore, moral identity has a private part and a public part[2] (See Table 2.1).

The private part of moral identity, internalisation, involves the extent to which moral characteristics are central to one's self-image. For moral identity, self-image refers to a mental image of what a moral person is likely to think, feel, and do. Internalisation refers to the process by which someone adopts and internalises values and norms from society or a specific group as part of their own personality. This can happen through upbringing, education, or observing the behaviour of others.

The public part of moral identity, symbolisation, refers to the extent to which moral characteristics are expressed through actions in the external world. Through behaviour, actions, and symbols, meaning is given to values and norms. Symbolisation is a powerful means of communicating and reinforcing moral beliefs, such as religious beliefs, political ideologies, or cultural traditions.

2.1.2 Identity Work

Scholarly debate exists around the nature of moral identity, with some researchers positing that it is fixed and stable, akin to our core values, which are seen as relatively unchanging throughout one's life. From this perspective, an individual's moral framework, the foundation of ethical behaviour and decision-making, remains consistent over time, irrespective of external circumstances. Conversely, contemporary scholars advocate for a more fluid conception of moral identity, suggesting it transforms over time and is influenced by diverse contexts and life experiences. This perspective is supported by research indicating that exposure to new situations, challenges, and reflective processes can lead to an evolution in one's moral reasoning, ethical priorities, and overall moral self-conception. Thus, according to this view, moral identity is not static but subject to continual development and reshaping through life's myriad experiences. The process through which individuals engage in forming, repairing, maintaining, strengthening, or revising their senses of self is called identity work. Identity work encompasses the myriad ways in which people actively construct and negotiate their identities in response to various social, professional, and personal challenges and experiences.

Finnish psychologist Mari Huhtala and colleagues highlighted the significance of moral identity work in organisational contexts, emphasising how individuals reflect upon and align their actions with their moral values and principles.[3] As people gain new experiences or are exposed to different moral perspectives, moral identity can also change over time through a process of introspection and reflection, as well as personal experiences such as witnessing injustice or experiencing moral dilemmas. The tension between context-dependent moral actions and moral identity, particularly at the top of companies (leaders), can lead to a reassessment of one's moral beliefs and values. Firstly, they may experience limitations or incentives that determine the options for their moral actions. For example, consistent ethical standards in the organisation may encourage moral actions. In contrast, less ethical standards, including focusing on short-term profit, may limit moral actions and provide little room for individual moral considerations and identity. Secondly, leaders may experience potentially conflicting expectations from different stakeholders due to their different responsibilities. This can be a threat to their own moral identity if personal moral values are not in line with the demands of an organisation. Such a moral conflict can lead to a reformulation of one's moral identity.

They identified four moral identity statuses of leaders (See Table 2.2.). Their classification of moral identity statuses among leaders was determined by the methods of leaders when engaging with and understanding moral dilemmas, as well as the impact of the organisational setting on their ethical decision-making. Achievement-oriented leaders have undergone self-exploration to establish a clear value framework, guiding their decisions fairly and responsibly, even amid conflicting demands. Moratorium leaders actively explore and refine their moral values, but ongoing uncertainty sometimes leads to compromises and internal conflict. Foreclosure leaders adhere to a predetermined moral framework without self-exploration, maintaining rigid stances and resisting alternative viewpoints. Finally, diffusion leaders lack a clear moral identity, struggle to reconcile competing interests, and fail to establish a guiding framework. These variations in moral identity statuses have significant implications for encouraging the development of moral identity in business leaders within the professional environment.

These different statuses require different approaches. For example, leaders with diffused moral identities need help to become more aware of moral issues and strengthen their values, possibly through ethics training. Those with a foreclosed moral identity, which can sometimes be too rigid, should be encouraged to consider alternative perspectives in a supportive environment. And leaders in a moral identity moratorium, where the self-exploration of one's moral identity is ongoing, can benefit from positive role models to help resolve their conflicts. Leaders with achieved moral identities should continuously develop their moral insights.

According to the researchers, organisations should move beyond rewarding loyalty and obedience to foster discussions on moral uncertainties and alternative viewpoints. This approach can drive the reformulation of moral identities, leading to richer and more coherent identities that contribute positively to the organisation and reduce the risk of immoral actions. Supporting managers in becoming moral leaders involves recognising their current moral identity and encouraging the development of personally meaningful moral

Table 2.2 Four statuses of moral identity

Achievement	Commitment to a personally meaningful moral value framework is established through a period of self-exploration. A clear value framework guides decision-making even when faced with competing demands. No avoidance of responsibility or unpleasant confrontations and actions that are seen as fair and aligned with their values
Moratorium	Actively processing and exploring values to (re-)establish a personally meaningful moral value framework in the employment context. Uncertainty about fully standing behind moral values and sometimes making a compromise, and thus experiencing an ongoing moral conflict
Foreclosure	Commitment to a given moral value framework is present with little or no personal self-exploration. A foreclosed moral identity may be resistant to identity development in a rigid way, avoiding or denying
Diffusion	No clear idea of what was central to their personal moral identity. An ongoing uncertainty about how to reach compromises between competing interests (for example, supporting employee autonomy versus following rules and formal policies) and no efforts to establish a moral framework

Adapted from Huhtala, Fadjukoff, and Kroger (2020)

convictions through exploration and commitment to moral values. Supervisors should be open to alternative moral values that challenge organisational norms and use insights from identity research to support leaders with different moral identities.

2.2 Measuring Moral Identity

Moral identity is a psychological construct. A psychological construct is an abstract concept that is not directly observable or measurable but describes what happens in human thinking and behaviour. It attempts to describe and explain specific mental processes, experiences, personality traits, behaviours, or other aspects of human psychology. Although a psychological construct is abstract and not directly observable, it is possible to measure it using validated instruments such as questionnaires, scales, or interviews. Several scales and questionnaires have been developed to measure moral identity. For example, the Moral Identity Questionnaire (MIQ), the Moral Identity Scale (MIS), the Moral Foundation Questionnaire (MFQ), and the Ethical Leadership Scale (ELS).[4] Such measurement instruments include questions and statements about various aspects of moral identity, such as the extent to which someone applies moral principles in their life, the extent to which someone identifies with their moral values, and the extent to which someone sees themselves as a moral person.

The Moral Identity Scale (MIS) developed by Aquino and Reed is one of these measurement instruments.[5] They first collected 376 concepts mentioned by a group of over 300 participants as attributes, characteristics, or qualities of a moral person. These concepts were then reduced to nineteen moral attributes by merging synonyms: 'caring, compassionate, conscientious, considerate, dependable, ethical, fair, forgiving, friendly, generous, giving, hardworking, helpful, honest, kind, loyal, religious, trustworthy, and understanding'. To avoid including concepts that not everyone saw as fitting for a moral person but, for example, fit another social identity, only concepts mentioned by at least 30 per cent of the participants were included. This resulted in nine attributes characterising a moral person: caring, compassionate, fair, friendly, generous, helpful, hardworking, honest, and kind (See Table 2.3). Although the authors acknowledge that these nine attributes may not be the only characteristics of a moral person, these nine attributes evoke a series of associations with other traits that align with one's moral self-image.

The MIS questionnaire asks participants to imagine a person with these attributes. This person can be the participant themselves or someone else. The

Table 2.3 Nine attributes of a moral person

Caring	Demonstrates empathy and prioritises the well-being of others
Compassionate	Actively seeks to alleviate others' suffering
Fair	Ensures decisions are based on justice and equality
Friendly	Exhibits warmth and openness in relationships
Generous	Offers resources or time beyond expectations, without seeking return
Helpful	Readily assists others in need or in reaching goals
Hardworking	Shows diligence and a strong commitment to tasks
Honest	Upholds truthfulness and integrity
Kind	Engages in considerate and supportive actions towards others

Attributes by Aquino and Reed (2002), definitions by author

participant must visualise the kind of person who possesses these attributes. How would that person think, feel, and act? After the participant has formed a clear picture, ten statements are presented, and the participant must indicate how much they agree with each statement. All items are answered on a 7-point scale from 1 = strongly disagree to 7 = strongly agree.

Five statements refer to the extent to which moral attributes are central to self-image (internalisation). For example, '*Being someone with these attributes is an important part of who I am*'. And five statements refer to the extent to which the attributes are expressed in the respondent's actions in the world (symbolisation), for example, '*The types of things I do in my free time (e.g., hobbies) clearly indicate that I have these attributes*'.

Scholars have widely used the MIS to measure moral identity. While measuring moral identity allows for insight, it is essential to emphasise that measuring moral identity is only an approximation of the complex and dynamic process of moral development and behaviour. As described earlier, one's moral identity can differ from situation to situation, as can how people express their moral identity. However, measuring moral identity can provide insight into how people see their own moral identity and how it relates to their behaviour and choices.

Notes

1. See amongst others: Aquino, K., & Reed, A., 2nd. (2002). The self-importance of moral identity. *Journal of Personality and Social Psychology, 83*(6), 1423–1440, Erikson, E. H. (1964). A memorandum on identity and negro youth. *Journal of Social Issues, 20*(4), 29–42, Huhtala, M., Fadjukoff, P., & Kroger, J. (2020). Managers as moral leaders: Moral

identity processes in the context of work. *Journal of Business Ethics, 172*(4), 639–652.
2. Erikson, E. H. (1964). A memorandum on identity and negro youth. *Journal of Social Issues, 20*(4), 29–42.
3. Huhtala, M., Fadjukoff, P., & Kroger, J. (2020). Managers as moral leaders: Moral identity processes in the context of work. *Journal of Business Ethics, 172*(4), 639–652.
4. See for the MIQ: Black, J. E., & Reynolds, W. M. (2016). Development, reliability, and validity of the moral identity questionnaire. Personality and individual differences, *97*, 120–129, the MIS: Aquino, K., & Reed, A., 2nd. (2002). The self-importance of moral identity. *Journal of Personality and Social Psychology, 83*(6), 1423–1440, the MFQ: Graham, J., Haidt, J., & Nosek, B. A. (2009). Liberals and conservatives rely on different sets of moral foundations. *Journal of Personality and Social Psychology, 96*(5), 1029–1046, and the ELS: Brown, M. E., Treviño, L. K., & Harrison, D. A. (2005). Ethical leadership: A social learning perspective for construct development and testing. *Organizational Behavior and Human Decision Processes, 97*(2), 117–134.
5. Aquino, K., & Reed, A., 2nd. (2002). The self-importance of moral identity. *Journal of Personality and Social Psychology, 83*(6), 1423–1440.

3

Moral Judgement

> The greatest happiness of the greatest number is the foundation of morals and legislation.
> —Jeremy Bentham 1748–1832

In the boardroom, directors frequently face decisions that require them to weigh the outcomes for various stakeholders, sometimes making difficult compromises on moral principles to achieve a higher purpose. While certain moral principles might seem non-negotiable—lying, cheating, and stealing are universally condemned—directors often navigate in a grey area where moral principles are subjective, may conflict, or are less universal. The challenge lies in finding the delicate balance between upholding ethical standards and pursuing outcomes that benefit the broader organisation and its stakeholders.

Even with the above-mentioned apparently non-negotiable moral principles, like lying, one could argue that they are acceptable in certain situations. For example, during negotiations about a takeover, lying or lying by omission might prevent panic and insecurity among employees and others, safeguarding morale and stability.

The way directors determine right and wrong can be influenced by the ethical framework they use in their moral judgements, either more focused on the consequences and impact of the decision or a stronger adherence to moral principles. What might be considered 'good' in one framework can easily be labelled 'wrong' in another. This delicate balancing act reflects the contrasting inclinations of consequences versus moral principles, either utilitarian or deontological ethics. While utilitarianism calls for maximising benefits for the greatest number, deontological approaches stress sticking firmly to moral rules.

For example, the balance of when lying is acceptable in the takeover example can vary among directors depending on the ethical frameworks they use. Directors with a utilitarian outlook may be more inclined to justify withholding information to maximise overall benefits (financial and non-financial) and avoid organisational turmoil. In contrast, those with a more deontological mindset might prioritise transparency and stick to moral principles, valuing honesty as an intrinsic duty regardless of the potential fallout.

With the public's increasing scrutiny of how directors reach their decisions in a moral dilemma, ethical leadership may involve considerations that extend beyond an individual's personal moral identity. Directors not only possess unique moral identities (see Chapter 2) but will also resolve moral dilemmas through distinct ethical frameworks. This chapter delves into the theoretical differences between utilitarian and deontological ethical frameworks. A more practical application of these two frameworks will be featured in a Moral Considerations Matrix in Chapter 10, which will be utilised in Part II to examine the boards' considerations in ten case studies.

3.1   Moral Development

Given directors' significant responsibilities, elevated levels of morality, moral judgement, and moral reasoning are crucial for effective leadership. Directors set the tone for the organisation, and strong ethical principles empower them to steer the company responsibly through the complexities of modern business. Their decisions can influence the livelihoods of employees, the satisfaction of customers, and the trust of investors, impacting a wide range of stakeholders. Advanced moral reasoning enables them to navigate complex situations where ethical principles may conflict, ensuring that decisions are made thoughtfully and compassionately.

Moral reasoning and moral judgement are closely related processes that involve thinking through and evaluating moral situations. However, they do slightly differ. Moral judgement is an evaluative process that determines the rightness or wrongness of actions or situations, serving as the basis for decision-making in moral contexts. Moral reasoning is the cognitive process that underlies how individuals arrive at moral judgements, involving the evaluation of reasons and principles to solve moral dilemmas.[1]

Directors with strong moral judgement and reasoning skills can build trust by fostering a culture of integrity, safeguarding the company's reputation, and enhancing its credibility in a world increasingly scrutinising corporate ethics. Elevated moral reasoning encourages a long-term perspective that emphasises sustainability over short-term gains, ensuring that ethical, environmental, and social factors are incorporated into strategic planning.

But what entails elevated moral reasoning? The Theory of Moral Development, developed by psychologist Lawrence Kohlberg, suggests three levels of the development of moral reasoning, each characterised by increasingly complex moral reasoning: the pre-conventional, conventional, and post-conventional levels, with two distinct stages in each level (See Table 3.1).[2] At the conventional level, a child's sense of morality is externally controlled, for example, by parents and teachers, and actions are judged by their consequences. At the conventional level, morality is tied to personal and societal relationships. Rules of authority figures are still leading, but mainly because this is necessary to ensure positive relationships and societal order. At the last level, the post-conventional level, morality is defined by more abstract principles and values.

The first and second levels of moral reasoning rely on external authorities to guide decisions between right and wrong, simplifying moral judgements by following societal norms or directives from authority figures. This approach, while clear, encourages a form of passivity in moral decision-making, where the individual doesn't profoundly engage with the principles behind their choices. Kohlberg placed most adults in stages three or four, where the laws of society and the viewpoints of important individuals greatly influence their moral reasoning.[3]

Transitioning to the third level, post-conventional morality, individuals move away from this reliance on external definitions of morality. Instead, they develop their own set of moral beliefs through independent thought, which they then apply creatively to moral dilemmas. This shift marks a significant change from adherence to external rules to an engagement with ethics based on personal principles.[4] The main difference refers to the determinants in the individual's reasoning, either determined by societal laws and opinions of significant others (the conventional level) or by universal moral principles (the post-conventional level). Ultimately, reaching this level reflects a more nuanced, autonomous, and principled engagement with moral questions, signifying a mature approach to ethics that transcends mere rule-following.

Some scholars suggest that corporate leaders are placed in the third, post-conventional level.[5] For example, professor in management Jill Graham described that transitioning to the third level of moral reasoning requires

Table 3.1 Six stages of moral development

Pre-conventional level	
Stage 1: Obedience and punishment orientation	Young children (typically up to age 7) see morality as external to themselves, governed by powerful figures like parents or teachers. They follow rules to avoid punishment, understanding right and wrong in terms of consequences to themselves
Stage 2: Individualism and exchange	As children start to interact more with peers (around age 7–10), they begin to understand that there is more than one right view. They recognise the importance of individual perspectives and the value of fairness in exchanges, learning to negotiate and compromise
Conventional level	
Stage 3: Good interpersonal Relationships	During preadolescence, children become increasingly concerned with social relationships. They make moral choices based on the desire to be seen as good by their peers and adults, focusing on being nice and earning approval
Stage 4: Maintaining the social order	As children enter adolescence, they start to understand the importance of the larger social order beyond personal relationships. They respect authority and rules because they maintain societal stability, which they recognise as important for the well-being of the group

(continued)

Table 3.1 (continued)

Post-conventional level	
Stage 5: Social contract and individual rights	Older adolescents and young adults begin to see laws and rules as flexible tools that can be changed to improve society. They appreciate the balance between individual rights and societal needs, understanding that social contracts are necessary for the welfare of all
Stage 6: Universal principles	Not all individuals reach this stage, but those who do, often in adulthood, base their moral reasoning on universal ethical principles. They prioritise justice, human rights, and equality, and are willing to challenge laws or social norms that conflict with these principles

Source Adapted from Kohlberg (1981)

individuals to actively engage in a balanced consideration of all interests and employ independent analysis and moral courage.[6] She also highlighted that these higher levels of moral reasoning require other leadership styles, transformational or servant leadership, essential for elevating organisational ethical standards. Transformational leadership improves the moral behaviour of both leaders and followers by upholding principles of justice, equality, and respect for individual dignity. Similarly, servant leadership emphasises meeting the crucial needs of those served, focusing on both internal and external stakeholders.[7]

3.2 Utilitarian Versus Deontological Moral Judgement Formation

In this book, moral judgement refers to the process of contemplating moral dilemmas. It involves identifying a moral dilemma, considering various perspectives and values, weighing the potential consequences of different choices, and selecting the most morally responsible option.[8]

This also happens with moral dilemmas in the boardroom, where directors also follow this process of contemplating individually and collectively as a team. To understand this process of weighing consequences and moral principles, it is also vital to understand the distinction between utilitarian and deontological moral judgement. While these concepts may initially seem rather theoretical, they significantly shape directors' decision-making, ultimately influencing outcomes and their impact. This book delves deeply into the distinction between these ethical frameworks, introducing the Moral Considerations Matrix in Chapter 10. This matrix later becomes a recurring tool used to analyse the varying perspectives of directors in the case studies featured in Part II.

3.2.1 Utilitarian Moral Judgement

Utilitarian ethics focuses on the outcomes of moral actions, with the core principle being to maximise overall well-being, happiness, or utility for the largest number of people. This philosophical approach, synonymous with assessing utility, traces its roots back to the Scottish thinker David Hume (1711–1776). It gained further momentum and development through the works of English jurist and philosopher Jeremy Bentham (1748–1832) and John Stuart Mill (1806–1873), an English economist and philosopher. These thinkers laid the groundwork for utilitarianism by arguing that the moral worth of actions is determined by their contribution to general happiness or utility.

In practical terms, utilitarian moral judgement necessitates thoroughly evaluating how different actions can promote well-being or minimise harm among all stakeholders in each ethical dilemma. This approach is characterised by a nuanced cost–benefit analysis, not in financial terms, but in utility, happiness, and overall well-being considerations. It's a misconception to assume that utilitarianism disregards moral norms; instead, it integrates critical ethical principles, including respect for individual rights and freedoms, alongside the imperatives of fairness and justice. From a utilitarian perspective, actions that infringe upon these rights and freedoms are seen as detrimental to the collective well-being.

Moreover, utilitarianism posits that a society grounded in fairness and justice is essential for optimising happiness or well-being across the community. This ethical framework encourages a balanced assessment of actions, where decisions are not merely transactional or self-serving but are made with the broader impact on society in mind. Utilitarianism, therefore, provides a compelling lens through which to navigate complex moral issues, advocating for decisions that strive to achieve the greatest good for the greatest number while upholding fundamental moral standards and promoting a just and equitable society.

3.2.2 Deontological Moral Judgement

Deontological ethics involve adhering to certain moral principles, such as justice, equality, and fairness, irrespective of the potential consequences of the action. Specifically, deontological moral judgement revolves around universal rules and duties that must be followed regardless of the context or consequences. Deontology, derived from the Greek words deon (duty) and logos (reason), underlies the works of the German philosopher Immanuel Kant (1724–1804). For moral dilemmas, this means that some moral principles are so fundamental that they cannot be sacrificed or ignored, even if following these principles may have overall negative consequences. In this sense, principle-based arguments can be persuasive as they focus on protecting fundamental moral values.

So, utilitarianism focuses on the consequences of an action by weighing costs and benefits, while deontology focuses on consistency with moral norms. From a utilitarian perspective, moral judgement can be determined by a simple rule: whether an action maximises the greatest total utility. Meanwhile, the deontological perspective describes a set of rules or principles that serve as constraints on morally permissible actions.[9] Utilitarian considerations are, therefore, more rational and primarily guided by cognitive processes, while deontological considerations are more emotional and driven by affective processes.

Table 3.2 summarises the differences between utilitarian and deontological moral judgement. In the boardroom, these perspectives cannot be easily separated. Directors are expected to uphold moral norms and values while simultaneously maximising the interests of a wide range of stakeholders. This will be further developed in Chapter 10.

Table 3.2 Utilitarian versus deontological moral judgement

Utilitarian	Deontological
Consequential ethics	Principle ethics
Weighing costs and benefits	Adhering to moral norms
Cognitive process	Affective process
Rational	Emotional
Slow	Fast
Deliberate	Intuitive
System 2	System 1

3.3 Moral Dilemmas

In this book, moral judgement refers to the process of contemplating moral dilemmas. It involves identifying a moral dilemma, considering various perspectives and values, weighing the potential consequences of different choices, and selecting the most morally responsible option.[10] Social psychological research focusing on choosing between more utilitarian or deontological options often employs moral dilemmas. Participants must determine whether they are more inclined to opt for the option that maximises overall utility or the option that adheres to universal moral norms. Moral dilemmas have become a standard method for studying moral judgement formation.[11]

A prominent example of such a moral dilemma is the trolley dilemma. Introduced by British philosopher Philippa Foot in 1967, the trolley dilemma was designed to investigate the ethical distinction between 'acting' and 'omitting to act', as well as whether the moral appropriateness of an action depends on the actor's intention. The dilemma explores the 'double effect' problem, where it might be morally acceptable to act with a bad outcome if a good outcome is also present, but only if the bad outcome is an unintended side effect and not the means to achieve the good outcome.

> **The Trolley Dilemma**
> Phillippa Foot (1967).[12]
>
> A runaway railway trolley is speeding towards five railway workers on the tracks. You are standing next to the tracks. The trolley will kill the five railway workers unless you pull a lever that switches the trolley to another track, saving the five workers. If the trolley is diverted to the other track, it will, however, kill one railway worker who is working on that track and would otherwise not have been killed.
>
> Is it morally appropriate to pull the lever to save the five railway workers?

The double effect in the trolley dilemma refers to the fact that the chosen action (pulling the lever) has two different consequences or effects:

- Saving five lives by diverting the train to the side-track.
- Causing the death of one person who is on the side-track.

The first is a positive effect, while the second is a negative effect. The dilemma arises because a choice must be made between these two effects, where one effect comes at the expense of the other. This raises questions about which moral principles should be followed and how to decide which effect carries more weight than the other. The decision to act and pull the lever, thereby saving five lives but simultaneously causing the death of another railway worker, is utilitarian; it weighs costs and benefits, depends on consequences, and is rational as it is less influenced by emotions. The decision not to act and not pull the lever is deontological because it gives more weight to the 'you shall not kill' principle.

Various variations of the trolley dilemma have been developed, involving different actions, emotional involvement with the victim, or varying the number of potential victims. Examples include the footbridge dilemma and the coastguard dilemma.

> **The Footbridge Dilemma**
>
> Judith Jarvis Thomson (1985).[13]
>
> A runaway railway trolley is heading at full speed towards five railway workers on the track. You are on a railway bridge above the track. The trolley will kill the five railway workers unless you throw something heavy in front of the trolley. Coincidentally, a heavy man is standing next to you; the only way to stop the trolley is to push this man off the bridge onto the track, causing his death but saving five lives.
>
> Is it morally appropriate to push the man off the bridge to save the five railway workers?

The footbridge dilemma is nearly identical to the trolley dilemma, and the potential consequences are also the same as in the trolley dilemma (five or one railway workers dying). However, there is a different response to this dilemma. The act of pushing the man, where the participant becomes directly involved in causing the death of the sacrificed victim, less frequently leads to the utilitarian choice. The English philosopher and BBC journalist David Edmonds refers to this dilemma in the title of his book 'Would You Kill the Fat Man', in which he describes numerous dilemmas and the considerations associated with them.[14]

In the coastguard dilemma, the researchers varied the number of people who could be saved (two, four, dozens, or hundreds) and the participant's relationship to the potential victim (stranger, brother, nephew, or friend. The hypothesis was that if more people benefit from the action, participants are more willing to abandon moral norms, thus preferring the utilitarian choice. However, if the fallen-overboard passenger, such as his brother, was emotionally closer to the participant, the choice would become less rational and utilitarian. Therefore, context also determines the chosen option.

> **The Coastguard Dilemma**
>
> Tassy et al. (2013).[15]
>
> A passenger fell off a coastguard boat of which you are the captain. If, as the captain, you decide to turn back to rescue the passenger, you would consequently be unable to reach and save the four sailors on a sinking boat that you were initially en route to assist.
>
> Is it morally appropriate to abandon the passenger to save the four sailors?

Research showed that when the cognitive system is more activated in a dilemma, which is necessary for utilitarian considerations, the choice becomes less intuitive, and the deontological option is less likely to be chosen.[16] This study presented dilemmas in the participants' native language, either with or without a foreign accent. Interestingly, a foreign accent prompted more utilitarian choices, attributed to factors like increased cognitive effort, diminished emotional response, and greater psychological distance. For example, an accent signals the speaker's external origins, potentially categorising them as belonging to a different social group, thereby introducing psychological distance and encouraging a more abstract, utilitarian approach to the dilemma.

Also, cultural nuances significantly impact how moral dilemmas are perceived in research. An original set of ten moral dilemmas,[17] widely utilised in various studies, was translated into Dutch for use in a Belgian context.[18] However, a pre-test revealed that certain dilemmas did not resonate within the Belgian context as expected. For instance, a dilemma about a teenager considering an abortion was not as contentious in Belgium as in the United States, leading to a unanimous pre-test response and indicating its limited usefulness in distinguishing between participants' moral positions in that context.

The use of stylised hypothetical moral dilemmas, such as the trolley problem, faces criticism for its lack of realism. These scenarios are often overly simplified, fictional, and predictable, offering little insight into the nuances of individual and cultural moral reasoning. Typically presenting only binary choices, these dilemmas fail to capture the complexity of moral decision-making. Incorporating more realistic scenarios might provide a richer understanding of moral complexities. Despite these limitations, moral dilemmas are valuable tools for exploring factors contributing to utilitarian or deontological moral judgement. In these dilemmas, participants' responses often reveal the underlying moral principles or intuitions that guide their decision-making process. In the boardroom, directors may face moral dilemmas that require them to navigate conflicting values, interests, and ethical considerations. Understanding and analysing these dilemmas from both utilitarian and deontological perspectives can contribute to more informed and responsible decision-making.

3.4 Measuring Utilitarian or Deontological Inclinations

Instruments designed to gauge inclinations towards utilitarian and deontological ethics often present dilemmas that pit these two principles against each other.[19] This approach enables the calculation of a conventional score, treating the principles as opposing forces, and a process dissociation (or dual process) score, which considers the principles as two separate, independent processes.

3.4.1 Traditional Score

In conventional studies of utilitarian and deontological ethics, moral dilemma choices are treated as opposites on a spectrum, meaning they are inversely related.[20] These studies employ a single measure that ranges from 0 to 1, with higher scores reflecting stronger deontological tendencies and lower scores indicating a utilitarian inclination.[21] This traditional score is calculated by tallying the instances where participants judge an action in a dilemma as 'inappropriate'. For example, if someone considers 2 out of 10 actions inappropriate, their score would be 0.2, signifying a lean towards utilitarianism. On the other hand, someone who finds 6 out of 10 actions inappropriate would score 0.6, showing a deontological inclination.

3.4.2 Process Dissociation Score

More recent studies assume that utilitarian and deontological considerations are two independent processes.[22] The first, associated with deontological thinking, is characterised as quick, intuitive, affect-driven, and emotionally based. The second, related to utilitarian thinking, is described as slow, deliberate, and reliant on cognitive reasoning, often viewed as more analytical.[23] This concept expands on the dual-process theory, as described by Daniel Kahneman, but in the context of moral judgements investigated by Greene et al.[24]

> **Thinking, Fast and Slow**
>
> Kahneman (2011).[25]
>
> The popular book *Thinking, Fast and Slow* by Nobel laureate Daniel Kahneman will be familiar to many. This book is also based on *dual-processing,* wherein Kahneman explores the psychology of human decision-making. In this book, he introduces two systems of thinking: System 1 and System 2. System 1 is the intuitive, automatic, and fast mode of decision-making, often relying on heuristics, mental shortcuts, and emotional responses. In contrast, System 2 is the reflective, slow, conscious, and rational process of decision-making, primarily driven by logical reasoning and analysis.

Using a process dissociation procedure, it becomes possible to analyse and understand the separate contributions of deontological and utilitarian factors in moral decision-making. This method typically involves presenting individuals with about ten moral dilemmas in two different forms: congruent and incongruent, to tease apart these distinct modes of moral judgement. With congruent moral dilemmas, both deontological and utilitarian perspectives align, resulting in a shared moral judgement. This alignment occurs when an action, based on moral principles (deontological), is deemed inappropriate, and simultaneously, the benefits fail to outweigh the costs (utilitarian). Conversely, incongruent moral dilemmas present a different dynamic, where the two ethical considerations diverge and yield conflicting decisions. In such cases, the action remains inappropriate from a deontological perspective, while from a utilitarian standpoint, the benefits now outweigh the costs, rendering the action acceptable.

For instance, consider the scenario of administering a drug with severe side effects to patients (See Table 3.3).

In the congruent version of this dilemma, both the deontological and utilitarian viewpoints converge in concluding that the action is inappropriate. This agreement arises from the recognition that the advantages (reduced flu suffering) do not outweigh the disadvantages (potential fatalities). In the example of administering the drug in its incongruent variation, a utilitarian viewpoint deems it appropriate due to the potential to save more lives than it may harm. However, from a deontological standpoint (which upholds the principle of not causing harm), it still deems the action as inappropriate.

This method provides a nuanced and insightful approach to examining how individuals navigate their moral decision-making processes, offering a deeper understanding of how moral principles interact with the calculation of potential gains and losses in complex moral dilemmas.

Table 3.3 Example of a moral dilemma: administering a drug with severe side effects

Administering a vaccine	
You are a doctor in a health clinic overrun by patients with a serious disease. You just received a shipment of drugs that can cure the disease, but the drugs have their own severe side effects	
Congruent moral dilemma	**Incongruent moral dilemma**
If you administer the drugs to your patients, a small number will die from the side effects, but most will live. If you do not, most will continue to suffer from the effects of the flu virus for some time	If you administer the drugs to your patients, a small number will die from the side effects, but most will live. If you do not, most will die from the disease
Is it appropriate for you to administer the drug to your patients?	Is it appropriate for you to administer the drug to your patients?

Adapted from Conway and Gawronski (2013)

Methodology

By conducting a comparative analysis of responses to congruent and incongruent moral dilemmas, researchers can quantitatively evaluate individual preferences for either utilitarian or deontological choices in isolation. This analytical approach has been embraced by numerous scholars in the field.[26]

Figure 3.1 provides a visual representation of potential outcomes when individuals are confronted with congruent or incongruent moral dilemmas. It delineates three distinct scenarios: one where utilitarianism guides the response (U), another where deontology steers the response (D), and a third where neither utilitarianism nor deontology significantly influences the response, computed as $((1 - U) * (1 - D))$. This analytical framework enhances our understanding of the multifaceted factors that underpin moral decision-making and the extent to which individuals lean towards utilitarian or deontological considerations when making ethical choices. Comparing responses to congruent and incongruent dilemmas allows for the separate quantification of preferences for utilitarian or deontological options. Just like with the traditional score, both process dissociation scores (PD-scores) are also discrete variables between 0 and 1. They are calculated by comparing the probability of rejecting harm in both the congruent and incongruent dilemmas.

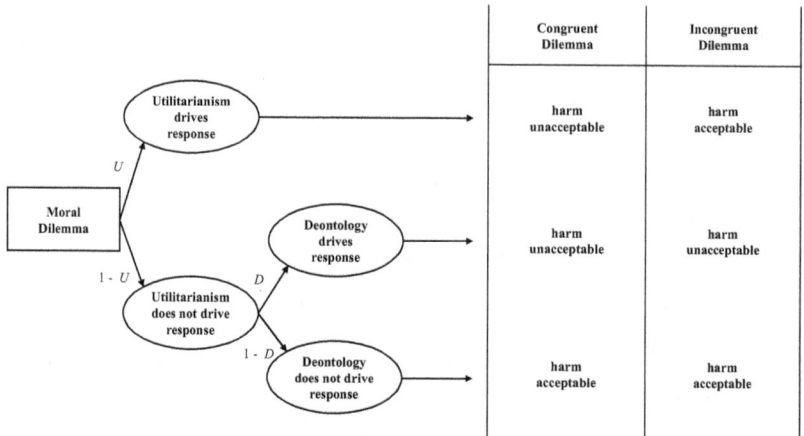

Fig. 3.1 Moral dilemmas and process dissociation (Derived from Conway & Gawronski, 2013, p. 220)

3.5 Moral Identity and Moral Judgement

Many studies that delve into the relationship between moral identity and moral judgement typically operate under the assumption that a stronger moral identity corresponds to heightened deontological inclinations and reduced utilitarian tendencies. Individuals with higher moral identity scores often exhibit a proclivity towards embracing deontological principles, opting for a rule-based approach in their moral decision-making processes rather than engaging in strict cost–benefit analyses.[27] The deontological moral schemes are readily accessible to individuals with stronger moral identities, leading them to prioritise moral considerations over other competing concerns when evaluating specific situations.

The concept of internalised moral identity was explored in relation to ethical leadership.[28] The researchers made a critical distinction between symbolisation, which they characterised as a social role, and internalisation, constituting the private dimension of moral identity. Within the context of their research, they posited that ethical leadership practices, when not rooted in an internalised moral identity, may be adopted solely due to external expectations, or motivated by Machiavellian or utilitarian motives.

> **Machiavellian Motives**
>
> Niccolò Machiavelli.[29]
>
> Machiavellian motives involve the use of strategic, manipulative tactics primarily aimed at acquiring and maintaining power. This approach, inspired by Niccolò Machiavelli's writings, particularly 'The Prince', suggests that achieving one's objectives by any means necessary, even at the expense of ethics or morality, is acceptable. Such motives are characterised by a pragmatic and often ruthless pursuit of power, where the ends are seen to justify the means. This concept is applied across various fields, including politics, business, and interpersonal relationships, highlighting a focus on effectiveness and success above moral or ethical considerations.

Given that deontological inclinations are often closely aligned with intuition, it logically follows that the internalisation facet of moral identity exhibits a stronger association with deontological tendencies, in contrast to the symbolisation aspect. Indeed, some research supported this premise, revealing a significant correlation between the internalisation (private) aspect of moral identity and a preference for deontological inclinations in moral judgement, whereas such a relationship was not observed for the symbolisation (public) aspect of moral identity.[30] Several researchers specifically chose to focus only on the internalisation subscale. This decision was mainly driven by the belief that the internalisation subscale possesses greater predictive power concerning prosocial behaviour, as it captures personal moral self-perceptions rather than public self-presentation. Due to the evolving nature of public discourse on business ethics, ethical leadership behaviour may be adopted for reasons beyond a genuine commitment to ethical norms and values. Given the heightened scrutiny by the public regarding how leaders arrive at their moral decisions, ethical leadership may encompass considerations beyond personal moral identity.

Notes

1. Conway, P., & Gawronski, B. (2013). Deontological and utilitarian inclinations in moral decision making: A process dissociation approach. *Journal of Personality and Social Psychology*, *104*(2), 216–235.
2. Kohlberg, L. (1981). The philosophy of moral development: Moral stages and the idea of justice. Harper & Row.
3. See amongst others McDevitt, R. E., & Maroney, J. J. (2008). The effects of moral reasoning on financial reporting decisions in a

post Sarbanes–Oxley environment. *Behavioral Research in Accounting*, *20*(2), 89–110 and Trevino, L. K. (1986). Ethical decision making in organizations: A person-situation interactionist model. *The Academy of Management Review*, *11*(3), 601–617.
4. Graham, J. W. (2015). Leadership, moral development, and citizenship behavior. *Business Ethics Quarterly*, *5*(1), 43–54.
5. McDevitt, R. E., & Maroney, J. J. (2008). The effects of moral reasoning on financial reporting decisions in a post Sarbanes–Oxley environment. *Behavioral Research in Accounting*, *20*(2), 89–110.
6. Graham, J. W. (2015). Leadership, moral development, and citizenship behavior. *Business Ethics Quarterly*, *5*(1), 43–54.
7. Graham (2015) refers to these definitions by citing Burns (1978) and Greenleaf (1977).
8. In scientific literature, a more precise distinction is made between different terms, including moral judgments, moral decisions, moral behaviour, and moral reasoning, see for an overview Ellemers, N., van der Toorn, J., Paunov, Y., & van Leeuwen, T. (2019). The psychology of morality: A review and analysis of empirical studies published from 1940 through 2017. *Personality and Social Psychology Review*, *23*(4), 332–366.
9. Bartels, D. M., & Pizarro, D. A. (2011). The mismeasure of morals: Antisocial personality traits predict utilitarian responses to moral dilemmas. *Cognition*, *121*(1), 154–161.
10. In scientific literature, a more precise distinction is made between different terms, including moral judgments, moral decisions, moral behaviour, and moral reasoning, see for an overview Ellemers, N., van der Toorn, J., Paunov, Y., & van Leeuwen, T. (2019). The psychology of morality: A review and analysis of empirical studies published from 1940 through 2017. *Personality and Social Psychology Review*, *23*(4), 332–366.
11. See for example, Tassy, S., Oullier, O., Mancini, J., & Wicker, B. (2013). Discrepancies between judgment and choice of action in moral dilemmas. *Frontiers in Psychology*, *4*, 250. Christensen, J. F., Flexas, A., Calabrese, M., Gut, N. K., & Gomila, A. (2014). Moral judgment reloaded: A moral dilemma validation study. *Frontiers in Psychology*, *5*, 607. Gawronski, B., Armstrong, J., Conway, P., Friesdorf, R., & Hutter, M. (2017). Consequences, norms, and generalized inaction in moral dilemmas: The CNI model of moral decision-making. *Journal of Personality and Social Psychology*, *113*(3), 343–376.

12. Foot, P. (1967). The problem of abortion and the doctrine of double effect. *Oxford Review*, *5*, 5–15.
13. Thomson, J. J. (1085) The trolley problem. *The Yale Law Journal*, *94*(6), 1395–1415.
14. Edmonds, D. (2015). Would you kill the fat man? The Trolley Problem and What Your Answer Tells Us About Right and Wrong. Princeton University Press.
15. Tassy, S., Oullier, O., Mancini, J., & Wicker, B. (2013). Discrepancies between judgment and choice of action in moral dilemmas. *Frontiers in Psychology*, *4*, 250.
16. Foucart, A., & Brouwer, S. (2021). Is there a foreign accent effect on moral judgment? *Brain Sciences*, *11*(12), 1631.
17. See for example: Lee, J. J., & Gino, F. (2015). Poker-faced morality: Concealing emotions leads to utilitarian decision making. *Organizational Behavior and Human Decision Processes*, 126, 49–64, and Patil, I., Zucchelli, M. M., Kool, W., Campbell, S., Fornasier, F., Calò, M., Silani, G., Cikara, M., & Cushman, F. (2021). Reasoning supports utilitarian resolutions to moral dilemmas across diverse measures. *Journal of Personality and Social Psychology*, *120*(2), 443–460.
18. Bostyn, D. H., Roets, A., & Van Hiel, A. (2016). Right-wing attitudes and moral cognition: Are right-wing authoritarianism and social dominance orientation related to utilitarian judgment? *Personality and Individual Differences*, *96*, 164–171.
19. Greene, J. D., Sommerville, R. B., Nystrom, L. E., Darley, J. M., & Cohen, J. D. (2001). An fMRI investigation of emotional engagement in moral judgment. *Science*, *293*(5537), 2105–2108.
20. See for example, Conway, P., & Gawronski, B. (2013). Deontological and utilitarian inclinations in moral decision making: a process dissociation approach. *Journal of Personality and Social Psychology*, *104*(2), 216–235, Conway, P., Goldstein-Greenwood, J., Polacek, D., & Greene, J. D. (2018). Sacrificial utilitarian judgments do reflect concern for the greater good: Clarification via process dissociation and the judgments of philosophers. *Cognition*, *179*, 241–265, Korner, A., Deutsch, R., & Gawronski, B. (2020). Using the CNI model to investigate individual differences in moral dilemma judgments. *Personality and Social Psychology Bulletin*, *46*(9), 1392–1407, and Patil, I., Zucchelli, M. M., Kool, W., Campbell, S., Fornasier, F., Calò, M., Silani, G., Cikara, M., & Cushman, F. (2021). Reasoning supports utilitarian resolutions to moral dilemmas across diverse measures. *Journal of Personality and Social Psychology*, *120*(2), 443–460.

21. Hannikainen, I. R., Machery, E., & Cushman, F. A. (2018). Is utilitarian sacrifice becoming more morally permissible? *Cognition, 170*, 95–101.
22. Conway, P., & Gawronski, B. (2013). Deontological and utilitarian inclinations in moral decision making: A process dissociation approach. *Journal of Personality and Social Psychology, 104*(2), 216–235. And Greene, J. D., Cushman, F. A., Stewart, L. E., Lowenberg, K., Nystrom, L. E., & Cohen, J. D. (2009). Pushing moral buttons: The interaction between personal force and intention in moral judgment. *Cognition,* 111(3), 364–371.
23. Conway, P., & Gawronski, B. (2013). Deontological and utilitarian inclinations in moral decision making: A process dissociation approach. Journal of Personality and Social Psychology, *104*(2), 216–235., Patil, I., Zucchelli, M. M., Kool, W., Campbell, S., Fornasier, F., Calò, M., Silani, G., Cikara, M., & Cushman, F. (2021). Reasoning supports utilitarian resolutions to moral dilemmas across diverse measures. *Journal of Personality and Social Psychology, 120*(2), 443–460, and Xu, Z. X., & Ma, H. K. (2015). How can a deontological decision lead to moral behavior? The moderating role of moral identity. *Journal of Business Ethics, 137*(3), 537–549.
24. Greene, J. D., Sommerville, R. B., Nystrom, L. E., Darley, J. M., & Cohen, J. D. (2001). An fMRI investigation of emotional engagement in moral judgment. *Science, 293*(5537), 2105–2108.
25. Kahneman, D. (2011). Thinking, Fast and Slow: Farrar, Straus and Giroux.
26. See for example Bostyn, D. H., Roets, A., & Van Hiel, A. (2016). Right-wing attitudes and moral cognition: Are right-wing authoritarianism and social dominance orientation related to utilitarian judgment? *Personality and Individual Differences,* 96, 164–171. Conway, P., & Gawronski, B. (2013). Deontological and utilitarian inclinations in moral decision making: A process dissociation approach. *Journal of Personality and Social Psychology, 104*(2), 216–235. Patil, I., Zucchelli, M. M., Kool, W., Campbell, S., Fornasier, F., Calò, M., Silani, G., Cikara, M., & Cushman, F. (2021). Reasoning supports utilitarian resolutions to moral dilemmas across diverse measures. *Journal of Personality and Social Psychology,* 120(2), 443–460.
27. Xu, Z. X., & Ma, H. K. (2015). How can a deontological decision lead to moral behavior? The moderating role of moral identity. *Journal of Business Ethics, 137*(3), 537–549.

28. Skubinn, R., & Herzog, L. (2014). Internalized moral identity in ethical leadership. *Journal of Business Ethics*, *133*(2), 249–260.
29. 'The Prince' (Il Principe) is a sixteenth-century treatise by Niccolò Machiavelli, structured as a practical guide for new rulers. Written by the Italian diplomat and political theorist, it famously endorses the view that achieving political power and success can justify the use of immoral tactics. The work is known for its direct approach to the mechanics of political power, emphasising pragmatism over ethical considerations in governance.
30. Xu, Z. X., & Ma, H. K. (2015). How can a deontological decision lead to moral behavior? The moderating role of moral identity. *Journal of Business Ethics*, *137*(3), 537–549.

4

Right-Right Dilemmas

> The really tough choices…don't centre upon right versus wrong. They involve right versus right. They are genuine dilemmas precisely because each side is firmly rooted in one of our basic, core values.
> —Rushworth Kidder, 1995

Adidas employees criticised their directors, accusing them of having 'turned off their moral compass' by ignoring years of harassment by Ye. The CEO of Carlsberg described his dilemma about leaving Russia during the Ukraine war as a 'Catch-22'. Meanwhile, Maastricht University's board referred to the challenge of paying ransom after a cyberattack as a 'Devil's Dilemma'. In these cases, metaphors like a one-direction-only compass or a more opposing-direction scale are employed to capture the complexity of these apparently moral dilemmas.

The often-used reference to the moral compass of directors, or the lack of a moral compass, can be used for dilemmas where directors must choose between ethical and unethical actions, a right-wrong dilemma, because it clearly points in a single direction. Much like a compass that consistently aligns with the magnetic north, one's moral compass guides decisions towards what is unequivocally 'right' or 'wrong'.

However, the metaphor of a moral compass is less suitable for dilemmas that involve two equally positive moral principles that often conflict and are mutually exclusive, a right-right dilemma. Here, a moral compass would not provide clear direction since both choices are ethically justifiable, leaving no 'true north' to follow. Instead, the metaphor of a moral scale is more appropriate. A scale requires careful weighing of both options to determine which aligns best with the core values of the individual or organisation. It acknowledges the complexity of prioritising between two valid moral principles and the need for a nuanced approach to balance conflicting positive ideals.

The founder of the Institute for Global Ethics, Rushworth Kidder, described right-right dilemmas as choosing between two options, both of which are ethically correct or positive but are mutually exclusive.[1] Solving a right-right dilemma requires deep ethical reasoning and reflection, as it involves analysing and prioritising core values. The decision-maker must consider the broader implications of their choice, including long-term effects and the impact on stakeholders. He argued that 'the really tough choices don't centre upon right versus wrong. They involve right versus right. They are genuine dilemmas precisely because each side is firmly rooted in one of our basic, core values'.

4.1 Four Categories of Right-Right Dilemmas

So, right-right dilemmas arise when two equally important values come into conflict, requiring a decision that sacrifices one value for the sake of another. These dilemmas often lack clear guidelines for resolution, making the decision-making process more subjective and dependent on personal or organisational values, ethics, and priorities. Although right-wrong dilemmas may still pose challenges, the presence of a clear ethical guideline or norm often makes the decision-making process more straightforward. The primary challenge may lie in the temptation or pressure to choose the wrong option due to personal gain, fear, or other factors. The complexity of right-right dilemmas lies in their inherent ambiguity and the need for nuanced ethical reasoning, while right-wrong dilemmas challenge individuals and organisations to adhere to ethical principles in the face of potential gains or pressures to do otherwise.

Kidder came up with four classic categories of right-versus-right dilemmas, Truth versus Loyalty, Individual versus Community, Short Term versus Long Term, and Justice versus Mercy(See Fig. 4.1).

These dilemmas are particularly challenging because they require balancing conflicting moral imperatives. Each dilemma represents a clash of fundamental moral principles, making decisions in such contexts especially difficult and often leading to significant ethical reflection and debate.

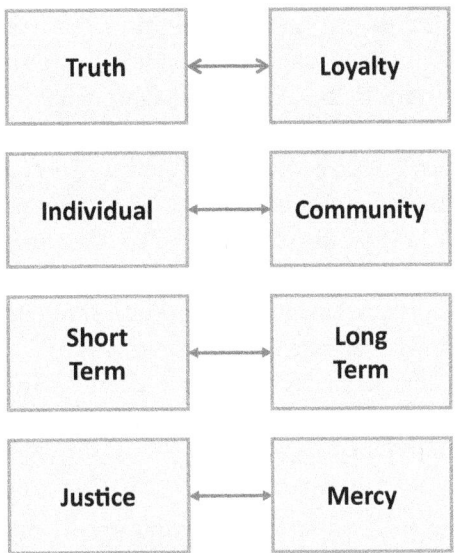

Fig. 4.1 Four right-versus-right dilemmas (Based on Kidder, 1995)

4.1.1 Truth Versus Loyalty

This dilemma arises when directors must choose between being transparent and honest, upholding the value of truth, and remaining loyal to a person, group, or institution. This scenario often arises in situations where disclosing certain information could have significant implications for the organisation or specific individuals within it.

On the one hand, the moral commitment to truth involves upholding principles of transparency and integrity in communication. This might mean sharing information about strategic decisions, challenges, or changes that, while not reflecting misconduct, could still cast a shadow on the perceived competence or decision-making of individuals like the CEO. The imperative to be truthful with stakeholders stems from a belief in the importance of honesty in building trust and credibility, not just within the organisation but also with the wider public and market.

Conversely, the value of loyalty, especially when it concerns individuals, involves a nuanced consideration of the impact that transparency might have on stakeholders and their personal dignity. Loyalty, as a moral value, refers to a commitment or fidelity to individuals, groups, or institutions driven by ethical principles and personal values. In cases where the reputation of the CEO or another key figure is at stake, loyalty might advocate for a more measured approach to transparency. This could involve framing information in a way that is still honest but also mindful of its potential impact, choosing to communicate challenges in the context of learning rather than as personal failings, or delaying communication until later when it is less damaging. This approach is driven by respect for the individual's contributions and an understanding that everyone faces challenges and makes mistakes.

Please note that in this context, the right-right dilemma refers to loyalty as a moral value, not as a legal duty, as defined in US company law. The duty of loyalty as a specific legal requirement is designed to ensure that those who govern and manage corporations do so in the best interests of the corporation and its shareholders, with clear legal ramifications for breaches. In contrast, loyalty as a moral value is guided by personal ethics and principles, which can vary significantly among individuals and contexts, and does not carry legal penalties for violations, though it may have personal or professional consequences.

The ethical challenge in balancing truth and loyalty might not be whether to be honest but in determining how and when to share information. It requires a deep understanding of the consequences of disclosure, not just for the organisation but for the stakeholders involved. Leaders may navigate this dilemma by focusing on the collective responsibility of the board and the executive team, sharing both successes and setbacks as part of the organisation's journey rather than highlighting individual blame.

> **Example: Disclose Investigation into Inappropriate Behaviour Director?**
>
> (see full description of this case in Part II of this book).
>
> In the case of Ajax Football Club, the board faced a significant 'truth versus loyalty' dilemma involving a fellow executive director. Unconfirmed rumours had surfaced regarding the director's inappropriate behaviour, necessitating an investigation. However, this situation coincided with the director's impending reappointment at the Annual General Meeting (AGM), scheduled just two days later. This example now does not relate to the later confirmed inappropriate behaviour (the directors send dick pics to female colleagues) but only to the dilemma of how to act when this behaviour was still a rumour.
>
> The board was caught between two conflicting ethical imperatives. On one hand, the commitment to truth, addressing the rumours by withdrawing his reappointment, posed a direct challenge to fairness and could lead to a premature judgement in the court of public opinion. Publicly associating the director with unverified accusations could unjustly tarnish his reputation, inflicting potentially irreparable personal and professional damage if the rumours were later found to be unfounded.

> Conversely, the principle of loyalty suggested a different path. By proceeding with the reappointment, the board would be extending a measure of trust and support to their colleague, allowing the due process of investigation to unfold without the complicating factor of public scrutiny. This approach would protect the director's reputation in the interim, fostering a presumption of innocence until proven otherwise. However, this would mean endorsing him at the AGM as 'the best candidate for the position', despite knowing about the ongoing investigation, and thus potentially compromising the board's integrity if the allegations were later substantiated.

4.1.2 Individual Versus Community

This type of dilemma pits the rights or needs of the individual against the welfare or needs of the community. It requires directors to evaluate the extent to which the interests of one or a few individuals can be sacrificed for the collective good. However, the concept of 'community' in this context is multifaceted, as it does not pertain to a single, homogeneous entity. Instead, communities can exist at various levels, from the more immediate and smaller groups, such as the workforce of an organisation, to the larger society that, in its own turn, also consists of diverse populations.

When emphasising the well-being of the individual versus that of the community, one must consider the often-competing interests at play. For example, within an organisation, a decision may benefit most of the workforce, such as a policy change that improves overall working conditions or efficiency but might be at the expense of a few individuals who may find their roles diminished or their working conditions adversely affected. In such instances, the welfare of the few is weighed against the benefits realised by the many within that specific community.

Expanding the lens to the larger society introduces additional layers of complexity. Decisions made by an organisation can have far-reaching implications beyond its immediate workforce, affecting local communities, consumers, environmental sustainability, and even global market dynamics. Here, the concept of community broadens, encompassing stakeholders who may not have a direct connection to the organisation but are nonetheless impacted by its actions. For instance, a company may decide to relocate its manufacturing operations overseas to leverage cost efficiencies, benefitting shareholders and potentially leading to lower product prices for consumers. However, this decision could detrimentally affect the local workforce and community from which the company relocates, highlighting the tension between the well-being of these distinct groups.

> **Example: Paying Ransomware?**
>
> (see full description of this case in Part II of this book).
>
> On December 23, 2019, Maastricht University faced a significant security breach when over 200 of its servers were encrypted with malware during a ransomware attack, with hackers demanding a ransom of 200,000 euros in bitcoins. The university's leadership was placed in a challenging position, having to weigh the immediate needs of their academic community against broader societal consequences and the global fight against cybercrime. The dilemma of whether to fulfil the ransom request presented a profound moral quandary for the university's board, described as a 'devil's dilemma'.[2] Failure to pay the ransom would result in an operational shutdown for three to four months, causing estimated financial damages of 20 to 25 million euros per month. This would lead to significant delays in students' education and disruptions in faculty research.[3] However, agreeing to pay the ransom was seen as undesirable, as it would support the economic model of cybercriminals and was considered improper for an institution, given it involved allocating public funds to pay off criminals.[4] Ultimately, prioritising the continuity of its educational and research activities, the university resolved to pay the ransom, thereby obtaining the decryption key needed to unlock the servers. By January 6, 2020, academic operations were able to resume.
>
> Conversely, after experiencing a hack in 2021, another large educational institution, ROC Mondriaan, decided against paying the demanded ransom of 100 bitcoins, equivalent to approximately four million euros at that time. The CEO deemed the ransom exorbitant but stated that payment was never an option, asserting a principled stance of non-payment.[5] This decision was also motivated by the desire to send a clear message, deter future attacks, and the recognition that the ransom constituted a significant amount of taxpayer money.[6]

4.1.3 Short Term Versus Long Term

This dilemma involves a conflict between immediate, short-term, and long-term goals. It involves navigating complex decisions where immediate moral imperatives may conflict with broader, future-oriented ethical considerations.

In the short term, moral dilemmas might revolve around pressing issues such as ensuring fairness, justice, and respect for current customers, employees, and society. On the other hand, long-term moral considerations require looking beyond the present to anticipate and mitigate potential ethical challenges that could arise for future stakeholders, even those not yet born. This could involve ethical stewardship, such as adopting sustainable business practices that protect the environment for future generations or investing in products and technologies that are expected to bring long-term benefits to society, even if they do not address immediate needs or generate quick returns.

Commitment to addressing present needs or current issues, which are vital for maintaining trust and integrity in the relationship between a company and its current stakeholders, may be reflected in actions that are guided by principles of doing no harm, actively doing good, and ensuring fairness and equity. Conversely, investing money, time, and effort in long-term initiatives might not yield immediate benefits for current stakeholders and could even require sacrifices, such as diverting funds from short-term projects, temporarily accepting an ongoing injustice or lower profit margins. However, they are driven by the principles to prevent future harm that today's activities could cause and to ensure that future generations inherit a world where they can thrive. This side of the dilemma is about legacy, stewardship, and the moral responsibility of leaving the world better than we found it.

> **Example: Leaving Russia in a Hurry or Buying Time?**
>
> (see full description of this case in Part II of this book).
>
> Several companies faced a short-term versus long-term moral dilemma after Russia's invasion of Ukraine in March 2022. On one hand, the impulse to immediately leave Russia was driven by the desire to make a clear and urgent moral statement: distancing from a regime led by Putin, which was guilty of human rights violations, and renouncing any financial benefit, direct or indirect, from this war. The immediate announcement by companies such as Heineken to leave Russia aligned with global calls for responsibility and justice, reflecting a commitment to ethical principles over short-term business interests.[87] However, a rapid exit also posed potentially severe consequences. Local employees and their families would lose their livelihoods, and local management faced a significant risk of imprisonment due to Russian legislation criminalising an abrupt departure. Moreover, a hasty exit could lead to the seizure of business assets, inadvertently benefiting Putin and his regime by transferring valuable property for free.
>
> A more measured withdrawal, aimed at responsibly selling off operations, was the longer-term option. This required continuing production, as otherwise, there would be no business unit to sell. This approach would protect the jobs of local workers and their families, prevent the imprisonment of local management, and reduce the risk of nationalisation and the resulting enrichment of the Russian regime, potentially making it a better option in the long term. Nonetheless, this strategy carried its own moral costs: it was seen as a lack of immediate condemnation of the war and Russia's actions, leading to criticism for prioritising financial results over a clear ethical stance.[8]

> The CEO of the Danish brewer Carlsberg, Cees 't Hart, referred to this in the Financial Times as a 'Catch-22'.[9] Nationalisation later proved to be a legitimate fear, with Carlsberg being nationalised by Putin in July 2023.[10] Heineken sold its Russian business unit for 1 Euro in August 2023, with a loss of 300 million Euros.[11]

4.1.4 Justice Versus Mercy

Here, the justice versus mercy dilemma is between, on the one hand, adhering strictly to rules and principles and doing justice when they are breached (justice) and, on the other hand, showing compassion or mercy for people who may have made a mistake but apologised. This dilemma refers to the contrast between a zero-tolerance policy and a permissive attitude towards making mistakes. A culture where mistakes are allowed encourages a merciful approach, recognising that errors are an integral part of learning and development. This philosophy acknowledges that to innovate, grow, and improve, individuals must feel safe to take risks, experiment, and, inevitably, sometimes fail. A zero-tolerance policy represents a firm commitment to justice, emphasising the importance of rules, standards, and consequences. In such a framework, actions that violate policies or expectations are met with predetermined, often strict, penalties, regardless of the circumstances or intentions behind the violation. This approach aims to deter less ethical or undesirable behaviour by demonstrating that such actions will invariably lead to sanctions, reinforcing a clear understanding of what is unacceptable within an organisation or community.

> **Example: Accept a Lie After (Sincere) Excuses?**
>
> (see full description of this case in Part II of this book).
>
> The case of Yahoo and its CEO, Scott Thompson, presents an example of the justice versus mercy dilemma faced by corporate boards. Thompson was found to have inaccurately stated his academic credentials on his resume, a revelation that placed the board in a difficult position. On one hand, they had the option to enforce justice by terminating Thompson for dishonesty, emphasising the importance of integrity and accountability at the highest levels of the company. Such a decision would serve as a clear statement that ethical breaches, regardless of their nature, would not be tolerated, aligning with the principle of justice that demands consequences for wrongful actions.

On the other hand, the board had the option to show mercy by allowing Thompson to apologise and remain in his role, also considering his strong performance as CEO. This decision would underscore the value of forgiveness and the belief in second chances, particularly when an individual demonstrates remorse and a commitment to change.[12]

If the board viewed the resume misrepresentation as a severe ethical violation, a strong stance like termination could be justified to underscore the non-negotiable nature of honesty and accountability within the organisation. Conversely, if the board considered the possibility of genuine remorse and saw value in Thompson's reflection and willingness to rectify his mistake, a less severe penalty (for example, withholding his bonus) coupled with a chance for redemption could embody a more merciful approach.

However, the situation took a decisive turn when Thompson's response to the controversy did not align with the board's expectations for accountability and contrition. Instead of displaying genuine remorse, Thompson's reaction was perceived as aggrieved and defensive. The pivotal moment came when he was implicated in a second deceit, further undermining his credibility and trustworthiness. This subsequent revelation shattered any remaining confidence the board might have had in his ability to lead with integrity. This second lie 'was the final straw', according to one of the directors.[13]

4.2 Dirty Hands

The concept of 'dirty hands' in ethical decision-making refers to moral dilemmas and the compromises individuals must navigate when their decisions involve significant ethical trade-offs. Traditionally, the 'dirty hands' problem is associated with situations where politicians face a choice between two morally questionable options, often referred to as wrong-wrong dilemmas. In 1973, political scientist, philosopher, and professor at the Institute for Advanced Study at Princeton explored the dilemmas faced by political leaders who must sometimes engage in morally questionable actions for the sake of a greater political good or necessity.[14] These are scenarios where every available option seems to involve some form of ethical compromise or violation, forcing leaders to choose the lesser of two evils.

> Why would someone with clean hands, a moral person, do something that is morally wrong? Because it is the right thing to do.
> —Michael Walzer, 2023

Fifty years later, in 2023, Walzer reacted to the criticism he received over the last 50 years, that his essay 'is used in introductory philosophy courses as an example of philosophical incoherence'.[15] Incoherence here refers to the main assertion of the essay that certain actions, though right to undertake, are simultaneously wrong. However, Walzer notes that 'dirty hands' was not meant 'to identify or condemn a perennial wrongdoer whose hands are always dirty; it's about someone with clean hands getting them dirty. How does one do that? By doing something it is morally wrong to do; moral wrongdoing dirties the hands. And why would someone with clean hands, a moral person, do something that is morally wrong? Because it is the right thing to do'.

4.2.1 Jean-Paul Sartre

The term 'dirty hands', originates from Jean-Paul Sartre's play 'Les Mains Sales'.[16]

> **Les Maines Sales, Jean-Paul Sartre[17]**
>
> "How desperately you cling to your purity, young man! How afraid you are to soil your hands! Well, remain pure! What good will it do you? Why did you come to us? Purity is an idea for a yogi or a monk... To do nothing, to stay motionless, arms at your side, wearing kid gloves. Well, I have dirty hands. Right up to the elbows. I've plunged them in filth and blood. But what do you hope? Do you think you can govern innocently?"

This quote is part of a crucial confrontation between Hugo, a young, idealistic member of the Communist Party, and Hoederer, a pragmatic, older party leader with whom Hugo has been living under the same roof, assigned to assassinate him. The dialogue unfolds in the context of political strategy and moral dilemmas faced by the party members during a fictional European conflict.

Just before this quote, Hugo and Hoederer engage in a tense and philosophical debate about the nature of political action, ethics, and the compromises required by revolutionary activity. Hugo is torn between his desire to remain morally pure and his assignment to kill Hoederer, who he sees as betraying the party's ideals by negotiating with the fascists. Hoederer, on the other hand, argues for a more pragmatic approach to politics, one that requires dirty hands because it deals with the complexity of real-life situations and the need to make hard choices for the greater good. Joseph Badaracco, a former professor of Ethics at Harvard, derived from this passage that 'men and women who have power over the lives and livelihoods of others will almost inevitably have to dirty their hands, not in the sense of rolling up their sleeves and working hard, but in the sense of losing their moral innocence'.[18]

4.2.2 Dirty Hands for Right-Right Dilemmas?

The existence of right-right dilemmas highlights the potential for moral standards to clash, forcing directors to make profound choices. When directors are torn between two ethically positive options, their decisions might be misunderstood or even morally compromising. So, why can the application of the 'dirty hands' concept not also be extended to right-right dilemmas? In such cases, the 'dirty hands' emerges from the feeling that, in selecting one right course of action, one inevitably neglects or compromises another equally valid moral principle. Therefore, even when selecting what seems to be the correct choice, directors might still encounter a feeling of ethical unease or discomfort, sensing that they have not completely adhered to all ethical principles. This sensation can intensify when stakeholders perceive a situation that originally presents a choice between two 'right' options as a conflict between right and wrong, especially if they believe that compromising on one of the ethical values is truly incorrect and unethical.

This broader interpretation of 'dirty hands' acknowledges the complexity of ethical decision-making in real-world contexts, where choices are rarely clear-cut and often involve navigating a labyrinth of competing moral values and practical considerations. It highlights the inherent challenges in striving for ethical leadership and the often unavoidable nature of moral compromise in the pursuit of the common good.

4.2.3 Moral Dilemmas Need Some Courage

Moral dilemmas, characterised by the necessity to choose between two morally compromising or conflicting options, demand more than just analytical skills or ethical reasoning; they require courage to act despite the inherent risks and moral burdens involved. Whether facing a right-right dilemma (choosing between two good but incompatible actions) or a wrong-wrong dilemma (choosing the lesser of two evils), courage is the linking pin that enables directors to take decisive action. It involves the readiness to make sacrifices, acknowledging that every choice might lead to some form of moral compromise or loss.

Directors are required to make tough choices and take responsibility for them, even when those decisions carry significant moral and ethical weight. Sometimes, doing nothing or sidestepping the issue might seem easier or less ethically demanding. The courage to choose in a moral dilemma with no clear-cut ethical solutions involves acknowledging the ethical ambiguity and accepting that any choice made will have its moral costs. It also requires taking responsibility: being prepared to bear the moral and sometimes public accountability for the decisions made. Directors must be ready to defend their choices, not just on pragmatic grounds but on moral ones, fully aware that their decisions might be scrutinised, criticised, or even condemned. Balancing various ethical imperatives, stakeholder interests, and the greater good demands the courage to make unpopular or difficult decisions while maintaining one's company values as well as one's own values.

Notes

1. Kidder, R.M. (1995), How Good People Make Tough Choices, William Morrow; First Edition (January 24, 1995).
2. 'Zeer grote morele bezwaren' tegen betaling losgeld ("Very strong moral objections" against paying ransom), Observant, February 5, 2020.
3. Als ik een beroep doe op mensen om te werken met kerst, dan moet ik er zelf ook zijn ('If I ask people to work on Christmas, then I must be there myself'), Riki Janssen, Observant, December 11, 2020.
4. Binnen zonder kloppen—Digitale weerbaarheid in het hoger onderwijs, ('Enter Without Knocking—Digital Resilience in Higher Education, Ministry of Education, Culture and Science, July 2021.
5. Overheid in actie tegen betalen van losgeld aan ransomware-criminelen ('Government Takes Action Against Paying Ransom to Ransomware Criminals'), Joost Schellevis, NOS, September 19, 2021.
6. Wat als je ICT-systeem wordt gehackt? Het gebeurde bij ROC Mondriaan ('What If Your ICT System Gets Hacked? It Happened at ROC Mondriaan), Interview with PO Council, December 23, 2021.
7. Heineken stops production and sale of Heineken beer in Russia, Heineken Press release, March 9, 2022.
8. See for example, 'Heineken breekt belofte en investeert toch in Rusland' ('Heineken breaks promise and invests in Russia anyway'), Olivier van Beemen, Follow the Money, February 21, 2023, 'Carlsberg-ceo Cees't Hart over vertrek uit Rusland'. 'Alsof de regels van het schaakspel werden herschreven' ('Carlsberg CEO Cees 't Hart on leaving Russia. 'As if the rules of the chess game were being rewritten'), Pieter Couwenbergh, het FD, July 14, 2022, and 'Hoekstra: Investeringen in Rusland moreel niet uit te leggen' ('Hoekstra:

'Investments in Russia morally indefensible'), BNR, February 21, 2023.
9. Carlsberg seeks buyback clause as it nears exit from Russia, Financial Times, February 7, 2023.
10. Russia seizes control of shares in Danone and Carlsberg subsidiaries, The Guardian, July 17, 2023.
11. Heineken completes exit from Russia, Press release, August 23, 2023.
12. In the Undoing of a C.E.O., A Puzzle, James B. Stewart, The New York Times, May 18, 2012.
13. Yahoo's Chief to Leave as Company Strikes Deal With Loeb, Michael J. De La Merced & Evelyn M. Rusli, The New York Times, May 13, 2012.
14. Walzer, M. (1973). Political action: The problem of dirty hands. Philosophy & public affairs, 160–180.
15. Walzer, M. (2023). Dirty hands revisited. *The Journal of Ethics*, 27(4), 441–460.
16. Badaracco, J. L. (1997). Dirty Hands. In defining moments: When managers must choose between right and right. Harvard Business School Press.
17. Sartre, J-P., (1948), Les mains sale, Gallimard. Parijs.
18. Badaracco, J. L. (1997). Dirty Hands. In defining moments: When managers must choose between right and right. Harvard Business School Press.

5

Stakeholderism

> When all is said and done, how do we measure better versus worse?
> —Michael Jensen in 2002

Previous chapters have highlighted that some directors might opt for choices maximising utility through cost–benefit analysis (utilitarian inclination), whereas other directors might adhere to moral principles (deontological inclination). Despite the apparent moral superiority of deontological reasoning due to its emphasis on universal moral norms, utilitarianism also may hold deep moral significance, while it is rooted in the moral duty to maximise well-being or happiness for the largest possible group.[1] The utilitarian approach requires that directors choose the option that maximises utility. But this leaves directors with a starting question: which utilities should be maximised? Or, 'when all is said and done, how do we measure better versus worse?'[2]

This book uses the concept of 'stakeholderism' to describe the commitment of directors to maximising the welfare of all stakeholders.[3] Stakeholderism is seen as a moral obligation to treat all stakeholders equitably and balance their interests, costs, and benefits. *Shareholderism* is defined as a motivated, principled approach to increasing shareholder value, and *stakeholderism* is an equally principled approach where there are multiple equally important stakeholders, of which the group of shareholders is just one. Stakeholderism implies that directors make and implement decisions that satisfy all groups that have a stake in the company as much as possible, including shareholders, employees, customers, suppliers, communities, and other groups. It is opposed to shareholderism that discourages unnecessary allocation of money, time, or other resources to other stakeholders: directors should maximise the return for shareholders.[4]

5.1 Maximising Which Utility

Individual directors may lean more towards a stakeholder or shareholder viewpoint (See Table 5.1). Those with a stakeholder orientation concentrate on harmonising the varied interests of different stakeholders, following the principles of Freeman's Stakeholder Theory.[5] Conversely, those favouring a shareholder perspective prioritise efficiency and profit maximisation for shareholders, aligning with Friedman's Shareholder Theory.[6] The stakeholder model advocates for fair and just treatment of all stakeholders, ensuring equitable consideration of their interests, costs, and benefits.[7] Thus, we could see this model as a form of utilitarianism, aiming to maximise overall utility or happiness, not just for shareholders but for all stakeholders. Directors must balance their own moral standards and those of the external environment with their duty to act in the company's and all stakeholders' interests.

In line with 'the greatest happiness of the greatest number' by Bentham, corporate law professor Loewenstein argued that the utilitarian approach in companies also ultimately comes down to maximising 'happiness' to all stakeholders because this is the only thing that ultimately makes life better.[8] He described the developments in the United States, stating that the primacy of the shareholder should no longer be leading and that companies should act in a more socially responsible way. Directors should consider the effect of their actions on stakeholders other than just shareholders and be guided by morality, doing the right thing, when making business judgements. Loewenstein illustrated that this could lead to surprising implications in the

Table 5.1 Stakeholderism versus shareholderism

Stakeholderism Freeman (1984)	Shareholderism Friedman (1970), Jensen en Meckling (1976)
• Creating value for all stakeholders • Stakeholders: employees, customers, suppliers, society, shareholders • Involvement through stakeholder dialogues • Performance measurement: financial, social, environmental, societal • Long term • Impact	• Maximising shareholder value • Stakeholders: shareholders • Decision-making in shareholders' meeting • Performance measurement: financial performance • Short term • Output

boardroom. The decision to dissolve a company, for example, would be a disadvantageous decision for the shareholder but could, on balance, create the greatest happiness in the world if it benefits other stakeholders (even future ones) and would be a good decision. And because no one's happiness should be given higher priority than that of someone else, directors who try to maximise this utility (happiness) might decide that dissolving the company is indeed the right choice.

On the other hand, Harvard professor Michael Jensen argued that directors should start with the questions: 'What are we trying to achieve?' Or: 'When all is said and done, how do we measure better versus worse?' Almost thirty years after his Agency Theory (1976), a theory that is primarily aimed at protecting shareholder interests, Jensen came up in 2002 in the context of increased attention to the stakeholder model with an 'enlightened view on value maximisation'.[9] It should be noted that the Agency Theory painted a rather negative and distrustful image of executive directors: if you do not give executive directors clear goals, partly driven by bonuses, and the non-executives do not properly monitor them, the executive directors will pursue their own interests. According to this theory, executive directors are opportunistic, self-enriching, and self-interest-pursuing managers whom non-executives, on behalf of the shareholders, must supervise.[10]

According to Jensen, directors should, therefore, only make decisions that increase the total market value of the company in the long term. Directors who claim to act from the perspective of all stakeholders, as long-term value creation models imply, pretend to make decisions that consider the interests of all stakeholders. One of the problems Jensen sees with this is that it is impossible to maximise more than one dimension at the same time unless the dimensions are monotone transformations of each other. Directors can, therefore, not make considered decisions, let alone that non-executives can meaningfully supervise this. According to Jensen, steering on multiple forms of value creation, therefore, increases the agency problem. It gives executive directors 'unlimited power' to do almost anything they want, and they are only deterred by the discipline of the financial markets. In non-profit organisations, this problem would be even greater, because for this group the discipline of a financial market does not exist.

Previous research suggested that especially profit organisations can have conflicting demands from different stakeholders, such as making the greatest profits in the best interests of shareholders, being a 'good community citizen' in communities where the company is represented, being a generous caretaker of employees, and producing and delivering the highest-quality product for the customer.[11] These conflicting demands can justify actions that others would call immoral or unethical.

In addition to the discipline imposed by financial markets, another influential form of disciplinary action exists that extends its reach beyond profit-driven entities to encompass both for-profit and non-profit organisations. This form hinges on the approval or disapproval of society at large, making it a powerful driver of decision-making. In numerous instances, both profit-oriented companies and non-profit organisations have found themselves compelled to reevaluate their choices in the wake of societal outrage or acclaim.

5.2 The Pyramid of Corporate Social Responsibility

The responsibilities of directors towards both shareholders and stakeholders can also be seen as not an either/or proposition but as a comprehensive, multifaceted approach to business ethics and social responsibility. In his 1991-pyramid model of Corporate Social Responsibility (CSR), emeritus professor in management Archie Caroll articulated a nuanced and layered approach to conceptualising the responsibilities of corporations[12] (See Fig. 5.1).

This pyramid posits four main types of responsibilities: economic, legal, ethical, and philanthropic, each layer building upon the previous layer to illustrate a company's broad spectrum of obligations. The model expands on the stakeholder-model idea that fulfilling responsibilities across these layers

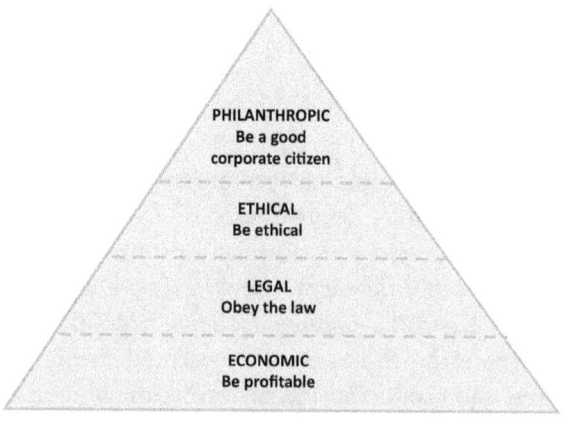

Fig. 5.1 Pyramid of corporate social responsibility. Adapted from Carroll (1991)

benefits a wider array of stakeholders, encompassing employees, consumers, communities, and the environment, thereby advocating for a more inclusive and sustainable approach to business operations.

At the base of the pyramid are the economic responsibilities of a corporation, which align closely with the traditional shareholder model. This foundation underscores that a company's primary duty is to be profitable; it's 'the foundation upon which all others rest'. Profitability is not just for the benefit of shareholders in terms of dividends and increased stock value but also serves as the engine that powers all other CSR activities. Without economic success, a corporation cannot fulfil additional responsibilities.

Building on this economic foundation, the pyramid includes legal responsibilities, which represent the company's obligation to comply with laws and regulations: 'law is society's codification of right or wrong, play by the rules'. These responsibilities are vital to both shareholder and stakeholder models, ensuring that the company operates within the bounds of legality, thus safeguarding the interests of all parties.

The next layer encompasses ethical responsibilities, beyond mere compliance with laws and focuses on doing 'what is right, fair and just, and avoid harm'. This level acknowledges the stakeholder model that companies operate as part of a broader social fabric and have a duty to conduct themselves in a manner that respects the rights and interests of all stakeholders, including employees, customers, suppliers, and the broader community.

At the pinnacle of the pyramid is philanthropic responsibility, which goes beyond what is expected or required by ethics or law and moves into the realm of corporate citizenship and benevolence. This top layer highlights voluntary actions by companies to improve the quality of life for employees, local communities, and society at large. It reflects the stakeholder model's principle that companies should contribute positively to society, reinforcing the idea that businesses have a role in supporting social causes and addressing global challenges.

In 2016, Carroll readdressed the CSR Pyramid by stating that businesses, and their directors, should simultaneously meet four key responsibilities: economic, legal, ethical, and philanthropic, rather than sequentially.[13] The role of business in society should be seen as a unified whole, where economic and legal duties are mandatory, while ethical and philanthropic efforts are expected and desired. He argued that essentially a firm's total social responsibility is the sum of these four areas, aiming to be profitable, law-abiding, ethical, and socially beneficial at the same time.

5.3 The Purpose of a Corporation

The Anglo-Saxon perspective on the purpose of a corporation, prevalent in countries like the United States and the United Kingdom, is characterised by a shareholder-centric approach: shareholderism. From this perspective, the primary goal of corporations is to maximise shareholder value, with corporate directors bound by a legal duty of loyalty to act in the best interests of shareholders. This duty reinforces a focus on financial returns, often driving decisions that prioritise short-term profits. The evidence of this approach can be seen in market-based financial systems where stock market performance is a key indicator of success, and corporate governance structures, such as executive compensation tied to stock performance, encourage strategies aimed at maximising shareholder returns.

Conversely, the European mainland perspective, seen in countries like Germany, France, and The Netherlands, leans more towards stakeholderism. These countries advocate for a balance in considering the interests of various stakeholders, including employees, customers, suppliers, the community, and the environment, in addition to shareholders. Legal and structural frameworks in these countries, such as Germany's 'Mitbestimmung' (co-determination) law that allows for significant employee representation on company boards, or the Dutch consensus-based decision-making model, embody this philosophy by ensuring that corporate decisions reflect a broader set of interests. The French corporate law incorporates the concept of 'intérêt social', which encourages directors to consider the company's interest in a way that balances the needs of all stakeholders. This stakeholder-centric approach often encourages a longer-term view of corporate success and sustainability, focusing on ethical practices and the broader social and environmental impacts of business operations.

The distinction between Anglo-Saxon shareholderism and European stakeholderism is not absolute, with both perspectives influencing practices across these divides. In the United States, the Business Roundtable's shift towards a broader stakeholder focus exemplifies a move away from strict shareholder primacy, indicating a blending of models. Similarly, European firms sometimes adopt shareholder value strategies to remain competitive globally. These examples highlight a growing convergence between the two approaches, suggesting a more nuanced corporate governance landscape where traditional models evolve to incorporate broader societal and economic considerations.

5.3.1 The US Business Roundtable

In August 2019, the US Business Roundtable released a statement that redefined the purpose of a corporation, shifting from prioritising shareholder interests to acknowledging a broader responsibility towards all stakeholders.[14] The Business Roundtable, established in 1972, is an association of CEOs of America's leading companies. While the Business Roundtable's statements are not legally binding, they serve as influential recommendations that can shape corporate governance trends and practices in the US Corporations may look to these guidelines when formulating their governance strategies, policies, and practices.

The 2019 declaration highlighted that corporations should serve not only their shareholders but also their customers, employees, suppliers, communities, and the environment. This move towards a stakeholder-oriented governance model marked a transition towards more inclusive and sustainable business practices, recognising the importance of a corporation's wider ecosystem of stakeholders for long-term success and societal welfare. It was signed by 181 CEOs, among who were Jeff Bezos of Amazon, Tim Cook of Apple, Mary Barra of General Motors, and Doug McMillon of Walmart.

Following this declaration, a mixed reaction came from various sectors. Critics argued that while the statement was a step in the right direction towards more ethical and sustainable business practices, actual implementation lagged. Some pointed out a lack of tangible change in corporate behaviour, suggesting that the statement was more of a public relations move than a commitment to real action. Concerns were raised about the vagueness of the commitments and the absence of accountability mechanisms to ensure corporations followed through on their promises. Moreover, sceptics highlighted that, despite these announced intentions, many companies continued to prioritise profits over people and the planet, questioning the sincerity of the commitment to stakeholder capitalism.

In April 2020, after observing the actions of several signatory companies in response to the COVID-19 pandemic, The New York Times published an article titled '*Big Business Pledged Gentler Capitalism. It's Not Happening in a Pandemic*', pointing out that the rhetoric of prioritising stakeholders hasn't fundamentally altered American capitalism.[15] It remains focused on 'where the money flows'. The article quotes Harvard professor Lawrence Katz, who argues that companies paying dividends or bonuses to executives are clearly violating the norms that the Business Roundtable vowed, saying, 'It just seems both inappropriate and short-sighted'.

> It just seems both inappropriate and short-sighted
> —Lawrence Katz in 2020

Despite the criticism, the Business Roundtable's statement has sparked ongoing discussions and debates about the role of corporations in society, the importance of sustainable and ethical business practices, and the need for genuine efforts to balance the interests of all stakeholders for the greater good. The debate continues on how best to operationalise this broader vision of corporate responsibility and ensure that companies genuinely adopt a stakeholder-oriented approach in their governance models.

> **Statement of the Purpose of a Corporation**
>
> US Business Roundtable (2019).
>
> Americans deserve an economy that allows each person to succeed through hard work and creativity and to lead a life of meaning and dignity. We believe the free-market system is the best means of generating good jobs, a strong and sustainable economy, innovation, a healthy environment, and economic opportunity for all.
>
> Businesses play a vital role in the economy by creating jobs, fostering innovation, and providing essential goods and services. Businesses make and sell consumer products; manufacture equipment and vehicles; support the national defence; grow and produce food; provide health care; generate and deliver energy; and offer financial, communications, and other services that underpin economic growth.
>
> While each of our individual companies serves its own corporate purpose, we share a fundamental commitment to all of our stakeholders. We commit to:
>
> 1. Delivering value to our customers. We will further the tradition of American companies leading the way in meeting or exceeding customer expectations.
> 2. Investing in our employees. This starts with compensating them fairly and providing important benefits. It also includes supporting them through training and education that help develop new skills for a rapidly changing world. We foster diversity and inclusion, dignity, and respect.
> 3. Dealing fairly and ethically with our suppliers. We are dedicated to serving as good partners to the other companies, large and small, that help us meet our missions.
> 4. Supporting the communities in which we work. We respect the people in our communities and protect the environment by embracing sustainable practices across our businesses.
> 5. Generating long-term value for shareholders, who provide the capital that allows companies to invest, grow, and innovate. We are committed to transparency and effective engagement with shareholders.

> Each of our stakeholders is essential. We commit to deliver value to all of them, for the future success of our companies, our communities, and our country.

5.4 Measuring Stakeholderism

The Stakeholderism vs Shareholderism-measurement tool, developed by Professor Renee Adams and colleagues, offers a way to assess how directors weigh the needs of various stakeholders.[16] Built on five distinct scenarios, respondents are required to evaluate two statements per scenario that pits shareholder interests against those of consumers, employees, creditors, and the broader community.

The first four vignettes are derived from specific cases. The *consumer scenario* refers to Dodge v. Ford (1919), where Ford Motor Company wanted to use its surplus funds to benefit consumers and employees, but the court ruled a corporation is primarily for the profit of the stockholders. The *employees' scenario* refers to Parke v. Daily News (1962) and involves a UK newspaper company deciding to liquidate and pay employees and pensioners beyond their legal entitlements. The court ruled the proceeds should only go to shareholders. The *creditors scenario* refers to Credit Lyonnais v. Pathé (1991) and MGM's financial distress, where the court suggested the board has duties to the corporate enterprise, especially near insolvency, implying actions might favour creditors over shareholders to avoid further financial distress. The community scenario refers to Shlensky v. Wrigley (1968), which involved the refusal to install lights at Wrigley Field for night baseball games, prioritising community impact over financial gain, with the court supporting this decision despite financial losses. For the fifth scenario, regarding *the corporate philosophy*, respondents are asked to choose between a monist shareholder-oriented philosophy and a pluralist stakeholder-oriented philosophy for a firm's website, exploring preferences for corporate governance orientations. This choice reflects more than theoretical preference; it reveals the participant's deeper corporate values and priorities.

Although the four real-life situations might seem a bit outdated, they still serve to examine attitudes towards the balance between shareholder interests and other stakeholder considerations in corporate decision-making. The two statements for each scenario are scored on a 1 to 6 scale, indicating the extent of consideration (agree-disagree) for each stakeholder group. This tool's comprehensive method seeks to understand the balance directors must strike, offering insight into how they prioritise stakeholder and shareholder interests.

5.4.1 An Example

The scenario where the interest of the consumer is weighed against the interest of the shareholder was derived by Adams and her colleagues from a 1919 lawsuit involving car manufacturer Henry Ford. Henry Ford advocated for cheaper cars so more people could enjoy them: 'I don't believe we should make such a huge profit on our cars. A reasonable profit is good, but not too much. I believe it is better to sell a large number of cars at a small profit. I hold this view because it allows a larger number of people to buy a car and enjoy its use and because it provides a larger number of people with good-wage jobs'.

> **Consumer as Stakeholder**
> Example adapted from Adams et al. (p.1354), based on Dodge v. Ford (1919).
>
> Corporation F is a manufacturer of consumer goods. Despite considerable competition, Company F is a very profitable corporation thanks to patented technology and manufacturing know-how. In recent years the company has been paying out only small amounts as regular dividends. The corporation now contemplates ways for using its very high capital surplus.
>
> Suppose you are a director in F. To what extent would you agree with the following statements?
> The company should …
> … distribute almost all of its undistributed profits to its shareholders.
> … reduce the price of its products to benefit consumers.
>
> * Answers on a scale of 1 = strongly disagree, 6 = strongly agree.

5.5 Stakeholderism, Moral Judgement, and Moral Identity

Several studies indicated that individuals possessing a strong moral identity are more inclined towards prosocial actions, like volunteering or aiding others, and less prone to engaging in deviant or unethical behaviours. Additionally, moral identity seems to influence a person's resolve to uphold personal beliefs, even when faced with social pressures to conform, such as the phenomenon of groupthink. Also, previous research revealed that as the number of lives saved in moral dilemmas increased, participants were more likely to make utilitarian choices, thus deviating from their earlier, more deontological inclinations.[17] This would lead to the hypothesis that a higher moral identity would correlate with elevated levels in both deontological and utilitarian metrics.[18] However, this anticipated positive link between moral identity and utilitarian thinking is not consistently observed. Researchers attribute this to potential conflicting influences: individuals might opt for utilitarian solutions due to underlying emotional deficiencies, such as a degree of psychopathy or Machiavellian tendencies (manipulation and deceit for personal gain). Conversely, some might choose utilitarianism out of a sincere concern for the well-being of others. This latter group might hold a reasoned belief that utilitarianism is the most effective means to achieve the goals of morality.[19] Directors with a higher level of stakeholderism feel a moral duty to pursue the general welfare of all stakeholders and make a cost–benefit analysis based on that. If this general welfare is at stake, directors with a relatively higher moral identity will also score higher on utilitarian considerations.

The results of the study of Adams suggested that directors' strategic decisions are influenced by their personal values and roles, significantly affecting their stance on shareholderism versus stakeholderism.[20] It emphasised that directors' choices are shaped by personal values rather than just external regulations. The research underscored the importance of considering individual motivations in corporate governance reforms, challenging the efficacy of reforms focused solely on formal measures. The authors called for an approach that integrates subjective factors, which could either support or challenge such reforms based on their underlying values.

Notes

1. Conway, P., & Gawronski, B. (2013). Deontological and utilitarian inclinations in moral decision making: A process dissociation approach. *Journal of Personality and Social Psychology*, *104*(2), 216–235.
2. Jensen, M. C. (2002). Value maximization, stakeholder theory, and the corporate objective function. *Business Ethics Quarterly*, *12*(2), 235–256.
3. Adams, R. B., Licht, A. N., & Sagiv, L. (2011). Shareholders and stakeholders: How do directors decide? *Strategic Management Journal*, *32*(12), 1331–1355.

4. Friedman, M. (1970). The social responsibility of business is to increase its profits. New York Times. And Jensen, M. C. (2002). Value maximization, stakeholder theory, and the corporate objective function. *Business Ethics Quarterly, 12*(2), 235–256.
5. Freeman, R. E. (1984). Strategic management: A stakeholder approach. Boston.
6. Friedman, M. (1970). The social responsibility of business is to increase its profits. New York Times.
7. Freeman, R. E. E., & McVea, J. (2001). A stakeholder approach to strategic management. *SSRN Electronic Journal,* 1–32.
8. Loewenstein, M. J., & Geyer, J. (2021). Shareholder primacy and the moral obligation of directors. *Fordham Journal of Corporate & Financial Law, 26,* 105–146.
9. Jensen, M. C. (2002). Value maximization, stakeholder theory, and the corporate objective function. *Business Ethics Quarterly, 12*(2), 235–256.
10. Jensen, M. C., & Meckling, W. H. (1976). Theory of the firm: Managerial behavior, agency costs and ownership structure. *Journal of Financial Economics, 3*(4), 305–336.
11. Brower, H. H., & Shrader, C. B. (2000). Moral reasoning and ethical climate: Not-for-profit vs. for-profit boards of directors. *Journal of Business Ethics, 26*(2), 147–167.
12. Carroll, A. B. (1991). The pyramid of corporate social responsibility: Toward the moral management of organizational stakeholders. *Business Horizons, 34*(4), 39–48.
13. Carroll, A. B. (2016). Carroll's pyramid of CSR: Taking another look. *International Journal of Corporate Social Responsibility, 1*(1), 1–8.
14. Statement on the purpose of a corporation, US Business Roundtable, August 19, 2019, BRT.org/OurCommitment.
15. Goodman, P.S., (2020), Big business pledged gentler capitalism. It's not happening in a pandemic, April 20, 2020, The New York Times.
16. Adams, R. B., Licht, A. N., & Sagiv, L. (2011). Shareholders and stakeholders: How do directors decide? *Strategic Management Journal, 32*(12), 1331–1355.
17. Tassy, S., Oullier, O., Mancini, J., & Wicker, B. (2013). Discrepancies between judgment and choice of action in moral dilemmas. *Frontiers in Psychology, 4,* 250.
18. See for example: Kunnari, A., Sundvall, J. R. I., & Laakasuo, M. (2020). Challenges in process dissociation measures for moral cognition. *Frontiers in Psychology, 11,* 559,934, and Xu, Z. X., & Ma, H. K.

(2015). How can a deontological decision lead to moral behavior? The moderating role of moral identity. *Journal of Business Ethics, 137*(3), 537–549.
19. See for example: Bartels, D. M., & Pizarro, D. A. (2011). The mismeasure of morals: Antisocial personality traits predict utilitarian responses to moral dilemmas. *Cognition, 121*(1), 154–161, Bostyn, D. H., Roets, A., & Conway, P. (2022). Sensitivity to moral principles predicts both deontological and utilitarian response tendencies in sacrificial dilemmas. *Social Psychological and Personality Science, 13*(2), 436–445, Patil, I., Zucchelli, M. M., Kool, W., Campbell, S., Fornasier, F., Calò, M., Silani, G., Cikara, M., & Cushman, F. (2021). Reasoning supports utilitarian resolutions to moral dilemmas across diverse measures. *Journal of Personality and Social Psychology, 120*(2), 443–460.
20. Adams, R. B., Licht, A. N., & Sagiv, L. (2011). Shareholders and stakeholders: How do directors decide? *Strategic Management Journal, 32*(12), 1331–1355.

6

Gender Differences

> Where would we be if women ran Wall Street?
> —New York Times, 2009

Apparently, the first time the question 'Would the world be in this financial mess if it had been Lehman Sisters' was asked was in February 2009 at the World Economic Forum (WEF) in Davos during one of the panels. It referred to Lehman Brothers, a global financial services firm. Its high-profile bankruptcy in 2008, which was the largest in US history at the time, is frequently cited as a pivotal moment of the 2008 financial crisis.

Journalist Katrin Bennhold described the WEF incident in the New York Times article titled *Where would we be if women ran Wall Street?* and noted that it 'certainly hit a nerve with some of the more defensive male participants at the WEF'.[1] She quoted people present at the Davos panels. Micro-financing pioneer Muhammad Yunus said the current crisis would almost certainly not have happened if women had shaped financial practices because women 'wouldn't have taken the enormous types of risks that brought the system down'. Neelie Kroes, the European competition commissioner, was 'absolutely convinced that testosterone was one of the reasons the financial system had been brought to its knees'. She added that 'in general terms, females are a bit less ego-driven and a bit more responsible than men'.

Christine Lagarde, at that time Minister of Finance in the French Government, commented on the very few women being present at the WEF and said that this 'illustrated two shortcomings of the past years, one, this is a world where there is too little diversity, and two, there is too much herding behaviour'.[2] In 2018, Lagarde, then Head of the International Monetary Fund (IMF), addressed the issue again, 'As I have said many times, if it had been Lehman Sisters rather than Lehman Brothers, the world might well look a lot different today' and warned that the male domination of banking could lead to another financial crisis.[3]

> If it had been Lehman Sisters rather than Lehman Brothers, the world might well look a lot different today
> —Christine Lagarde in 2018

Two studies among Fortune 500 companies, with data from respectively 2007 and 2010, showed that as the number of female directors increased, the likelihood of a company being listed on Ethisphere's World's Most Ethical Companies also increased.[4] As one of the studies mentioned, this raises an interesting question: 'Do more ethical companies choose women to be on their boards of directors, or do women influence how ethical a company is?' Another study among 350 top executives by Altares, Dun & Bradstreet, a company specialising in business data and analytics, revealed that one in five male top executives found it irrelevant whether their business relations committed fraud or money laundering as long as these business relations met their financial obligations to the company. For female top executives, this figure was one in ten.[5]

6.1 Gender and Moral Identity

Research into whether women and men differ in moral judgement has produced varied insights, often reflecting broader debates on gender, socialisation, and moral reasoning.

Organisational psychologist and professor Jessica Kennedy and colleagues analysed multiple scientific studies, a meta-study, and showed that several studies found that women exhibited more ethical behaviour and held higher ethical standards in a business context.[6] Women lost interest in their job, unlike men when ethical values such as honesty or loyalty had to be sacrificed for money or social status at work. In a study that found women's moral reasoning to be significantly superior to men's, even after adjusting for variables such as education level, academic major, and the religious nature of the institution, it was unexpectedly found that sex role orientation, a social construct of gender attributes, did not markedly impact moral reasoning.[7]

They hypothesised that there are gender differences in moral identity, positing that women tend to incorporate moral traits, such as being caring, compassionate, fair, and kind, more strongly into their self-concepts than men do. This concept, defined as moral identity strength, refers to the extent to which individuals internalise moral traits as part of their identity. The paper hypothesised that these gender differences in moral identity strength underlie variations in unethical negotiating behaviours, with a specific focus on the internalisation part of moral identity rather than the symbolisation part. The emphasis on internalisation was chosen for its consistent prediction of moral cognition and behaviour across both private and public contexts and its relevance to explaining gender differences in ethical actions. The authors suggested that gender differences in moral identity may stem from differing self-constructs between men and women, with women more likely to see relationships as central to their identities and, therefore, more inclined to adopt moral goals and values that emphasise others' welfare. Consequently, women are expected to have a stronger moral identity than men.

Furthermore, they discussed moral disengagement, a cognitive process that allows individuals to act unethically without feeling guilt, as another factor where gender differences might play a role. Prior research showed that women engage in less moral disengagement than men, which is consistent across various contexts. Their study hypothesised that gender differences in moral disengagement, alongside moral identity, predict ethical behaviour.

6.2 Ethic of Care Versus Ethic of Justice

In 1982, feminist, psychologist, and professor Carol Gilligan introduced the distinction between the Ethic of Care and the Ethic of Justice[8] (See Table 6.1). The Ethic of Care emphasises interpersonal relationships, compassion, and the responsibility to care for others. It values context and the nuances of specific situations over abstract principles, and this approach is more relational and situational, concerned with the needs of individuals and the dynamics of relationships. The Ethic of Justice focuses on abstract principles such as fairness, rights, and justice and is associated with Lawrence Kohlberg's stages of moral development.[9] This mode of reasoning is about applying universal principles to resolve moral dilemmas.

Her book *In a Different Voice* emerged as a critique of Kohlberg's Theory of Moral Development, which she believed was biased towards male patterns of moral reasoning and overlooked moral perspectives that were more commonly associated with women. Gilligan argued that due to differences in socialisation and experiences, women are more likely to use the ethic of care in their moral reasoning, while men are more inclined towards the ethic of

Table 6.1 Ethic of care and ethic of justice

Ethic of care	Ethic of justice
Interpersonal relationships	Abstract principles
Compassion	Fairness
Care for others	Rights
Empathy	Justice
Context	Impartiality
More likely with women	More likely with men

justice. She suggested that this difference was not about moral superiority but about different perspectives on morality, shaped by gendered experiences. So, moral identity can be constructed through different lenses of moral reasoning. For women, moral identity might be deeply intertwined with notions of care, relationships, and empathy, reflecting a more relational approach to ethics. For men, moral identity might be more closely associated with principles of justice, autonomy, and rights, reflecting a more principled approach to moral dilemmas.

Gilligan's theory has been both influential and controversial. A meta-study has challenged the notion of significant gender differences in moral reasoning, suggesting that both men and women can and do employ both of Gilligan's ethical frameworks.[10] The importance of context, cultural influences, and individual differences has been emphasised in later studies, suggesting a more nuanced view of moral identity that transcends gender binaries. For example, New Zealand philosopher and feminist Annette Baier argued that Gilligan's dichotomy between the ethic of care and justice is overly simplistic and that it reinforces gender stereotypes by associating women predominantly with care.[11] She emphasised that a truly effective moral theory emerges from the collaborative efforts of both genders, merging the principles of justice and care. This unified approach demands the integration of insights from both traditional masculine and newly acknowledged feminine moral viewpoints, highlighting the importance of every individual's contribution, regardless of gender. If Gilligan's findings on the distinct moral strengths of women are accurate, women's inherent empathy and diplomatic skills will likely spearhead this unification. This merger could facilitate a mutual exchange of moral skills between genders, progressively narrowing the gap in moral perspectives that Gilligan identified through a process of shared learning and understanding.

6.3 Social Role Theory

Contrary to the Ethic of Care, which offers a more prescriptive approach to ethics, suggesting *how* men and women consider care, relationships, and justice in their moral decision-making, the Social Role Theory of social psychologist Alice Eagly is more descriptive. It aims to explain *why* men and women behave differently based on the roles they are socialised into.

Eagly argues that gender differences primarily arise from the different social roles traditionally fulfilled by men and women in society.[12] Social role theory primarily examines the social and psychological effects of societal roles on behaviours and attitudes, including but not limited to moral reasoning. According to Eagly, gender differences in behaviour and personality are not primarily determined by biological factors but by the social roles that men and women take on. For example, girls and young women are encouraged to be caring and empathetic, while boys and men are encouraged to be independent and competitive. These cultural norms and expectations can contribute to the development of different moral identities. Traditionally, women are responsible for tasks more related to caring for others, while men are responsible for tasks more focused on achievement and power. These traditional roles can lead to different values and attitudes in men and women, as well as different skills and interests. These roles influence how people behave, think, and feel, contributing to the formation of gender stereotypes and prejudices.

6.4 Gender Differences in Utilitarian or Deontological Choices

Numerous studies have delved into the impact of gender on individuals' preferences for utilitarian or deontological choices.[13] As described earlier, utilitarian considerations primarily stem from cognitive processes characterised by their rationality and deliberate nature, often requiring more time for deliberation. In contrast, deontological considerations are predominantly driven by affective processes, characterised by emotional and empathetic responses, and are typically made intuitively and swiftly. It is often posited that women tend to be more receptive to messages that appeal to their emotions, experience stronger emotional reactions, and exhibit higher levels of empathic concern. Consequently, women are inclined to resolve moral dilemmas with greater empathy, considering the welfare of others (reflecting the ethic of care perspective), whereas men tend to approach them from a more rational standpoint, focusing on individual rights and justice (reflecting the ethic of justice perspective).[14]

A comprehensive meta-analysis of forty studies has supported these claims, revealing that women indeed scored significantly higher on deontological choices.[15] However, men exhibited only a slight, nonsignificant preference for utilitarian choices. Researchers attribute this to the fact that women's moral judgements are more profoundly influenced by affective processes, resulting in higher deontological scores. However, both men and women tend to evaluate the consequences of their decisions, similarly, leading to nearly equal levels of utilitarian assessments.

6.5 Gender Differences in Stakeholderism

Previous research indicates that there are signs that female directors focus more on elements of corporate social responsibility (CSR) than their male colleagues. Male directors would be more concerned about economic performance,[16] and female directors would be more interested in philanthropic activities and community service.[17] Female directors consider a wider range of stakeholders and have values that align better with the social performance of companies.[18] Female non-executive directors also seem to have a less frequent business background and, therefore, offer non-business perspectives and expertise from other community groups. A meta-study combining multiple studies showed that the presence of female directors in the boardrooms was positively related to CSR and to the social reputation and performance of companies.[19] Other studies also concluded that female directors are more focused on elements of CSR than men.[20]

Notes

1. Where would we be if women ran Wall Street?, Katrin Bennhold, February 1, 2009, The New York Times.
2. Lückerath-Rovers, M. (2014). Five years after Lehman brothers: Still too few sisters—Gender Diversity in the Board in the Netherlands. *SSRN Electronic Journal*.
3. 'If it was Lehman Sisters, it would be a different world', Richard Partington, September 5, 2018, The Guardian.

4. See Larkin, M. B., Bernardi, R. A., & Bosco, S. M. (2013). Does female representation on boards of directors associate with increased transparency and ethical behavior? *Accounting and the Public Interest*, *13*(1), 132–150, and, Bernardi, R. A., Bosco, S. M., & Columb, V. L. (2009). Does female representation on boards of directors associate with the 'Most Ethical Companies' List? *Corporate Reputation Review*, *12*(3), 270–280.
5. Altares, D., & Bradstreet (2021). Zakendoen op gut feeling kan echt niet meer. Over het belang en prioriteiten binnen bedrijfsscreening. (Doing business based on gut feeling is no longer acceptable. On the importance and priorities within corporate screening.).
6. Kennedy, J. A., Kray, L. J., & Ku, G. (2017). A social-cognitive approach to understanding gender differences in negotiator ethics: The role of moral identity. *Organizational Behavior and Human Decision Processes*, *138*, 28–44.
7. Elm, D. R., Kennedy, E. J., & Lawton, L. (2016). Determinants of moral reasoning: Sex role orientation, gender, and academic factors. *Business & Society*, *40*(3), 241–265. doi.org/10.1177/
8. Gilligan, C. (1982). In a different voice: Psychological theory and women's development. Harvard University Press.
9. Kohlberg, L. (1981). The philosophy of moral development: Moral stages and the idea of justice. Harper & Row.
10. Jaffee, S., & Hyde, J. S. (2000). Gender differences in moral orientation: A meta-analysis. *Psychological Bulletin*, *126*(5), 703–726.
11. Baier, A. C. (2020). The need for more than justice. *Canadian Journal of Philosophy*, Supplementary Volume, *13*, 41–56.
12. Eagly, A. H. (1987). Sex Differences in social behavior: A social-role interpretation. Hillsdale, NJ: Lawrence Erlbaum.
13. See for example Aldrich, D., & Kage, R. (2003). Mars and Venus at twilight: A critical investigation of moralism, age effects, and sex differences. *Political Psychology*, *24*(1), 23–40. Armstrong, J., Friesdorf, R., & Conway, P. (2018). Clarifying gender differences in moral dilemma judgments: The complementary roles of harm aversion and action aversion. *Social Psychological and Personality Science*, *10*(3), 353–363. Arutyunova, K. R., Alexandrov, Y. I., & Hauser, M. D. (2016). Sociocultural influences on moral judgments: East–west, male–female, and young–old. *Frontiers in Psychology*, *7*, 1334. and Friesdorf, R., Conway, P., & Gawronski, B. (2015). Gender differences in responses to moral dilemmas: A process dissociation analysis. *Personality and Social Psychology Bulletin*, *41*(5), 696–713.

14. Kennedy, J. A., Kray, L. J., & Ku, G. (2017). A social-cognitive approach to understanding gender differences in negotiator ethics: The role of moral identity. *Organizational Behavior and Human Decision Processes, 138*, 28–44.
15. Friesdorf, R., Conway, P., & Gawronski, B. (2015). Gender differences in responses to moral dilemmas: A process dissociation analysis. *Personality and Social Psychology Bulletin, 41*(5), 696–713.
16. Terjesen, S., Sealy, R., & Singh, V. (2009). Women directors on corporate boards: A review and research agenda. *Corporate Governance: An International Review, 17*(3), 320–337.
17. Block, K., Croft, A., & Schmader, T. (2018). Worth less? Why men (and women) devalue care-oriented careers. *Frontiers in Psychology, 9*, 1353.
18. Adams, R. B., Licht, A. N., & Sagiv, L. (2011). Shareholders and stakeholders: How do directors decide? *Strategic Management Journal, 32*(12), 1331–1355, and Byron, K., & Post, C. (2016). Women on boards of directors and corporate social performance: A meta-analysis. *Corporate Governance: An International Review, 24*(4), 428–442.
19. Byron, K., & Post, C. (2016). Women on boards of directors and corporate social performance: A meta-analysis. *Corporate Governance: An International Review, 24*(4), 428–442.
20. Edmonds, D. (2015). Would you kill the fat man? The trolley problem and what your answer tells us about right and wrong. Princeton University Press.

7

Moral Values in the Boardroom

> Do not do unto others what you would not want others to do unto you.
> —Confucius (551 BC)

Is the emphasis on morality in the boardroom a recent development, or has the convergence of corporate scandals and a more informed society simply amplified its relevance? While moral considerations in corporate governance aren't new, today's focus is heightened by several debacles, which shattered public trust and underscored the far-reaching consequences of unethical practices. This scrutiny has placed boards under intense pressure to balance moral leadership with business goals and long-term value creation for all stakeholders. Navigating this terrain requires greater transparency, as society increasingly demands moral accountability and expects boards to establish strong moral standards that steer their organisations in a responsible direction.

The role of moral values, moral judgement, and the integration of ethical considerations into the practices of corporate boards and directors is now increasingly recognised as a crucial element for the integrity and success of businesses. Moral values are essential not only for navigating the aftermath of corporate scandals but also for guiding the overall direction, culture, and values of an organisation. The responsibility of boards to embody ethical leadership and set a moral standard is fundamental, affecting everything from public trust to the corporation's ability to attract investors, customers, and talent.

According to the Australian Institute of Company Directors (AICD), every decision in the boardroom, including decisions about what to omit from discussion, reflects the ethical approach of executive and non-executive directors in the boardroom.[1] Directors might avoid ethical discussions, fearing judgement by their peers. This concern can inhibit open discussions and prevent the addressing of potentially contentious ethical issues. Additionally, there exists a belief among some directors that ethical behaviour is inherently obvious, stemming from an assumption that moral principles are universal and require no debate. This may lead to significant oversights in addressing complex ethical dilemmas. The subjective nature of ethics often leads to hesitancy in giving these issues the same weight as legal or economic factors. This underestimates the importance of ethics in sustaining a reputable and trustworthy organisation. Concerns that ethics could be used to mask improper actions superficially or that introducing ethics into discussions could bring unforeseen difficulties further complicate open dialogue about moral considerations in decision-making. It could also create a cynical view towards the genuine integration of ethics in decision-making. Moreover, the apprehension that incorporating ethics might unveil new challenges or complicate decision-making processes acts as a deterrent to their inclusion, fearing that it could introduce unpredictability or vulnerability.

7.1 Corporate Mission and Core Values

The embedding and dissemination of moral values by directors and their integration into the corporate ethos and decision-making are increasingly achieved through defining and publishing the corporate mission and core values. By communicating the mission and core values, companies aim to demonstrate to their employees, customers, suppliers, and other stakeholders their purpose, their moral principles, and their desired conduct. These items are part of a hierarchy (see Fig. 7.1) where a compelling articulated mission (1st layer) is expanded into a vision and corporate core values (2nd layer), which are then developed into a strategy focused on long-term value creation (3rd layer). Ultimately, this strategy should lead to specific and operational objectives (4th layer).[2] In this final stage, involving distinct actions, products, and services, and where behaviour and culture are both observed and experienced, it becomes evident if a company truly embodies its mission and core values, and whether its leadership mirrors these values.

The flow from corporate mission and purpose down to operational objectives transitions from wide-ranging and general ideas to detailed, specific

Fig. 7.1 Pyramid with mission, core values, strategy, and operational control. Adapted from Lückerath-Rovers (2020)

actions. Each step in this process not only refines the preceding broad concept but also necessitates a greater level of detail. Consequently, as actions become more specific, they require a broader base of information and detail, expanding the next layer of the pyramid to encompass these complexities and ensure actionable plans are well-supported. When there's a misalignment between these layers, the integrity and effectiveness of the entire structure are undermined. Misalignment results in a narrative that lacks credibility because the company claims to value certain ideals (like innovation, quality, and ethics) but its actions, strategies, or objectives do not support these claims. This dissonance can erode trust among stakeholders, leading to a perceived lack of integrity in the company's operations and leadership.

> **Example: Misalignment in Four Layers**
>
> A hypothetical technology company, GreenTech Innovations, provides an example of how misalignment across the four layers can manifest.
>
> **Compelling Articulated Mission (1st Layer):** GreenTech's mission is 'to drive sustainable innovation in technology, improving global environmental practices'. This ambitious mission sets a clear direction for making a positive environmental impact through technology. If GreenTech starts investing heavily in technologies that are more profitable in the short term but harmful to the environment, such as non-renewable energy projects, it directly contradicts its stated mission.
>
> **Vision and Corporate Core Values (2nd Layer):** Building on its mission, GreenTech outlines its vision and core values as 'promoting sustainability', 'encouraging green technology', and 'acting with integrity towards the planet'.

Suppose GreenTech, despite its green pledge, sources materials from suppliers engaged in deforestation or fails to ensure its products are recyclable. This behaviour would contrast with its commitment to sustainability and integrity.

Strategy Focused on Long-Term Value Creation (3rd Layer): GreenTech's strategy involves developing and marketing eco-friendly products, with plans to become a market leader in sustainable technology over the next decade. If the company decides to cut research and development funding for sustainable products in favour of more traditional, high-polluting gadgets that yield immediate financial returns, it's not staying true to its strategic commitment to long-term value creation through sustainability.

Specific and Operational Objectives (4th Layer): The operational objectives include launching a new line of solar-powered devices and achieving a 40% reduction in carbon footprint for all products by 2025. If GreenTech sets these ambitious objectives but then allocates minimal budget and resources towards achieving them, or worse, increases its carbon footprint through expanded operations without environmental considerations, it fails to operationalise its strategy and core values.

In this scenario, GreenTech's narrative of being a champion for environmental sustainability loses credibility due to the misalignment between its declared mission, core values, strategic focus, and actual operational objectives and actions. Stakeholders would see a company that talks about environmental responsibility but walks a different path, eroding trust and potentially harming its reputation and market position.

7.1.1 Mission

The mission or purpose of a company, typically encapsulated in a single sentence, articulates the reason for its existence and is aligned with the industry it operates in. This statement goes beyond guiding internal strategies to become a vital part of marketing efforts and public speeches, aiming to inspire. It crafts a narrative that connects with employees, customers, and partners, embodying the company's goals and driving its ambitions forward. Used effectively in various communication platforms, the mission statement elevates the company's profile, distinguishing its brand and reinforcing its commitment to its foundational goals in a way that resonates broadly.

Consider Nike, which frames its mission as 'to bring inspiration and innovation to every athlete in the world', specifying that it views 'anyone with a body as an athlete'. This statement not only guides the company's strategy but also serves as a message in marketing, broadening its appeal. Similarly, the US retailer Walmart articulates its mission as 'to save people money so they can live better', a goal closely mirrored by another major retailer, Ahold

Delhaize, which adopts a slightly different phrasing: 'Eat well. Save time. Live better'. These similarities underscore the possibility for mission statements to share abstract yet powerful themes, even among different companies.

Google's mission 'to organize the world's information and make it universally accessible and useful', showcases a commitment to information accessibility, while Apple's 'to bring the best user experience to its customers through its innovative hardware, software, and services', highlights its focus on innovation and customer experience. These missions, though specific to each company's core competencies, reveal a shared aim of improving lives through services or products.

These examples illuminate how mission statements can be both unique and abstract, sometimes seeming interchangeable due to shared universal values. Importantly, a company's mission or purpose may evolve, reflecting shifts in strategic focus, market conditions, or societal expectations, ensuring the company remains aligned with its core values while adapting to new challenges and opportunities. This was, for example, the case with Facebook that became Meta in 2021 and formulated a new mission statement.

> **Example: Facebook Became Meta, and Changed Its Mission**
>
> Facebook, a leading social media platform, underwent a significant rebranding in 2021 by changing its corporate name to Meta. This rebranding was part of a strategic shift to reflect the company's broader ambitions beyond social media, focusing on building the 'metaverse', a collective virtual shared space created by the convergence of virtually enhanced physical reality, augmented reality, and the internet.
>
> This transformation also coincided with a change in the company's mission statement, reflecting a shift in focus and responding to criticism of its business practices. Until 2021, Facebook's ethos could be summarised by its well-known motto, 'Move fast and break things'. This phrase encapsulated the company's approach to rapid innovation and disruption, emphasising speed and progress, albeit with the recognition that such a pace could lead to mistakes or oversights.
>
> However, as Facebook transitioned to Meta and faced scrutiny over its business model, including concerns about privacy, misinformation, and the social impact of its platforms, the company adopted a new mission statement: 'Give people the power to build community and bring the world closer together'. This shift represents a move towards emphasising the positive role the company aspires to play in society—fostering community building and enhancing global connections. It suggests a more deliberate and responsible approach to innovation, with a focus on creating spaces that encourage meaningful social interaction and collaboration.

> The change in the mission statement reflects Meta's response to criticism and its attempt to realign its corporate identity and values towards more socially constructive goals. It indicates an awareness of the company's significant influence on global communication and a commitment to leveraging this influence to support community building and bring people closer together, marking a strategic pivot in how the company perceives and presents its role in the digital age.

7.1.2 Core Values

The mission or purpose gains more specificity when a company's vision and core values are outlined, answering what the company aims to be and what it stands for. Essentially, an organisation's core values are the beliefs, philosophies, and principles that drive it. These values significantly influence employee engagement and shape interactions with customers, partners, and shareholders.

Companies and organisations refer to the core values as their 'ethical compass', their 'identity', the 'foundation', or their 'DNA'. For example, Walmart described that their values in action define their culture, and this culture 'is the foundation of everything we do at Walmart'. For Meta the core values 'guide how we work, each and every day'.

Core values must meet several conditions to be effective. First, they must be relevant to the company and align with the vision and mission of the organisation. Second, core values must be clearly and understandably formulated, so that everyone inside and outside the company can understand them. In addition, the core values should be inspiring and motivating for the employees and encourage them to identify with the organisation. Also, core values must be consistently applied in the daily practice of the company, so they are credible and not just on paper. Finally, core values must be measurable and verifiable, so that the company can determine whether it is successful in adhering to these values.

> **Conditions for Core Values**
>
> Relevant to the company and aligns with vision and mission.
> Clearly and understandably formulated.
> Inspiring and motivating.
> Consistently applied in daily practice.
> Measurable and verifiable.

Core values are often formulated in such a way that they are broadly applicable and leave room for different interpretations and implementations. They are usually formulated in general terms and are not always concrete. Therefore, it can be difficult to make a clear and unambiguous translation to concrete behaviour or to provide direction in the choice of moral dilemmas. For example, what one person considers to be a core value such as 'integrity', 'connecting', 'courage', or 'individuality' can have a different meaning for another person.

> **Examples: Core Values**
>
> 'Service to the customer. Respect for the individual. Strive for excellence. Act with integrity'.
> **Walmart**
>
> 'Courage. Integrity. Teamwork. Care. Humour'.
> **Ahold Delhaize**
>
> 'Move fast. We build and learn faster than anyone else. Focus on long-term impact. Build awesome things. Live in the future. Be direct and respect your colleagues. Meta, metamates, me'.
> **Meta**

Most of these values, see, for example, the last value of Meta, 'Meta, metamates, me', need some clarification. This specific value is described on Meta's website as: 'We are stewards of our company and our mission. We have a sense of responsibility for our collective success and to each other as teammates. It's about taking care of our company and each other'. Another core value, 'Be direct and respect your colleagues' is described as a culture where employees are straightforward and willing to have hard conversations with each other, but at the same time, employees are respectful when feedback is shared.

So, core values are often not linked to specific behavioural norms or rules. For example, when 'respect' is adopted as a core value, its specific behavioural implications and how it applies to a company's daily operations may not be immediately evident. The absence of distinct and measurable objectives in the core values may result in diminished accountability and responsibility. It could help to establish clear norms and rules based on the core values so that employees know what is expected of them. Most companies do this often briefly to give direction to the core values. The inclusion of a unique core value, like humour at Ahold Delhaize, necessitates further clarification to avoid any ambiguity regarding its meaning. Questions naturally arise, such as who defines the nature of humour? Are certain jokes deemed inappropriate, and if so, who makes this judgement? According to Ahold Delhaize's elaboration, humour is embraced to offer perspective on their actions and to encourage them not to be overly self-serious. This clarification is vital to understand how humour functions within this company's culture and its intended purpose.

Examples: Explanation of Core Values

Be direct and respect your colleagues (Meta)
'We create a culture where we are straightforward and willing to have hard conversations with each other. At the same time, we are also respectful and when we share feedback, we recognize that many of the world's leading experts work here'.

Humour (Ahold Delhaize)
'We are humble, down-to-earth, and we don't take ourselves too seriously'.

It is thus essential to recognise that core values can often be ambiguous and subject to varying interpretations. The conduct and actions of directors, even amidst moral dilemmas, significantly shape how employees understand and adhere to the core values, how these values are communicated, the process of making pivotal decisions, and the accountability of the organisation in upholding these values. The 'Tone at the Top' is thus essential in both adhering to and promoting core values. Directors act as exemplars for other employees. Should they themselves fail to align with the core values, it becomes challenging to expect the same from the employees.

In the cases in Part II of this book, the core values of the implicated companies are always presented for illustrative purposes. In some organisations, these core values indeed influenced the decisions, while in others, not in the least.

7.2 Moral Values in the Boardroom

In the aftermath of the corporate scandals, Professor of Business Ethics Mark Schwartz and colleagues identified in 2005 four reasons for the increased attention towards moral value in the boardroom.[3] Firstly, they observed that the corporate scandals unveiled severe ethical breaches at the board level, highlighting how these failures can erode public trust and damage the corporation's reputation. Secondly, they pointed out that the essence of board functions necessitates a commitment to ethical obligations, as boards are pivotal in setting the moral compass for the entire organisation, influencing its culture and values. Thirdly, given that boards bear the ultimate charge of safeguarding their organisation's ethical standards, they must, in turn, embody ethical leadership, serving ethical role models themselves that inspire employees and stakeholders alike. Lastly, they argued that it is fundamentally beneficial for the prosperity of corporate businesses when directors adhere to ethical practices, as this fosters a culture of trust and reliability, attracting investors, customers, and talent who value ethical conduct.

To foster a meaningful discourse among directors regarding ethical standards and principles, it is imperative to have a well-defined understanding of these moral values. In 2002, Schwartz identified six fundamental moral values, which he refers to as ethical values: trustworthiness, respect, responsibility, fairness, caring, and citizenship.[4] Recognising the evolving landscape of corporate governance, Schwartz and colleagues adapted these moral values specifically for boardroom application. This adaptation led to six moral values tailored for directors' roles and responsibilities: honesty, integrity, loyalty, responsibility, fairness, and citizenship.[5]

In this book, these six moral values serve merely as a foundational framework and are subject to further enhancement and contextualisation (See Text Box). For example, they should include the consideration of the stakeholder model instead of the shareholder model and could also include more general descriptions of moral values between individuals. In the original framework, there is a notable emphasis on shareholders, as illustrated in their interpretation of 'fairness', which advocates for the equal treatment of all shareholders but does not extend this principle of fairness to other stakeholders. In their discussion on 'loyalty', they reference the US Company Law's 'duty of loyalty', suggesting that directors prioritise the company's interests above all, thereby avoiding conflicts of interest. However, an extended moral dimension of loyalty is used, encompassing support or protection for relationships or individuals, such as safeguarding a director's reputation or valuing long-standing partnerships with suppliers.

Also, for 'responsibility', the original framework predominantly focuses on directors maintaining professional standards through continuous professional education, voicing differing viewpoints, or self-assessment, and does not delve deeply into responsibility as making challenging decisions, displaying courage, or issuing apologies for past mistakes. In the Text Box, our elaborations and extensions have been incorporated into Schwartz's original set of moral values and are emphasised in italics. This approach may ensure a more comprehensive and practical application of these ethical principles in the complex and dynamic environment of corporate governance.

> **Moral Values for Directors**
>
> Adapted from Schwartz, Dunfee, and Kline (2005).
> *italicised sentences* and the points of attention are supplemented.
>
> **Honesty**
>
> 'Directors have an ethical obligation to act with honesty. The hallmark of honesty is truthfulness and forthrightness. It requires speaking up frankly when required to prevent a false impression. The honest director eschews half-truths and other linguistic devices intentionally used to create misunderstandings'.
>
> *Directors communicate clearly and honestly to all stakeholders and ensure that information stakeholders need to make informed decisions is available.*
>
> **Points of Attention**
>
> Is the truth being told? If not, why not? Is the truth twisted? Are half-truths or untruths contradicted? How is sensitive information safeguarded against misuse? Are measures in place to ensure that the dissemination of information is both responsible and does not compromise the company's integrity or stakeholders' trust?
>
> **Integrity**
>
> 'Directors have an obligation to act with integrity. This requires that directors act with honour, always ensuring that they are acting in accordance with their firms' espoused principles and values'.
>
> *Integrity also includes the concepts of reliability and confidentiality. However, confidentiality can also be at odds with other moral norms such as honesty and loyalty. Directors then have a responsibility to make a trade-off. Directors demonstrate by exemplary behaviour that they act by the core values of the company.*
>
> **Points of Attention**
>
> Is the decision in line with the core values? Are the core values also propagated? Is confidentiality breached? If so, why? Are we a reliable partner? How are the trade-offs justified? Is there a process in place for evaluating and making these difficult decisions, ensuring that they are made with the greatest ethical consideration?
>
> **Loyalty**
>
> 'Directors have an obligation to act with loyalty, in the best interests of the corporation as opposed to one's personal interests. To be considered acting with loyalty, directors should avoid self-dealing; taking advantage of corporate opportunities; engaging in potential or apparent conflict of interest transactions; and insider trading. They should maintain objectivity in decision-making and protect confidential and proprietary information'.

Loyalty as a moral value also applies to loyalty to relationships or individuals, for example when it is morally appropriate to support the director or other relationships. 'Misplaced loyalty' must be avoided.

Points of Attention

Is action being taken in the interest of the company? Is there possibly a case of (unwanted) conflict of interest or opposition of interests? How are potential or existing conflicts of interest disclosed and managed? Is action being taken in the interest of a person or relationship? If so, why? Is there a case of misplaced loyalty?

Responsibility

'Directors must fulfil their responsibilities as established by the company and corporate law in a transparent manner by which they can be held accountable'.

Responsibility also means that directors take responsibility for their own actions and decisions and can explain the consequences thereof. Not only taking responsibility for successes, but also for mistakes and failures. It requires courage, decisiveness, and a straight back.

Points of Attention

Is responsibility being taken to decide in the best interest of the company and stakeholders? Even if this requires courage in unpopular decisions. Is responsibility taken in explaining a decision? Or in possibly adjusting a decision?

Fairness

Directors must treat others and make decisions based on fairness. Fairness involves balancing the interests involved in all decision-making including any decisions related to hiring, firing, and executive compensation. It also implies ensuring that all classes of shareholders are treated fairly and deal fairly with stakeholder interests.

In the stakeholder model, this explicitly includes the fair treatment of all stakeholders and independent considerations of different interests, without bias and without obligation to consult or seek approval.

Points of Attention

Are shareholders treated equally? Are the interests of all stakeholders considered? Is there an independent consideration of interests? Is a justified weight given to the interests of all stakeholders?

Citizenship

'Directors must act as good citizens, which includes ensuring that they and their companies are complying with laws and regulations and the standards of the communities in which they operate. Acting as a good citizen means not only individual compliance with the law, but as a director, ensuring that mechanisms are in place, so that all of the company's agents are in compliance with the law and acting ethically'.

Directors who pursue good citizenship, acknowledge that they are not only responsible for maximising profit for shareholders, but also for maintaining a wide range of social, ecological, and economic values that are important to society as a whole.

Points of Attention

Is relevant law and regulation complied with? Is society not unnecessarily harmed on a social, economic, or environmental level? Is there a robust framework for compliance that is regularly reviewed and updated in response to changing laws and ethical expectations?

7.3 Ethics in Corporate Governance Codes

Since the early twenty-first century, following corporate scandals such as Enron, Worldcom, Parmalat, and Ahold, there has been a global implementation of codes of good governance across various sectors and industries. These codes place a strong emphasis on the necessity of well-defined roles and responsibilities. The instances of poor decision-making by directors have contributed to a growing consensus that corporate governance extends beyond mere structures and processes; it also encompasses the behaviour and role of both executive and non-executive directors within that framework.

Despite this recognition, there has been no formal movement to incorporate provisions for behaviour and corporate culture into governance codes. An analysis of 88 national governance codes conducted in 2020 revealed that most of them, specifically 55 codes, at that time did not address the impact of directors on corporate culture.[6] This study evaluated how national codes integrated corporate culture by identifying three dimensions of such integration: referring to the three layers of corporate culture (values, norms, and behaviour), the alignment of corporate culture within the organisation, and the board's roles regarding corporate culture. The analysis revealed significant variances among individual codes and identified five codes as 'best practice' (Brazil, Jordan, The Netherlands, New Zealand, and the United Kingdom) based on their comprehensive approach to incorporating corporate culture. These 'best practice' codes explicitly outlined the board's responsibility in defining, implementing, and monitoring corporate culture. The code of Brazil (2016) even added corrective measures in case of deviation.

> **Brazil Corporate Governance Code 2016**
>
> **Principle 2.1: Duties of the Board of Directors**
>
> The board of directors is the collective body in charge of the decision-making process of an organisation with regard to its strategic direction. It serves as the guardian of the principles, values, purpose, and system of governance of the organisation, being its main component.
>
> Practice b): The board of directors is responsible for identifying, discussing, and ensuring the dissemination of the organisation's values and principles. It should define strategies and make decisions that protect and raise the organisation's value, optimise the return on long-term investment, and seek to balance the expectations of all stakeholders. It should promote an organisational culture focused on the organisation's values and principles and promote an environment where people can express dissenting thoughts and discuss ethical dilemmas.
>
> Practice c): The board of directors should establish mechanisms to permanently monitor whether the business decisions and actions (and their results, as well as direct and indirect impacts) are aligned with its principles and values. In case of deviations, it should propose the application of corrective and, ultimately, punitive measures, as provided by the code of conduct.
>
> Please note, this is not the complete text of Principle 2.1.

In the United Kingdom, as early as 2011, the Financial Reporting Council, the same organisation responsible for the UK Corporate Governance Code, introduced a Guidance on Board Effectiveness. This guidance, aimed at addressing the role of culture and behaviour within corporate governance, will be detailed in the following sections. Before exploring this guidance in detail, a short description of the ethics within the OECD Principles of Corporate Governance and the Sarbanes–Oxley Act will be provided.

7.3.1 OECD Principles of Corporate Governance

The OECD Principles of Corporate Governance were first published in 1999 and have since been revised to reflect the evolving corporate governance landscape, with significant updates made in 2004, 2015, and lastly in 2023. These principles were developed in response to the financial crises of the late 1990s, with the aim of establishing a benchmark for good corporate governance practices worldwide. The OECD definition of corporate governance (p.6) refers to 'a set of relationships between a company's management, board, shareholders, and stakeholders' and that it provides 'structure and systems through which the company is directed, and its objectives are set, and the means of attaining those objectives and monitoring performance are determined'.

In 2023 the update aimed at alignment with the latest trends and expectations, now incorporating sustainability as a key focus.[7] The revision addressed the changing global landscape, including stakeholder concerns about environmental and social issues, to ensure the principles continue to provide relevant and effective guidance for sustainable growth and financial stability.

Principle V.C., titled 'The board should apply high ethical standards', states that the board plays a crucial role in defining a company's ethical framework.

> **OECD Principles of Corporate Governance**
>
> **Principle V.C. The Board Should Apply High Ethical Standards.**
>
> The board has a key role in setting the ethical tone of a company, not only through its own actions, but also in appointing and overseeing key executives and consequently the management in general. High ethical standards are in the long-term interests of the company as a means to make it credible and trustworthy, not only in day-to-day operations, but also with respect to longer-term commitments. To make the objectives of the board clear and operational, many companies have found it useful to develop company codes of conduct based on, among others, professional standards, and sometimes broader codes of behaviour, and to communicate them throughout the organisation. (...).
>
> Company-wide codes serve as a standard for conduct by both the board and key executives, setting the framework for the exercise of judgement in dealing with varying and often conflicting constituencies. At a minimum, the code of ethics should set clear limits on the pursuit of private interests, including dealings in the shares of the company. An overall framework for ethical conduct goes beyond compliance with the law, which should always be a fundamental requirement.
>
> Please note, this is not the complete text of Principle V.C.

7.3.2 Sarbanes–Oxley Act

The Sarbanes–Oxley Act of 2002 (SOX) aimed to restore public confidence in the financial reporting of publicly traded, companies, also in the wake of the high-profile financial scandals involving major corporations like Enron and WorldCom. It introduced reforms to enhance corporate accountability, improve the accuracy and reliability of financial disclosures, and combat corporate and accounting fraud. Key provisions of the act include the requirement for CEOs and CFOs to personally certify the accuracy of financial statements, the imposition of enhanced penalties for financial fraud, the strengthening of internal controls on financial reporting, and the protection of whistle-blowers who report fraud.

The establishment of the Public Company Accounting Oversight Board (PCAOB), an independent body charged with overseeing the audits of public companies to ensure the accuracy and integrity of financial statements, was intended to prevent conflicts of interest that were believed to have contributed to the accounting scandals.

Although SOX significantly impacted how companies conduct their financial reporting and governance practices, it also promoted ethical business practices. It implicitly incorporates ethical mandates that extend beyond mere compliance with the law. For example, by mandating the disclosure of codes of ethics for senior financial officers, providing protections for whistle-blowers, and holding top executives personally accountable for the accuracy of financial reports, it fosters a culture of integrity and transparency.

7.4 Code of Ethics for Non-Executives

Due to the lack of explicit attention to behaviour and culture in the Corporate Governance Codes, in 2009 the possibility of a 'Code of Ethics for non-executive directors and supervisors was investigated'.[8] The motivation behind developing such a code of conduct was largely influenced by the myriad of unwritten rules that are traditionally followed. Although there has been a trend towards formalising these rules through codes of best practices, most governance rules remain informal and influence behaviour and decisions.[9] Our code of ethics comprised ten principles, drawing upon the moral values as identified by Schwartz,[10] the topics from CEPLIS, and principles from the Dutch Institute of Chartered Auditors.

The European Council of the Liberal Professions (CEPLIS) has delineated eight topics that ought to be encompassed in professional codes of conduct.[11] The guidelines stress the importance of confidentiality, continuous skill development, objective decision-making, honesty, integrity, proper staff management, adherence to codes of conduct, and securing liability insurance. They also highlight the need for ethical guidance in resolving conflicts between professional duties and personal beliefs.

While recognising codes of conduct as self-regulatory without legal status, the code of ethics started with an introduction that adherence to laws and regulations is fundamental, with the code's compliance being an additional commitment voluntarily accepted by non-executives (See Table 7.1).

These principles were aimed to guide non-executives in navigating their roles with ethical integrity, ensuring their actions align with both the spirit and the letter of the code, thereby fostering trust and accountability in corporate governance. Rather than listing specific do's and don'ts, such a code of ethics should articulate the foundational principles of proper conduct and mindset. It may cover what seems to be elementary principles, and it does not claim to reveal novel insights. The principles governing appropriate behaviour

Table 7.1 Code of ethics for non-executive directors

1. Tasks and Role: It stressed the importance of ethical decision-making and the non-executives' significant influence over management and stakeholders, advocating for a proactive, critical engagement with executive boards.
2. Independence: The code insisted on non-executives operating without external influence, maintaining impartiality and objectivity, and preparing to resign if necessary to preserve independence.
3. Integrity: Non-executives were called to act with respect, loyalty, and integrity, balancing their duties to third parties and stakeholders while avoiding actions that could damage the profession's reputation.
4. Confidentiality: Emphasised the importance of keeping sensitive information confidential, barring public knowledge, and finding a balance between confidentiality and the need for independence and integrity.
5. Board Composition: The code encouraged a diverse and optimal board composition, underlining the necessity of selecting members based on objective criteria to prevent the board from becoming too static or dependent.
6. Evaluation: It highlighted the necessity of regular, possibly externally assisted evaluations of non-executives performance to ensure transparency, accountability, and quality of board functioning.
7. Remuneration: Stressed that non-executives should be adequately compensated without affecting their independence or willingness to intervene, with adjustments linked to workload rather than company performance.
8. Knowledge and Experience: Non-executives were expected to maintain and update their competency through continuous professional development, ensuring they meet the specific needs of the organisation, its market, and stakeholders.
9. Responsibility: The code recognised the importance of ethical behaviour next to legal liability, emphasising the role of non-executives in taking responsible actions.
10. Accountability: Lastly, it demanded transparency and accountability from non-executives to a broad group of stakeholders, requiring at least an annual report detailing performance, board composition, evaluation methods, and professional development efforts.

Adapted from Lückerath-Rovers and De Bos (2011)

are broadly recognised. Such a code could mainly serve as a guiding framework for ethical behaviour, emphasising the individual responsibility and accountability of directors. The aim was to establish ethical norms and values in a manner that gained consensus from both the directors and the wider society and stakeholders on what constitutes effective oversight.

7.5 UK Guidance on Board Effectiveness

In 2011, the Financial Reporting Council (FRC) deemed it essential to augment the UK Corporate Governance Code with a 'Guidance on Board Effectiveness', with an increased focus on moral standards, behaviour, and boardroom culture.[12] The FRC has been issuing the UK Corporate Governance Code since 1992, but observed that in the development of the Governance Code, significant emphasis was placed on clarity of roles and responsibilities, alongside accountability and transparency. Nevertheless, it has become increasingly evident that while these are necessary components of good governance, they are not solely sufficient. Directors must thoroughly consider how they execute their roles and the behaviour they exhibit, both individually and collectively. This reflects the 'Tone from the Top'.

> Well-informed and high-quality decision-making does not happen by accident.
> —FRC, 2018

Therefore, the Guidance, last updated in 2018, encouraged directors to reflect on their decision-making processes and how these influence the quality of outcomes. It underscored that 'well-informed and high-quality decision-making does not happen by accident' and that poor decision-making is often predictable and avoidable. By dedicating time to the decision-making process, the likelihood of poor decisions can be minimised.

The Guidance placed significant emphasis on ethics, exemplary behaviour, and values, and their impact on decision-making. Following its 2018 revision, it now not only includes principles guiding behaviour but also specific questions that directors can ask themselves or management to evaluate their leadership, decision-making, and strategic objectives from an ethical standpoint (See Table 7.2). According to the FRC, values need to be embedded at every level of the organisation to have an impact on behavioural outcomes and influence the way business is done. For instance, the Guidance prompts considerations about whether the culture being fostered supports the company's mission and long-term success, or if the behaviours driving strategy and financial objectives are appropriate. It also questions whether the key performance indicators (KPIs) align with these aspects.

Furthermore, the Guidance outlines various risks that can compromise prudent decision-making. These risks encompass issues like a lack of diverse perspectives resulting in 'groupthink', the failure to heed or respond to raised concerns, and not identifying leaders who act out of self-interest or exhibit poor ethical standards. It also highlights specific behaviours of executive directors or management towards non-executives as potential risks. These include management's lack of transparency, hesitance to engage non-executives in the decision-making process, and the propensity to approach the non-executives merely for 'approval' rather than engaging in thorough discussion.

As of 2024, after the publication of the new UK Corporate Governance Code in January 2024, the Guidance on Board Effectiveness is now replaced by a more general and online 'guidance', that incorporates multiple previously published FRC guidances: the Guidance on Board Effectiveness, the

Table 7.2 Examples of questions for boards themselves, and for management

Questions for Boards
- How do we demonstrate ethical leadership and display the behaviours we expect from others?
- To what extent is our own way of operating a reflection of the values we are promoting? Can we give good and bad examples?
- Is the board clear on what sort of culture is needed to underpin the company's purpose and its long-term success?
- How do we articulate and communicate what we consider to be acceptable business practices?
- What behaviours are being driven when setting strategy and financial targets?
- How consistent is company strategy with our purpose and values, and our responsibilities for long-term success and to contribute to wider society?
Questions for Management
- How have the values and expected behaviours been reinforced in our recruitment, promotion, reward, performance management, and other policies, processes, and practices?
- Do reward structures produce appropriate incentives that encourage desired behaviours and responsible risk-taking?
- What steps has management taken to communicate values and expected behaviours widely and clearly across the company?
- What assurance is there that the code of conduct and ethics training programmes are up to date, adequately communicated, and understood by the workforce?
- What steps has management taken to ensure that suppliers meet expected standards of behaviour?
- Has management identified appropriate KPIs that are properly aligned with desired outcomes and behaviours

Adapted from FRC (2018), p. 5 and 6

Guidance on Audit Committees, and the Guidance on Risk Management and Related Financial and Business Reporting.[13]

Notes

1. Australian Institute of Company Directors (AICD). (2019). Ethics in the Boardroom. A decision-making guide for directors.
2. Lückerath-Rovers, M. (2020). Langetermijnwaardecreatie in tijden van corona. MeJudice, April 22, 2020.
3. Schwartz, M. S., Dunfee, T. W., & Kline, M. J. (2005). Tone at the Top: An ethics code for directors? *Journal of Business Ethics*, 58(1–3), 79–100.
4. Schwartz, M. S. (2002). A code of ethics for corporate code of ethics. *Journal of Business Ethics*, 41(1/2), 27–43.
5. Schwartz, M. S., Dunfee, T. W., & Kline, M. J. (2005). Tone at the top: An ethics code for directors? *Journal of Business Ethics*, 58(1–3), 79–100.
6. Lobry, M.-F., Kaptein, M., & Lückerath-Rovers, M. (2020). What national governance codes say about corporate culture. *Corporate Governance: The International Journal of Business in Society*, 20(5), 903–917.
7. OECD (2023), G20/OECD Principles of Corporate Governance 2023, OECD Publishing, Paris.
8. Lückerath-Rovers, M., & De Bos, A. (2011). Code of conduct for non-executive and supervisory directors. *Journal of Business Ethics*, 100, 465–481.
9. Huse, M. (2005). Accountability and creating accountability: A framework for exploring behavioural perspectives of corporate governance. *British Journal of Management*, 16(s1), 1–366.
10. Schwartz, M. S. (2002). A code of ethics for corporate code of ethics. *Journal of Business Ethics*, 41(1/2), 27–43.
11. CEPLIS (2007), 'European Council of Liberal Professions; Common Values of the Liberal Professions in.
    the European Union. Preamble'.
12. Financial Reporting Council (FRC). (2018). Guidance on Board Effectiveness 2018. London.
13. https://www.frc.org.uk/library/standards-codes-policy/corporate-governance/corporate-governance-code-guidance/#section.951eef83

8

Decision-Making in the Boardroom

> We can be blind to the obvious, and we are also blind to our blindness.
> —Daniel Kahneman, 1934–2024

Directors' decision-making processes are often scrutinised for their perceived 'limited view', suggesting a disconnection from the broader context of their actions. This critique is encapsulated in questions like 'What world are they living in?' or 'Are they out of touch with reality?', pointing to a gap between boardroom decisions and societal expectations. Such criticism becomes especially pronounced when decisions, deemed reasonable within the confines of the boardroom, spark public outcry for seeming disconnected or morally short-sighted. This disconnect underscores the ongoing tension between decision-making in the boardroom and broader societal values, with often directors themselves acknowledging in public their 'limited perspective' as a reason to rethink and even reverse their decisions due to initial poor judgement. Psychologist and Nobel laureate for economy Daniel Kahneman was known for his research on biases, our unconscious preconceptions, that influence our thought processes, and he argued that these are difficult to overcome: 'we can be blind to the obvious, and we are also blind to our blindness'.[1]

To mitigate these challenges, directors should actively broaden their decision-making perspective. This includes seeking diverse perspectives and integrating feedback from a wide array of stakeholders, thereby ensuring a more inclusive consideration of the potential impacts of their decisions. By doing so, they not only address their own biases and the critiques levied against them but also align their decisions more closely with ethical standards and public expectations, showing decisions that are both responsible and responsive to the changing societal landscape.

8.1 Different Outcomes in Decision-Making in the Boardroom

In the boardroom, the decision-making process is not just a reflection of the board's governance style but also a process that is especially nuanced when navigating moral dilemmas, revealing a spectrum of potential outcomes that range from groupthink to irreconcilable differences (See Fig. 8.1). At one end of this spectrum, directors might share identical views, leading to minimal discussions because what is deemed obvious does not seem to require debate. This unanimity, while efficient, risks falling into the traps of groupthink or tunnel vision, where a lack of critical analysis and the dismissal of alternative viewpoints can lead to flawed decision-making. Conversely, the boardroom can also be a venue for opposing views, where even after thorough discussion, directors find their differences irreconcilable. In such cases, some directors may feel the need to distance themselves from the final decision, reflecting the complexity and diversity of thought that characterises effective boards. Between these two extremes lies a productive middle ground where healthy debate flourishes. Here, directors engage in meaningful discussions that may lead to a consensus, where a shared decision is reached, or to an agreement to disagree, acknowledging the validity of differing viewpoints without forcing a unified stance.

This range of outcomes, from groupthink to irreconcilable differences, with consensus and agree-to-disagree in between, underscores the varied nature of boardroom dynamics. Each of these decision-making types has its implications for the effectiveness of the board. Understanding and navigating these dynamics is essential for ensuring that boards can make decisions that are in the best interest of the organisation they govern.

8.1.1 Groupthink and Tunnel Vision

Groupthink occurs when a board makes decisions without sufficient critical evaluation of different viewpoints, often due to a high emphasis on unanimity and cohesion. This phenomenon can manifest in various ways, from no discussion at all to some level of discussion that still lacks dissenting opinions. At one end of the spectrum, there's the scenario where no discussion

8 Decision-Making in the Boardroom

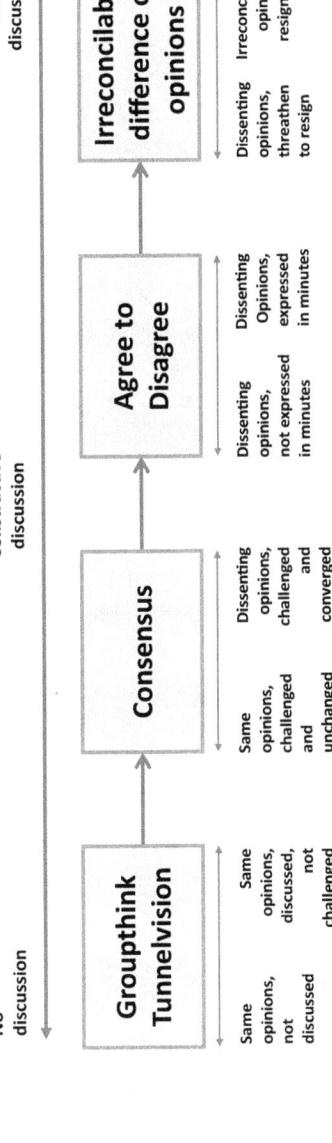

Fig. 8.1 Increasing intensity of discussion in boardroom decision-making

takes place because all members seemingly agree, deeming it too obvious to warrant any debate. This could be a result of a shared mindset where the need for deliberation is overlooked, as everyone appears to be on the same page. On the other hand, there are situations where there is some level of discussion, but it remains superficial and unchallenged. In these cases, while deliberations do occur, they lack depth and critical questioning. Dissenting opinions, if any exist, are either not voiced or are quickly dismissed. This still falls under the umbrella of groupthink, as the focus remains on preserving harmony and agreement, rather than rigorously exploring diverse perspectives and potential alternatives. In both instances, the underlying issue is the same: a preference for consensus and harmony over a thorough and critical exploration of different ideas. This approach can lead to decisions that are not fully explored or challenged, potentially overlooking risks and innovative solutions, and ultimately affecting the effectiveness of the board and the health of the organisation.

In 1972, psychologist Irving Janis introduced the concept of groupthink, a theory that emerged from his analysis of foreign policy decisions made by the US government, including the Bay of Pigs Invasion and the Pearl Harbor attack.[2] Janis's interest in these historical events led him to explore how groups could make critical errors in judgement despite the collective intelligence and expertise of their members. Janis identified groupthink as a psychological phenomenon that occurs within a group of people when the desire for harmony or conformity in the group results in an irrational or dysfunctional decision-making outcome. He proposed that groupthink is more likely to occur in highly cohesive groups where there is a strong preference for consensus, which can suppress dissenting viewpoints and lead to a deterioration in mental efficiency, reality testing, and moral judgement among group members. The eight symptoms of groupthink may lead to defective decision-making, as the group tends to ignore alternatives, take excessive risks, and overlook warnings about the potential dangers of their decisions.

> **Eight Symptoms of Groupthink**
>
> Adapted from (Janis, 1972)
>
> **Illusion of invulnerability**
> The group ignores danger, takes extreme risks, and is too optimistic.
>
> **Collective rationalisation**
> Ignoring warnings which could lead to reconsidering decisions taken earlier.
>
> **Illusion of the moral**
> The unquestioned belief in the morality of the group, whereby the ethical and moral correctness of decisions is ignored.
>
> **Excessive stereotyping**
> The group has an image of negative stereotypes of other 'types' outside the group.
>
> **Pressure for conformity**
> Members of the group who object to the stereotyping, illusions, or obligations of the group, are clearly made aware that this goes against the expected loyalty.
>
> **Self-censorship**
> Members of the group tend to minimise the importance of any possible divergent opinion or doubt.
>
> **Illusion of unanimity**
> The incorrect observation is that everyone agrees, particularly because of self-censorship, and thereby that silence is taken as agreement.
>
> **Self-appointed mind guards**
> Some members of the group protect the group against negative information, which might constitute a threat to the self-respect (the satisfaction) the group has about the effectiveness and morality of the decisions.

According to Janis, the eight symptoms of group thinking give rise to three risks: an exaggerated feeling of self-esteem, the creation of tunnel vision, and a strong pressure within the group to achieve consensus. Janis suggested several preventive measures to combat groupthink, including encouraging open debate, inviting external experts to challenge group perspectives, and appointing a 'devil's advocate' to question the group's assumptions and decisions. He also recommended that leaders should refrain from expressing their opinions too strongly at the outset to avoid influencing the group unduly.

> **Example: Groupthink at the IMF[3]**
>
> In 2011, the Independent Evaluation Office (IEO) of the International Monetary Fund (IMF) indicated groupthink and tunnel vision as one of the causes of the financial crisis in 2008. The IEO concluded that the IMF did not perceive the increasing risks because of a high degree of groupthink and intellectual capture, and a general mindset that a major financial crisis was unlikely, also due to the lack of incentives to raise contrarian views.

> 'The IMF's ability to detect important vulnerabilities and risks and alert the membership was undermined by a complex interaction of factors, many of which had been flagged before but had not been fully addressed. The IMF's ability to correctly identify the mounting risks was hindered by a high degree of groupthink, intellectual capture, a general mindset that a major financial crisis in large, advanced economies was unlikely, and inadequate analytical approaches. Weak internal governance, lack of incentives to work across units and raise contrarian views, and a review process that did not "connect the dots" or ensure follow-up also played an important role, while political constraints may have also had some impact'.
>
> The IEO then produced several solutions for avoiding group thinking including creating an environment in which frankness and expressing divergent views are encouraged. The silo mentality within the IMF also needs to be changed by striving for more diversity in recruiting new staff.
>
> 'Looking forward, the IMF needs to (i) create an environment that encourages candour and considers dissenting views; (ii) modify incentives to "speak truth to power"; (iii) better integrate macroeconomic and financial sector issues; (iv) overcome the silo mentality and insular culture; and (v) deliver a clear, consistent message on the global outlook and risks'.

8.1.2 Consensus

Consensus and groupthink or tunnel vision represent distinctly different outcomes in the decision-making process within boardrooms, with the former being a product of constructive discussion and the latter a result of critical oversight. Unlike groupthink or tunnel vision, where a lack of scrutiny and an unquestioning acceptance of the initial consensus prevails, consensus-building is marked by an openness to dissenting opinions and a willingness among directors to engage in constructive discussions.

The differentiation between consensus and groupthink lies primarily in the process and the mindset of the participants. In scenarios prone to groupthink or tunnel vision, board members might prematurely align with a common viewpoint, often out of a desire for harmony or conformity, inadvertently bypassing the critical evaluation of alternative perspectives. In contrast, aiming for consensus involves a deliberate process of engaging with and exploring a variety of viewpoints. This process can start from a point where some members might already share similar views, but it crucially remains open to evolution through discussion. It is distinguished by the readiness of participants to shift their stances based on new information or arguments, reflecting a genuine commitment to reaching the best possible decision rather than simply maintaining consensus. This openness to changing one's mind is a critical element that sets consensus apart from groupthink.

Furthermore, the consensus approach fosters a culture of open debate and careful deliberation, where every director is encouraged to voice differing opinions without fear of dissent being dismissed. Such a culture ensures that decisions are not just a reflection of a majority view or the loudest voice in the room but are instead the result of a collective accord that has carefully considered all perspectives. This makes the outcome of a consensus-driven process inherently more robust and reflective of the collective wisdom of the board, rather than the unchallenged acceptance of a singular viewpoint that characterises groupthink or tunnel vision.

Boards frequently announce that they have reached their decisions unanimously. This practice serves multiple purposes: it projects a unified stance to the outside world, reinforces the strength and cohesion of the board's position, and aims to preclude any speculation about internal disagreements or dissenting views. By presenting decisions as unanimous, boards seek to convey an image of solidarity and consensus, suggesting that after thorough discussion, all members align behind the final decision.

Example: 'Unanimity After Extensive Deliberations' at Harvard's Board

Amidst the conflict in Gaza in 2023, Harvard President Gay faced scrutiny during a congressional hearing on antisemitism in higher education on December 5, 2023. Alongside the presidents of Penn and MIT, she defended her stance and the principle of free speech on campus. To the question: 'Does calling for the genocide of Jews violate Harvard's rules on bullying and harassment?' she responded: 'The rules around bullying and harassment are quite specific and if the context in which that language is used amounts to bullying and harassment, then we take, we take action against it'. By referring to 'the context', criticism was directed at her for not explicitly stating that advocacy for the genocide of Jewish people would contravene Harvard's policies. Additionally, Gay faced allegations of plagiarism.

A few days later, the board of the Harvard Corporation issued a statement in which they stated that they had 'extensive deliberations', acknowledged some of the critics, and noted that 'President Gay has apologised for how she handled her congressional testimony'. They conclude that their 'extensive deliberations affirm our confidence that President Gay is the right leader' and that 'they unanimously stand in support of their President'.[4]

Note: President Gay resigned on January 2, 2024. The Board accepted her resignation 'with sorrow'.[5]

8.1.3 Agree-to-Disagree

In decision-making processes, especially in board meetings, there is often a need to acknowledge the existence of differing opinions. This scenario arises when, after thorough discussion, members still hold different views, but these differences don't pertain to core principles. The board collectively agrees to acknowledge these differences but chooses not to let them hinder the decision-making process. This approach is constructive as it respects the diversity of opinions and still enables progress based on majority voting. The minority, while not in agreement, accepts the majority's decision.

The question of whether to document dissenting opinions in the meeting minutes is nuanced. While board members with differing viewpoints can request their stance to be formally recorded, this should be done judiciously. Over-requesting the inclusion of dissenting views can be seen as a fallback strategy or a way to place on record an 'I told you so' for decisions that may not work out. This approach can create an atmosphere of distrust or suggest a lack of unity in decision-making. Moreover, it might overshadow the fact that even those who initially disagreed benefit from the successful outcomes of decisions. Thus, recording dissenting opinions should be reserved for significant issues where the record of the divergence in views holds substantial importance for future reference or accountability, rather than as a routine practice for every disagreement.

Publicly disclosing the identities of those who held dissenting opinions is not recommended. Doing so could be perceived as an attempt to evade collective responsibility, and harming solidarity and support for the decision within the organisation and in the public eye. Highlighting individual dissenters could undermine this unity, potentially weakening the board's collective authority and effectiveness.

> **Example: Majority Vote, with Not All Trustees in Agreement, at British Museum**
>
> In December 2023, the British Museum announced a new multi-year partnership deal with 'long-term supporter BP'. For years, this sponsorship was a heavy debated deal and public protests, accusing BP of using its sponsorship to 'greenwash' its public image, given the company's environmental impact (See Part IV for a detailed description of the case).
>
> The British Museum's board meeting minutes revealed that the decision to continue the sponsorship deal with BP was made through a majority vote, with not all trustees in agreement. However, those who disagreed did not have such principled objections that they considered resigning at that time. 'Some

> Trustees indicated strong personal disagreement about accepting money from companies in the sponsor's line of business but resolved that these were not such as to require them to recuse themselves from acting as trustees in the decision to be made'.[6]
>
> When the deal was made public, one of the trustees, Dame Mary Beard, confirmed that she was one of the trustees who had opposed the sponsorship deal. She responded by email to questions from The Sunday Times: 'I only have this to say. I accepted as a Board member the view of the majority of the Trustees (who I know looked long and hard at this). But it was not my view and speaking personally this would not have been my decision'.[7]

8.1.4 Irreconcilable Differences of Opinions

Occasionally, fundamental, and irreconcilable differences in viewpoints among directors can escalate to a point where a director considers resigning. This development is significant, as it signals deep-seated disagreements that go beyond normal, healthy debate, often arising in situations involving moral dilemmas where the conflict is rooted in stark contrasts with personal values and beliefs. In such scenarios, the prospect of continuing to serve on the board may become untenable for a member, due to a profound misalignment with their ethical principles or conscience.

These potential resignations might signify more than a procedural change; they could indicate a major shift within the organisation while most likely it results in a significant decrease of diversity in perspectives, and this can reshape the organisation's strategic direction, reflecting a transformation in its core values or methodologies. Moreover, these resignations send a visible signal to the external public, emphasising the existence of significant doubt or disagreement regarding the board's decisions, values, or direction.

Just before the end of this spectrum of disagreement is the tactic of threatening resignation. This step is of course considered before actual resignation, serving as a final, powerful tool to prompt the other directors to seriously reconsider their stance. However, this threat should be used judiciously, while probably it can only be used once. If a director more frequently threatens to resign as a mere tactic in debates, it loses its seriousness and impact. Overuse of this strategy can be perceived as manipulative, undermining the genuine intent behind such a profound action. Therefore, the threat of stepping down should be reserved for moments of deep, principled conflict, and not reduced to a tactical ploy in boardroom discussions. It's a powerful statement, one that should reflect true ethical or value-based dissent, rather than being a recurring strategy to influence debate outcomes.

> **Example: Resignations (2) at the British Museum**
>
> In the case of the sponsor contract between the British Museum and BP, trustee Ahdaf Soueif resigned in July 2019 from the British Museum's Board of Trustees.[8] She had been a trustee for seven years. In an open letter,[9] she described that her 'resignation was a cumulative response to the museum's immovability on issues of critical concern' and that 'the world is caught up in battles over climate change, vicious and widening inequality, the residual heritage of colonialism, questions of democracy, citizenship, and human rights. On all these issues the museum needs to take a clear ethical position'.[10]
>
> Four years later, in November 2023, another trustee, Vice-Chair Muriel Gray resigned, just before the decision to renew the sponsor deal was made public. The minutes of the meeting stated that 'she had made a personal decision to submit her resignation as a Trustee to the government'.[11] She had also been a trustee for seven years.
>
> The Board of Trustees now decided on a majority vote, as illustrated by the previous example. However, this resulted in a board lacking its most critical members, which will undoubtedly impact future decisions as well.

8.2 Upper Echelon Theory

Decisions involving moral dilemmas are inherently subjective, uncertain, and complex; if they weren't, they wouldn't be considered dilemmas. Additionally, they are influenced by an individual's moral identity and personality traits. Although aimed at strategic choices by top executives and not at moral dilemmas, the 'Upper Echelon Theory' proposed by Professor of Business Policy Donald Hambrick and co-author Phyllis Mason offers valuable insights into understanding this influence[12] (See Fig. 8.2). This theory posits that the backgrounds, experiences, education, personality traits, moral values, and life experiences of top executives significantly shape their perceptions, decision-making processes, and ultimately, their strategic choices. These personal characteristics are especially important in uncertain and complex situations, where the strategic options are less clear and there are more risks than in situations where objective data are known. Even in environments that appear objective, the personal lens through which senior managers view these situations can lead to diverse outcomes in decision-making.

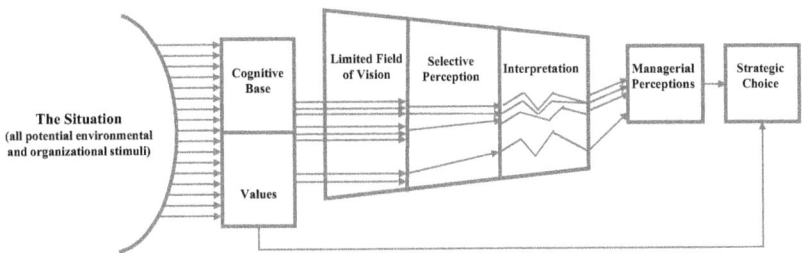

Fig. 8.2 Strategic choice under conditions of bounded rationality. Adapted from Hambrick and Mason (1984, p. 195)

Strategic decisions (at the far right) originate from 'the situation' (at the far left), encompassing all possible relevant factors from the environment and the organisation. As illustrated in the figure, not every factor is perceived, nor in the same manner, by the individual director or board member. Furthermore, their cognitive competencies (such as knowledge and expertise) and moral values also influence which elements are factored into their deliberations.

The cognitive abilities in this context relate to how directors process information and arrive at decisions, shaped by their education, work experience, knowledge, and problem-solving styles. A richer and more diverse cognitive skill set can lead to the contemplation of a broader selection of choices and, potentially, to more effective decision-making. Directors' (moral) values exert both an indirect and a direct effect (as indicated by the lower arrow in the diagram) on the strategic choices made. The ethical convictions of a director or board member can shape the aims and priorities of the organisation. For instance, if a director places a high value on environmental sustainability, it will likely affect decisions regarding manufacturing processes or material sourcing. A director's final perception of the strategic or ethical choice at hand is shaped by three factors: 1) the inherently limited perspective that subconsciously constrains the perceived field of view, 2) the selective focus on just a handful of elements within this field, and 3) the unique interpretation of these elements. Our inherent biases partly drive this process.

8.3 Biases

Biases are unconscious tendencies, preconceptions, or cognitive shortcuts that influence our thought processes, often eluding our awareness. These biases present a considerable challenge in decision-making environments like the boardroom, especially in the context of making moral judgements. Behavioural economists have shown that even when we believe our decisions are logical and evidence-based, our thought processes can deviate from rationality. The risk in boardroom decision-making is believing in the soundness of our choices while inadvertently ignoring contradictory evidence.

In a notable instance from 2014, a Delaware Court of Chancery justice pondered how a group of experienced, competent, and seemingly independent directors and advisors could oversee a significant oversight.[13] In the case he referred to, despite his conviction that the directors played a role in the oversight, they were legally absolved. He pinpointed five biases that disastrously swayed boardroom behaviour: dependence on initial estimates (anchoring), uncritical acceptance of options presented in a positive light (framing), preference for information that reinforces pre-existing beliefs (confirmation bias), a push towards unanimity (groupthink), and ethical standards being compromised by allegiance to leadership (misplaced loyalty). He further proposed that understanding behavioural tendencies should be an integral part of assessing director liability in legal contexts.

Behavioural economists Dan Lovallo and Olivier Sibony have identified numerous biases and organised them into five categories: action-oriented biases, interest biases, pattern-recognition biases, stability biases, and social biases.[14]

Five Categories Bias

Adapted from Lovallo and Sibony (2010)

Action-oriented bias
These include making hasty decisions driven by overoptimism, excessive confidence, or underestimation of competitive threats.

Interest bias
This involves prioritising personal interests or issues because of emotional connections, leading to an unbalanced focus on these aspects.

Pattern-Recognition bias
This refers to the erroneous recognition of familiarity in situations or procedures, which results in an overemphasis on confirmatory evidence and neglect of discrepancies.

Stability bias
This is the inclination to avoid making decisions in uncertain situations, placing more value on potential losses than on possible gains, or sticking with previous decisions despite new uncertainties.

Social bias
This denotes a preference for agreement over dissent, leading to groupthink or sunflower management, where decisions are overly influenced by the leader's views. In the realm of moral decisions, there's also the hazard of misplaced loyalty.

These insights highlight the complexity of boardroom decision-making and underscore the importance of vigilance against biases that can lead to flawed judgements and decisions.

8.3.1 Misplaced Loyalty

In the context of moral judgement and biases, the issue of misplaced loyalty warrants special consideration. This refers to the tendency of employees to show a strong sense of loyalty towards the CEO or other directors, even in the face of unethical or illegal behaviour. Such loyalty might originate from biases like the halo effect, where a leader's positive qualities are overemphasised, obscuring their negative traits, or the champions bias, where an idea is judged based on the proponent's past successes rather than objective facts. It could also be driven by sunflower management (akin to a sunflower always turning towards the sun), where the CEO fosters a culture that values flattery and rewards loyalty over competence or ethical conduct. When misplaced loyalty occurs, moral boundaries are breached. Subordinates may then ignore or rationalise unethical conduct, concealing illegal actions or even engaging in them themselves.

8.3.2 Mores

Like biases, mores also influence human behaviour and decision-making, often below the conscious level. The determination of what is considered morally appropriate is deeply influenced by a community's prevailing moral standards, the 'mores'. Mores are collective societal norms with a moral dimension that promote social cohesion.

'Mores', derived from the Latin word 'mōs' (with its plural form 'mores'), encompasses the customs, etiquette, and practices intrinsic to a society, including the uncodified rules and social behaviours that members of a particular group or society adhere to.[15] These mores often develop organically, not initially intended to serve as formal rules. They typically consist of minor actions that evolve into established customs through consistent repetition within a community. Being largely unwritten, these norms must be communicated directly to newcomers, as they cannot simply be learned from written sources. For those outside a particular group, merely observing these mores without understanding their significance can lead to feelings of alienation.

On an individual scale, biases display greater flexibility; with increased consciousness, educational insights, and dedicated endeavour, individuals are more capable of identifying and amending their personal biases than altering the deeply ingrained societal mores. William Graham Sumner, a nineteenth-century sociologist from the United States, introduced the term 'mores' in Sociology in 1898.[16] Mores are the unwritten but widely accepted norms, values, and conventions that govern social behaviour within a community. They include customs, traditions, and ethical standards facilitating social harmony and cohesion. Mores are inherently cultural, reflecting a society's collective preferences and values. They serve as a guide for acceptable and expected behaviour within a group. Mores often have a moral or ethical component, delineating right from wrong within a societal context. They help maintain order and social cohesion by setting standards for behaviour. Mores can evolve over time as societal values shift, but such changes usually occur slowly, reflecting gradual shifts in collective attitudes and beliefs. Sumner outlined several characteristics of mores.

> **Characteristics of Mores**
>
> **Adapted from Sumner (1906)**
> - Mores have authority; they are seen as facts because one has grown up with them, and the mores are not questioned.
> - Mores are unwritten and often apply unconsciously and unnoticed. Only in contact with other groups, in which other mores apply, does one become aware of one's mores.
> - Mores are rigid and slow to change. They do not give rise to reflection, on the contrary.
> - Mores provide stability to the social order where they are understood, common, and undisputed.
> - Mores can change from generation to generation because as the mores are received, they may not be passed on identically.
> - Mores do not suddenly change due to external intervention. They can only change by slowly trying again and again.

Moresprudence

Sharing the ethical considerations of directors when facing moral dilemmas, termed 'moresprudence', can be invaluable. Moresprudence involves applying moral norms and considerations to navigate such dilemmas, mirroring the way jurisprudence compiles judicial decisions in similar cases to guide future legal interpretations and decisions under analogous circumstances. In Part II of this book, various cases are explored, and the ethical deliberations of directors in moral dilemmas are detailed. These narratives serve as practical examples of moresprudence, demonstrating how decision-making is inherently subjective, varies across different organisations, and often triggers public controversy. Through these cases, the concept of moresprudence is enriched, offering insights into the complex interplay between corporate decision-making, moral values, and societal expectations. This extension of moresprudence emphasises the significance of recording and reflecting on the ethical dimensions of leadership decisions, contributing to a broader understanding of how moral considerations are integrated into corporate governance.

8.3.3 Four Perspectives of Moral Decision-Making

The necessity for directors to undertake a more diligent and inclusive approach in their ethical decision-making is evident. Not only must they seek to understand and weigh the implications of their decisions from multiple angles and stakeholders, but they must also foster an organisational culture that values ethical considerations and stakeholder welfare as paramount. Such an approach not only mitigates the immediate risks associated with public backlash but also positions the corporation on a sustainable path aligned with societal values and expectations.

The Australian Institute of Company Directors (AICD) introduced four distinct lenses or perspectives through which directors can examine moral dilemmas (See Table 8.1).[17] These perspectives range from a broad societal view to a director's specific individual viewpoint. This approach encourages a varied examination of ethical issues, urging consideration of the boardroom culture, the organisation's values, and personal biases and beliefs.

In the first, general perspective, directors focus on which aspects of the dilemma affect the organisation's environment, such as climate change, working conditions at suppliers, or work automation. This involves all internal and external stakeholders, and the question is also relevant to how the organisation wants to position itself, as a leader or as a follower.

From the second, organisational perspective, directors focus on the culture in the organisation when analysing the moral dilemma. From this perspective, the purpose, the values, and the principles of the organisation should be involved in analysing the moral dilemma.

In the third, boardroom perspective, the interpersonal relationships, the individual decision-making style, and the personal relationships between the directors play a role. They must be aware of the need to hear different views and be alert to processes such as groupthink or *boardroom dynamics*, where unconventional perspectives are not heard. The chairman has an important role in optimally utilising diversity and diverse perspectives.

Table 8.1 Four perspectives ('lenses') in moral decision-making

1. General perspective

Focus:
What aspects of the organisation's strategic environments are relevant to the decision?

Subjects:
- Are there factors that lie beyond the scope of the board papers? What is the connection between this choice and the long-term prospects of the organisation?
- Whose interests deserve to be considered?
- What are their interests? To what extent are those interests aligned?
- How do we wish to position the organisation? As a leader on such matters? As a close follower? Doing the minimum required by law or regulation?

2. Organisational perspective

Focus:
Does the board have a culture that enables and supports ethical considerations, including calling on the organisation's ethical framework?

Subjects:
- To what extent is the decision before the board clearly linked to the organisation's purpose, values, and principles?
- What impact will the board's decision have on the culture of the organisation?
- Is the board's decision framed in language that will resonate within the organisation?
- Where are the potential 'ethical blind spots' on the board? For example, is the proposed course of action being recommended for no better reason than 'everyone does it'?

3. Boardroom perspective

Focus:
Have you considered how group dynamics impact on board discussions, including how your own default decision-making style fits in?

Subjects:
- Is there too comfortable a drift towards agreement? Or is there an active effort to promote and manage diversity, and recognise and encourage differences of perspective?
- Are the opinions of some directors too easily dismissed because they are not subject matter experts? Are the opinions of some directors given too much weight because they are subject matter experts?
- Does the board identify and question the assumptions on which recommendations are based? Are directors given the time and opportunity to offer critiques of their own arguments?

4. Individual perspective

Focus:
Is each director aware of their personal ethical position and how it might differ from that of the organisation?

Subjects:
- Do your personal values and principles align with those of the organisation?
- Do you understand your own motivations and biases?
- How would your motivations look from an external perspective?
- Do you recognise your own preferred style of decision-making?
- Are you open to different approaches?
- Are you able to recognise and declare when you are 'out of your depth'? If so, have you sought counsel (if appropriate)? Are you prepared for a potentially difficult debate?

Adapted from AICD (2019, p.7)

Finally, the fourth, individual perspective is about the personal input of individual directors. This narrowest perspective recognises that each person has their own moral identity. Awareness of individual motivations, prejudices, and moral norms and values can help understand what the contribution in the boardroom is.

Notes

1. Kahneman, D. (2011). Thinking, Fast and Slow: Farrar, Straus and Giroux.
2. Janis, I. L. (1972). Victims of groupthink; a psychological study of foreign-policy decisions and fiascos. Boston: Houghton, Mifflin.
3. Independent Evaluation Office (IEO) of the International Monetary Fund, (2011). IMF Performance in the Run-Up to the Financial and Economic Crisis: IMF Surveillance in 2004–07, January 10, 2011.
4. Statement from the Harvard Corporation: Our President, December 12, 2023, https://www.harvard.edu/blog/2023/12/12/statement-from-the-harvard-corporation-our-president/
5. Statement from the Harvard Corporation: President Gay, January 2, 2024, https://www.harvard.edu/blog/2024/01/02/statement-from-the-harvard-corporation-president-gay/
6. Minutes of The British Museum Board Meeting, June 29, 2023.
7. Trustee quits British Museum over record £50 m sponsorship deal with BP, David Sanderson, The Times, December 19, 2023.
8. Minutes of The British Museum Board Meeting July 4, 2019.
9. On Resigning from the British Museum's Board of Trustees, Ahdaf Soueif, July 15, 2019.
10. Trustee resigns from British Museum over its stance on sponsorship and repatriation, Geraldine Kendall Adams, website Museums Associations, July 16, 2019.
11. Minutes of The British Museum Board Meeting November 27, 2023.
12. Hambrick, D. C., & Mason, P. A. (1984). Upper echelons: The organization as a reflection of its top managers. *The Academy of Management Review, 9*(2), 193–206.
13. Oesterle, D. A. (2014). Should courts do behavioral analysis of boardroom conduct? *Journal of Business & Technology Law, 9*(1), 51–58.
14. Lovallo, D., & Sibony, O. (2010). The case for behavioral strategy. McKinsey Quarterly, March 2010.

15. Lückerath-Rovers, M. (2010). Learning Mores. Soft Controls in Corporate Governance. Inaugural Speech, Nyenrode University.
16. Sumner, W. H. (1906). Folkways. A study of Sociological Importance of Usages, Manners, Customs, Mores and Morals. Ginn and Company.
17. Australian Institute of Company Directors (AICD). (2019). Ethics in the Boardroom. A decision-making guide for directors.

9

The Interplay Between Legality, Morality, and Opinions

> One has not only a legal but a moral responsibility to obey just laws. Conversely, one has a moral responsibility to disobey unjust laws.
> —Martin Luther King, 1963

This book explores moral dilemmas in the boardroom, exploring moral choices instead of the more black and white, legal versus illegal actions. Now, this chapter describes the complex dynamics between legal permissibility, moral acceptability, and the impact of public perception.

Although the legal system provides a framework for distinguishing right from wrong, it does not necessarily always mirror moral righteousness. For example, society might recognise a certain law as morally incompatible with principles of equality and human dignity. In such cases, individuals, activists, and even some conscientious public officials may refuse to comply with or enforce these unjust laws. They may engage in civil disobedience, protests, and advocacy campaigns to challenge and overturn discriminatory legislation. But also companies should not hide behind any laws which have not yet been adapted to new knowledge. If a manufacturing company is legally allowed to emit a certain level of pollutants into the atmosphere based on outdated regulations, but new scientific research reveals the severe health and environmental impacts of these emissions, the company cannot morally justify continuing its practices solely because they are within legal limits. This discrepancy between legality and morality highlights the limitations of legal guidelines in capturing the full range of ethical complexities and vice versa. Or, as stated by Martin Luther King in 1963 in one of his *Letters from a*

Birmingham Jail: 'One has not only a legal but a moral responsibility to obey just laws. Conversely, one has a moral responsibility to disobey unjust laws'.[1]

Morality, being inherently subjective, varies significantly from one individual to another. What is considered morally acceptable can shift dramatically across different cultural and societal contexts, illustrating the challenge of aligning legal, moral, and societal expectations. Furthermore, due to the increasing belief in the concept of stakeholderism, society demands a more activist and advocacy-oriented role from CEOs, too. This chapter describes the interplay between these different and, in the meantime, overlapping themes.

9.1 Legally Permissible? Or Morally Acceptable?

Legally permissible actions are those that align with the letter of the law; they are actions that regulations and legal frameworks explicitly allow or do not prohibit. In contrast, morally acceptable actions align with ethical principles and societal values, focusing on what is considered right, just, or good in a broader, often more subjective, sense. This 'moral compass' is frequently influenced by cultural, religious, and social standards, as well as personal beliefs and values.

The relationship between legality and morality is complex. While laws are often grounded in moral principles, they do not cover the full spectrum of what society considers morally acceptable or unacceptable. The legal system and societal moral standards are not always aligned (See Fig. 9.1).

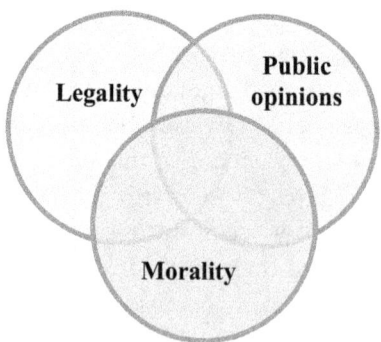

Fig. 9.1 Legally permissible, morally acceptable, and public opinion

Certain actions may be legal but are broadly viewed as immoral by society: 'Lawful but awful', such as exploiting legal loopholes for financial gain or engaging in practices that, while legal, go against public ethical standards.

> **Example: Lawful but Awful, Overnight Price Increase of a Life-Saving Drug**
>
> The board of Turing Pharmaceuticals became a focal point of intense public and media scrutiny when they decided to raise the price of Daraprim, a life-saving drug, overnight by over 5,000%, from 13.50 dollars to 750 dollars.[2] They operated within the legal frameworks governing pharmaceutical pricing. This decision was justified by Turing and CEO Shkreli on several grounds, including the need for funds to research new treatments and the assertion that the high price would be largely absorbed by insurers and healthcare programmes rather than directly impacting patients. However, the justification did little to quell the outrage, as the price hike posed a significant burden on healthcare systems and potentially restricted access to a vital medication for vulnerable populations. CEO Martin Shkreli was often referred to in the media as 'the most hated man in America' due to this incident and became a symbol of the ethical responsibilities of pharmaceutical companies.[3]

Morality is subjective, varying widely among individuals, unlike legality, which is based on universally recognised rules. This distinction becomes clear through various scenarios in daily life and business, where what is legal may not always align with what some consider moral. Laws that seem to discriminate or fail to protect vulnerable groups can prompt individuals to break them for what they believe is a morally just cause, leading to civil disobedience to spur change or draw attention to issues. Similarly, in business, practices that are legal but seen as unethical, such as low wages, tax avoidance, or contributing to environmental harm, can attract public criticism and harm a company's reputation. This highlights the need for businesses to consider the ethical implications of their actions in addition to legal compliance, to avoid public backlash and potential damage to their standing.

9.2   Public Opinions

Public opinion serves as a dynamic intersection between legality and morality, reflecting societal attitudes and the prevailing ethical consensus. It can validate or challenge the morality of legally permissible actions, influencing both legislative changes and shifts in ethical perspectives. While legality is grounded in statutory and regulatory norms, and morality in ethical principles, public opinion embodies the evolving social narrative, often acting as a catalyst for reconciling legal standards with ethical expectations. This interplay underscores that an action's acceptance by society hinges not only on its adherence to law but also on its alignment with contemporary moral and societal norms.

The CEO of the Danish brewer Carlsberg, Cees 't Hart, demonstrated the difficulties when balancing the different perspectives: 'Companies are now being asked more than politics sets requirements'. They are forced to take a broader consideration about the countries in which they are active. The question is how this will develop, and he adds, 'It feels like rewriting the rules of the chess game'.[4]

> It feels like rewriting the rules of the chess game
> —CEO Carlsberg, Cees 't Hart, 2022

The public's perception of morality is crucial, as it not only influences legislative changes but also shapes societal norms around what behaviours are considered ethically acceptable. Lawmakers often consider public sentiment on moral issues, which has led to significant legal reforms in various domains. For instance, the legal recognition of same-sex marriage in numerous countries reflects a shift in societal attitudes. Similarly, in corporate governance, public pressure has led to the enactment of laws aimed at enhancing diversity (for example gender quota laws) and regulating executive compensation.

Moreover, existing laws and corporate governance regulations may not fully ensure ethical behaviour among directors. While stricter regulations and potential sanctions can improve compliance, they often fail to address the spirit of the law, revealing loopholes that permit legal adherence without genuine ethical engagement. This underscores the complexity of aligning legal frameworks with moral expectations and the ongoing challenge of fostering a culture of integrity within and beyond the corporate sphere.

9.2.1 The Risk of Ignoring Outside Perspectives

When considering the different options in a moral dilemma, directors must consider the multiple perspectives of different stakeholders. The necessity for directors to assimilate the diverse perspectives of all stakeholders into their decision-making processes cannot be overstated. Numerous instances have shown that corporate boards frequently encounter difficulties when their decisions do not reflect public expectations or ethical norms.

9 The Interplay Between Legality, Morality, and Opinions

> A group of dedicated, everyday New Yorkers and their neighbours defeated Amazon's corporate greed
> —Alexandria Ocasio-Cortez in 2019

This misalignment typically stems from a significant oversight: the failure to adequately consider and integrate a broad spectrum of viewpoints, especially those that might challenge the board's initial inclinations or reveal unseen risks.

> **Example: Amazon Withdrew Plans for Headquarters in New York.**
> Amazon announced in 2018 a high-profile search for a location for its second headquarters, inviting cities to compete with tax breaks and incentives. When Amazon chose New York City for a new location, there was a strong backlash from local residents and politicians who criticised the decision to offer substantial tax incentives to one of the world's richest companies at the expense of local communities and infrastructure.[5] The public debate highlighted concerns over corporate responsibility and the ethical implications of leveraging public resources for private gain. On February 14, 2019, Amazon withdrew its plan to build a significant portion of its headquarters in New York, citing opposition from local politicians as a key reason.[6] Politician Alexandria Ocasio-Cortez (@AOC) tweeted on the same day: 'Anything is possible: today was the day a group of dedicated, everyday New Yorkers & their neighbours defeated Amazon's corporate greed, its worker exploitation, and the power of the richest man in the world'

The failure of boards to consider multiple perspectives exposes corporations to several risks. At the forefront is reputational damage, a peril that can undermine years of brand building and loyalty, effectively eroding stakeholder trust overnight. Public backlash, amplified in the digital age by social media, can swiftly translate into significant financial downturns, as consumers choose to dissociate from brands that fall short of ethical standards.

> The "moral compass of the company" was not pointing in the right direction
> —CEO Dara Khosrowshahi in 2018

Moreover, legal actions may follow, as regulatory bodies and watchdog organisations step in to scrutinise and penalise malpractices overlooked in the board's decision-making process. Finally, a deeper risk might manifest in the erosion of corporate culture.

> **Example: Uber CEO Resigned, Initially Defended by Board.**
> In 2017, the board of Uber initially defended Uber's practices after allegations of a toxic workplace culture, including sexual harassment, discrimination, and aggressive business practices.[7] In an interview with CNN, Uber board member Arianna Huffington commented that CEO Travis Kalanick should 'absolutely not' resign, arguing that individuals should not be assessed based on 'their worst moments'.[8] Only after the public outcry was intensified by a viral blog post by a former employee, an investigation revealed systemic issues within the company. The board's initial defence was met with public backlash, questioning the company's moral compass and the board's oversight of corporate culture and ethics. The controversy led to significant changes at the executive level, including the resignation of the CEO. The new CEO Dara Khosrowshahi later said that 'The "moral compass of the company" was not pointing in the right direction'.[9]

9.3 CEO Activism

CEO activism can play a pivotal role in shaping and broadcasting a company's stance on societal issues, underscoring the importance of leadership in driving corporate social responsibility. The actions and voices of CEOs can amplify a company's commitment to societal concerns, providing a human face to corporate initiatives and enhancing their impact.

CEO advocacy refers to situations where CEOs use their visibility, influence, and platform to speak out on social, environmental, political, or economic issues that may or may not be directly related to their company's immediate business interests. It can shape public discourse, influence policy, and impact a company's brand and stakeholder relationships.

> It's time we acknowledge that brands, like ours, play a role in influencing culture.
> —Gilette in 2019

A typology of CEO activism was developed by associate professor in crisis management Layla Branicki and her colleagues.[10] Their typology has two dimensions: the extent of corporate self-interest tied to the issue and the moral intensity of the problem within the broader society. These dimensions influence the form and intensity of CEO activism, affecting CEOs' readiness to make public moral declarations. Furthermore, they determine how activism influences broader societal moral transformations. From these dimensions emerge four distinct categories of CEO activism: Token, Servant, Strategic, and Citizen Activism.

Token Activism arises with issues of low moral intensity and business relevance, often reacting to mature social issues with broad consensus. It typically involves minimal actions like signing collective letters and crafting a desired moral identity for CEOs and their companies without profoundly impacting social change. Servant Activism features high moral intensity with little direct business connection, focusing on societal over corporate benefits. CEOs driven by personal values adopt stances on divisive topics, risking scrutiny but potentially significantly influencing public moral discourse. Strategic Activism is centred on issues critical to business but low in moral intensity. It aims to promote business interests while masquerading as moral action. It poses a low risk and aligns with CSR efforts, focusing on creating favourable social and political conditions for business success. Citizen Activism combines high moral intensity with strong business relevance, integrating strategic and servant activism features. CEOs engage in public debate on controversial issues, balancing moral and economic logic to reduce risks and align ethics with financial interests, enabling a pragmatic approach to moral leadership that accommodates shareholder concerns.

CEO activism is often seen as a double-edged sword: it can bolster a company's reputation and align it with socially responsible values, but it can also lead to backlash from customers, investors, or employees who have different views.[11]

> We didn't expect universal praise
> —CEO Starbucks Schultz in 2015

CEO activism illustrates the powerful role that business leaders can play in societal issues. However, the mixed outcomes of such advocacy underscore the need for CEOs to carefully consider the implications of their public statements and actions, ensuring they align with their company's values and stakeholders' expectations.

> **Examples: CEO Activism with Positive Impact**
>
> Former Unilever CEO Paul Polman has been widely praised for integrating sustainability into the core of Unilever's business model. He championed the Sustainable Living Plan, aiming to decouple the company's growth from its environmental footprint while increasing its positive social impact. Polman's advocacy for sustainability and responsible business practices not only bolstered Unilever's reputation but also set a benchmark in the industry for ESG efforts.

> Jesper Brodin, CEO of IKEA, has been vocal about supporting refugees, advocating for their right to work, and integrating them into society.[12] IKEA has committed to hiring refugees in its stores and production lines, particularly in Europe and the United States. This stance not only supports humanitarian values but also benefits IKEA by diversifying its workforce and fostering community goodwill, showcasing how social advocacy can align with business objectives and societal benefits.

CEO activism and messaging should be consistent because they build trust, support brand integrity, boost employee morale, attract investors, maintain consumer loyalty, and mitigate the risk of backlash. Stakeholders are more likely to support a company when they believe its leaders are genuinely committed to their values and statements. Inconsistency can lead to perceptions of insincerity, opportunism, or a lack of genuine commitment, all of which can undermine trust and credibility with stakeholders.

> **Example: CEO Activism that Backfired**
>
> CEO Howard Schultz of Starbucks campaign 'Race Together' encouraged baristas to start conversations about race with customers,[13] but faced significant backlash. Critics argued that it placed an unfair burden on employees and was not an appropriate venue for complex discussions about race, leading to a swift end to the initiative, within less than a week. CEO Schultz reacted that 'while there has been criticism of the initiative, and I know this hasn't been easy for any of you, let me assure you that we didn't expect universal praise'.[14]

CEO activism, therefore, should reflect and reinforce the corporate values. Consistency in advocacy ensures that the CEO's messages are aligned with the company's brand and values, enhancing its integrity. Inconsistent messaging can confuse the public and employees about what the company stands for, potentially diluting the brand and weakening its position in the market. Employees often look to their leaders for cues on the company's direction and values. A CEO who consistently advocates for issues that align with the company's values can inspire employees, improve morale, and increase retention. Inconsistent advocacy can lead to disillusionment and a lack of engagement among employees, who may feel disconnected from the company's purported mission and values.

Consistency might also be important for investors and shareholders, who increasingly consider ESG factors in their investment decisions. A CEO's consistent commitment to these issues can attract like-minded investors and enhance the company's reputation in the financial community. Conversely, inconsistency can signal risk and volatility, potentially deterring investment. Also, consumers are more inclined to support brands that consistently demonstrate commitment to causes they care about. Inconsistent advocacy can lead to scepticism and erode consumer loyalty, as it suggests that the company's engagement with social issues is superficial or merely a marketing strategy.

Other actions can nullify that positive impact proves the case of Jes Staley, the former CEO of Barclays.

> **Example: Inconsistent CEO Activism**
>
> A prominent example of positive CEO advocacy that was later nullified due to inconsistency involves BP's former CEO, Tony Hayward. In the mid-2000s, Hayward made significant public commitments towards environmental responsibility and sustainability, aiming to move BP 'Beyond Petroleum' by investing in renewable energy sources and reducing the company's carbon footprint. His advocacy for environmental sustainability and corporate responsibility was initially well-received, positioning BP as a forward-thinking energy company committed to addressing climate change. However, this positive advocacy was dramatically nullified following the Deepwater Horizon oil spill in April 2010, one of the largest environmental disasters in history. The spill resulted in the release of millions of barrels of oil into the Gulf of Mexico, causing extensive environmental damage, killing wildlife, and affecting the livelihoods of local communities.
>
> The inconsistency between Hayward's advocacy for environmental responsibility and the reality of BP's operations, highlighted by the disaster and the company's response to it, led to significant public and political backlash. Hayward's comments during the crisis, particularly the infamous 'I want my life back' remark,[15] further exacerbated the situation, making him seem out of touch with the severity of the disaster (11 people died) and the suffering of affected communities.[16] He lost his job only a month after he made this remark.[17]

When CEOs speak inconsistently on social issues, they risk backlash from all sides. Those who support the cause may feel betrayed if the CEO's actions do not match their words, while those opposed to the cause may view any advocacy as unnecessary or intrusive. This can lead to public relations challenges and damage the company's reputation.

Consistency in CEO advocacy is demonstrated by steadfastly standing by the message even in the face of backlash, underscoring a commitment to the cause despite public criticism.

> **Example: Consistent CEO Activism, Even After Backlash**
>
> Gillette's 'The Best Men Can Be' campaign, a variation on to their well-known slogan 'the best a man can get', sought to challenge toxic masculinity and promote positive behaviour among men, aligning with the #MeToo movement. Despite its intentions for social responsibility, the campaign faced backlash for seemingly generalising all men's behaviour, leading to accusations of virtue signalling and alienating its customer base.[18] Critics called for boycotts, expressing their discontent on social media. British broadcaster Piers Morgan accused the razor company on Twitter of contributing to the so-called 'global assault on masculinity'. @piersmorgan
>
> Nevertheless, Procter & Gamble, Gillette's parent company, stood by the campaign, emphasising its commitment to societal change. 'It's time we acknowledge that brands, like ours, play a role in influencing culture. And as a company that encourages men to be their best, we have a responsibility to make sure we are promoting positive, attainable, inclusive, and healthy versions of what it means to be a man'.[19] A website 'the best a man can be', under the umbrella of Gillette, is still in the air, focusing on role models.

Due to the increasing belief in the concept of stakeholderism, society demands a more activist and advocacy-oriented role from CEOs. This call has recently even more intensified especially due to the increasing visibility and urgency of global challenges, such as climate change, inequality, the war in Ukraine and the conflict between Gaza and Palestine, and human rights issues. As visible leaders, CEOs are more and more expected to use their platforms and influence to drive change. The rise of social media has amplified voices and accelerated the spread of information. Conversely, social media also means that companies and their leadership are under constant scrutiny, with their actions and inactions publicly analysed and discussed.

Notes

1. Letter from a Birmingham Jail, Martin Luther King, April 16, 1963.
2. Drug Goes From $13.50 a Tablet to $750, Overnight, Andrew Pollack, September 20, 2015, The New York Times.
3. Who is Martin Shkreli - 'the most hated man in America'?, Zoe Thomas & Tim Swift, August 4, 2017, BBC.
4. 'Carlsberg-ceo Cees 't Hart over vertrek uit Rusland. 'Alsof de regels van het schaakspel werden herschreven' ('Carlsberg CEO Cees 't Hart on leaving Russia. 'As if the rules of the chess game were being rewritten'), Pieter Couwenbergh, het FD, July 14, 2022.

5. A $2 Billion Question: Did New York and Virginia Overpay for Amazon?, Ben Casselman, November 13, 2018, The New York Times.
6. Amazon Pulls Out of Planned New York City Headquarters, J. David Goodman, February 14, 2019, The New York Times.
7. Uber's scandals, blunders and PR disasters: the full list, Sam Levin, June 28, 2017, The Guardian.
8. Uber board member Arianna Huffington said Travis Kalanick must 'absolutely not' go, Shona Ghosh, March 21, 2017, Business Insider.
9. Moral compass' was off at Uber under co-founder Kalanick, says new CEO Dara Khosrowshahi, Matthew J. Belvedere, January 23, 2018, CNBC.
10. Branicki, L., Brammer, S., Pullen, A., & Rhodes, C. (2020). The morality of "new" CEO activism. *Journal of Business Ethics*, *170*(2), 269–285.
11. Larcker, D. F., Miles, S., Tayan, B., & Wright-Violich K. (2018). The Double-Edged Sword of CEO Activism. Stanford Closer Look Series.
12. Ingka Group approaches 500 companies to integrate refugees, press release, May 26, 2022, ingka.com and 'At debate in Davos: Investing in social jobs and integrating refugees into the labour market', Ian Lewis, May 31, 2022, Impact Investor.
13. Starbucks Baristas Encouraged To Write 'Race Together' On Cups To Spark Dialogue On Race Relations With Customers, March 18, 2015, CBS.
14. Starbucks Ends Conversation Starters on Race, Ravi Somaiya, March 22, 2015, The New York Times.
15. BP CEO apologizes for "thoughtless" oil spill comment, June 2, 2010, Reuters.
16. BP's Tony Hayward and the Failure of Leadership Accountability, Rosabeth Moss Kanter, June 7, 2010, Harvard Business Review.
17. BP CEO Tony Hayward to step down and be succeeded by Robert Dudley, July 27, 2010, press release BP.
18. Why Gillette's New Ad Campaign Is Toxic, Charles Taylor, January 15, 2019, Forbes.
19. Our commitment enabling access to positive role models around the world, Gilette.com, gillette.com/en-us/about/the-best-men-can-be.

10

A Five-Step Ethical Decision-Making Model

> Wisdom begins with wonder.
> —Socrates in Plato's Theaetetus

The Greek philosopher Socrates was known for his quest for truth and knowledge. With his statement, 'wisdom begins with wonder', he meant that asking questions and wondering why the world is as it is, is the first step in the process of gaining wisdom. Various disciplines and scholars have developed multiple frameworks to guide individuals and organisations in navigating moral dilemmas. These models often share common elements, such as identifying the ethical issue, considering the stakeholders involved, evaluating the options from multiple ethical perspectives, deciding, and reflecting on the outcome.

Ethical decision-making models are models that guide people in a systematic and standardised manner to analyse and determine a defensible outcome when making a decision that has ethical implications. Over 150 such models have been published, these models vary from three to seventeen steps.[1] In this book, the five-step approach of the Australian Institute of Corporate Directors[2] is used as a basis. However, to demonstrate both the utilitarian and deontological considerations of directors, this AICD model is notably enriched by integrating a Moral Considerations Matrix in the third, evaluation, step.

10.1 Ethical Decision-Making Models

To arrive at a balanced decision in moral dilemmas, it is useful to introduce some structure. As with so many topics in the boardroom, simply collecting answers to these questions will probably result in a list of possible options without structure, without analysis, and without weights or priorities. It could also be the case that more weight is given to the opinion of a director who reacted most violently or emotionally than to a director who made rational considerations in the dilemma. A structured approach is, therefore, essential.

Several ethical decision-making models provide practical tools to evaluate moral dilemmas and come to a judgement. Most models consist of three to ten steps in which first the problem is clarified, then the different stakeholders are identified, the possible options are weighed against each other, and finally, a decision is made. This is usually followed by an evaluation or reflection. As a guideline for evaluating the ethicality of decisions in business and personal contexts, renowned authors about ethical decision-making Ken Blanchard and Norman Peale introduced in 1988 three ethical questions: Is it legal?, Is it balanced?, and How does it make me feel?[3] (See Table 10.1).

Table 10.1 Three ethical questions

Is it legal?
This question asks whether the action or decision complies with either civil law or company policy. It encourages individuals to consider all relevant legal frameworks, regulations, and rules. The aim is to ensure that the decision does not violate any legal boundaries, understanding that legality is a fundamental aspect of ethical conduct
Is it balanced?
This question focuses on fairness to all concerned, both in the short and in the long term. It prompts the individual to consider if the decision promotes win–win relationships. The idea is to strive for decisions that do not unduly favours one party over another but instead aim for a balance of interests, ensuring that no stakeholder is disproportionately affected
How does it make me feel?
This question is about self-reflection on the personal impact of the decision. Questions involved are: 'Will it make me proud', Will I feel good if my decision was published in the newspaper', and 'Would I feel good if my family knew about it?'. It encourages individuals to listen to their conscience and consider how the decision aligns with their personal values and principles. The question serves to remind that ethical decisions should not only be legally sound and balanced but also personally and morally satisfying

Adapted from Blanchard and Peale (1988)

10 A Five-Step Ethical Decision-Making Model

These questions are particularly useful for navigating grey areas in moral dilemmas, where the right course of action may not be immediately clear. The three questions encourage directors to think beyond the immediate benefits of a decision and consider the broader impact on all stakeholders and their own moral integrity.

These three questions also relate to the Ethical Triangle Model (see Fig. 10.1) developed by Jack Kem, a former military intelligence colonel and now a professor at the US Army Command and General Staff College.[4]

Kem developed this model to provide a comprehensive and practical framework for ethical decision-making, particularly in the context of military leadership and education. In the military environment, where decisions often have significant and far-reaching consequences, it's crucial for leaders to make choices that are not only legally sound but also ethically justified and aligned with military values and principles. Kem recognised the complexity of ethical dilemmas faced in such settings and sought to offer a model that facilitates a well-rounded approach to resolving these challenges.

> Doing the right thing is good. Doing the right thing for the right reason and with the right goal is better
> —Jack Kem, 2016

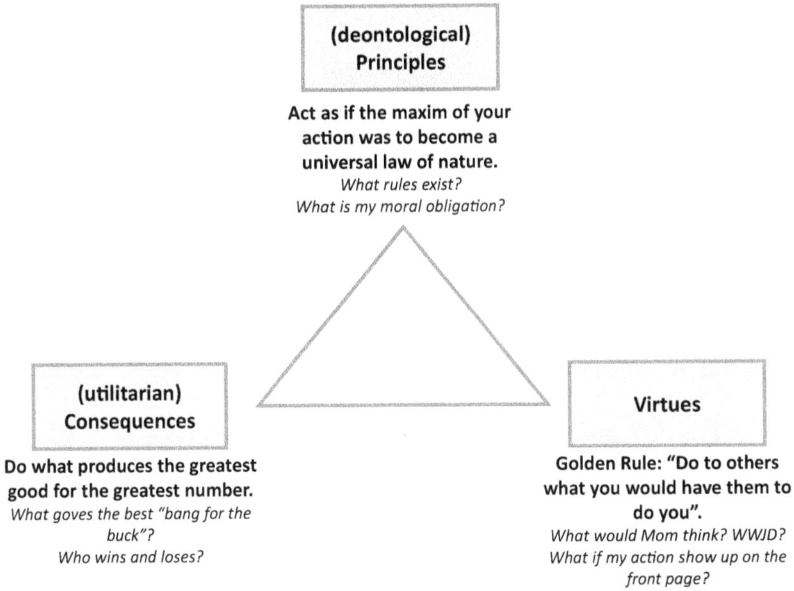

(deontological) Principles
Act as if the maxim of your action was to become a universal law of nature.
What rules exist?
What is my moral obligation?

(utilitarian) Consequences
Do what produces the greatest good for the greatest number.
What goves the best "bang for the buck"?
Who wins and loses?

Virtues
Golden Rule: "Do to others what you would have them to do you".
What would Mom think? WWJD?
What if my action show up on the front page?

Fig. 10.1 The ethical triangle. Adapted from Jack Kem (2016)

He aimed to equip leaders, especially those in the military, with a tool that balances legal compliance, consequences of actions, and moral duties. His publication starts with a quote from de US Army Leadership (par 3.27): 'Doing the right thing is good. Doing the right thing for the right reason and with the right goal is better'. His ethical triangle model encourages leaders to consider the legal aspects, the impacts of their decisions, and their moral and ethical duties. Together, these questions form a comprehensive framework for ethical decision-making, encouraging individuals and organisations to consider legal, balanced, and personal aspects of their actions. Unlike deontological ethics and utilitarian ethics, virtue ethics centres on what it means to be a good person and the virtues that constitute good character. It suggests that the moral worth of an action is determined not just by its adherence to principles or its consequences but by the character of the person performing the action and the intention behind it.

The five-step approach of AICD focuses on guiding directors through moral decision-making processes. This plan is detailed in the AICD publication 'Ethics in the Boardroom: A decision-making guide for directors'. (A more detailed outline can be found in Table 10.6 in the appendix to this chapter.) In this book, this five-step approach is enhanced with the inclusion of a Moral Considerations Matrix in the third step, showcasing both utilitarian and deontological considerations. The five steps do not determine the outcome or give a judgement but provide a structured approach to a moral dilemma. According to the AICD, it contributes to defensible decisions from the boardroom, even if these are controversial in the eyes of certain stakeholders.

The five steps that the AICD uses are:

1. *Frame*: define the dilemma
2. *Shape*: explore all options
3. *Evaluate*: evaluate the best options
4. *Refine*: refine the choice
5. *Act*: implement the choice

10.2 Defining the Dilemma (Frame)

The initial Frame phase involves clearly identifying the nature of the moral dilemma. This requires gathering facts, scrutinising assumptions, identifying key stakeholders, and aligning the issue with the organisation's core values while also ensuring compliance with laws and regulations. In this phase, it is important that questions are asked in a Socratic way.

10.2.1 Socratic Questions

The method named after Socrates is a process of asking questions and critical thinking to arrive at a deeper understanding and insight. Socrates encouraged people to remain critical and always look beyond their current knowledge and understanding. The Socratic method is aimed at exploring ideas, views, and beliefs through the asking of open and challenging questions. By asking open questions and challenging underlying assumptions and beliefs, the method can help to bring these hidden assumptions and thinking errors to light and thus gain a deeper understanding of the situation. Instead of simply providing answers, the Socratic method tries to help people find their own answers by asking questions that encourage them to think about their own beliefs and reasoning.

This way of asking questions is also relevant for the boardroom. For example, it assists directors to ask questions that are exploratory, rather than directive, thereby challenging management to explain and justify their decision-making proposals in a different way and gain new insights. It creates a culture of openness and transparency as directors are encouraged to share and explore their thoughts and beliefs. Examples of Socratic questions for the boardroom are: *What is the problem we are trying to solve and why is it important? How would different stakeholders view this problem and how can we incorporate their perspectives into our decision-making?* or *How have we made decisions in the past and what have we learned from that?*

In this phase, where the focus is on jointly investigating what the core of the moral dilemma entails, it is even more important to ask questions without prejudice. *What are the consequences for multiple stakeholders? What might be different perspectives? How do these perspectives relate to each other? What is the most important principle at stake here (individually and collectively)? How can we consider the interests of different stakeholders? What alternative solutions are there, and how would these alternatives relate to the core values and moral convictions of our organisation?*

Furthermore, in this phase, it is essential to recognising and mitigate biases, as they can cloud judgement and influence the framing of the dilemma.

10.2.2 Preventing Biases

There are several methods to prevent or at least reduce biases. A diverse composition of the group is important so that multiple perspectives are brought to the table. Also, contributions to discussions should be made based on expertise, not based on hierarchical positions. Good preparation based on complete, correct, and independent information is also of great importance. Psychologist and Nobel laureate for economy Daniel Kahneman, with colleagues Lovello and Sibony, formulated twelve questions that directors can use to help detect and neutralise biases[5] (See Table 10.2). Their questions are divided into three categories: preliminary questions to yourself, challenging questions to the team, and, ultimately, the evaluation of the proposal.

10.3 Exploring All Options (Shape)

This second Shape phase is dedicated to the exhaustive exploration of potential solutions, fostering an environment where creativity flourishes and no idea is off-limits. The AICD emphasises this as both the most liberating and challenging step, encouraging the consideration of all possibilities, however unconventional. It's also a time to discern genuine dilemmas from 'amoral temptations', such as the lure of unethical advantages. The discovery of 'inflection points', moments where conflicting values and principles intersect, can be pivotal. Identifying or creating these moments allows for the re-evaluation of the dilemmas' components, opening new avenues for resolution. This is particularly valuable in situations where the decision seems impossible, providing a way to navigate through the complexity.

The possible questions should encourage creative and out-of-the-box thinking to identify novel approaches and a thorough examination of the short-term and long-term outcomes associated with each potential solution. Also, looking at how similar dilemmas were handled in the past can provide valuable insights and help predict the consequences of different actions. Of course, ensuring consistency with the organisation's core values and mission is crucial for maintaining integrity and public trust. And sometimes, the best solution isn't immediately apparent and requires creative thinking to identify a middle ground. Challenge the initial perception of the dilemma to uncover alternative solutions, for example, by exploring the potential for partnerships or joint efforts in resolving the dilemma. Finally, exploring ways to lessen any adverse effects can help find a more palatable solution for all stakeholders involved.

Table 10.2 Detecting and neutralising biases

1. Preliminary questions to yourself

Check on self-interested biases
Are there perverse incentives present that steer the decision in a certain direction? Evaluate the proposal extra carefully, especially for overoptimism

Check on interest bias
Is the team 'in love' with the proposal? Thoroughly go through all requirements on the checklist

Check for groupthink
Were there dissenting opinions within the preparatory team? If yes, was this adequately responded to? Look for differing opinions, if necessary, discreetly

2. Challenge questions to the team

Check for false analogy
Could the underlying diagnosis have been too much influenced by a (false) analogy with another memorable success, by anecdotes or other striking examples? Ask for more analogies and analyse these for comparisons with the current situation

Check for confirmation bias
Have plausible alternatives been considered? Confirmation bias: ignoring signals that contradict claims. Demand multiple options/alternatives

Check for availability bias
If you had to make the same decision again in a year, what information would be needed and is this information already available? Availability bias: information that comes up quickly and easily, is used more often when making that decision. Use a checklist for information that is needed

Check for anchoring bias
Do we know where the underlying data comes from? Anchoring bias: sticking to a certain starting value. Restart by requesting a new analysis, based on figures from other models or benchmarks

Check for halo effect
Does the team assume that a person, organisation, or approach that was successful before, will be just as successful in a different situation? Eliminate false inferences and ask for additional comparable examples

Check for sunk costs
Is the proposal too much influenced by or attached to previously made decisions? Look at the situation as if you are a new CEO

(continued)

Table 10.2 (continued)

3. Evaluation of the proposal
Check for overconfidence, for overoptimism, for poor planning, and for ignoring competitors
Is the basic scenario too rosy? Bring the outside view in. Use wargames: look at it from the perspective of the competitor
Check for the ignoring disaster scenario
Is the worst-case scenario severe enough? Do a pre-mortem: looking ahead, imagine the worst that can happen, and then describe how it could have happened. This is the opposite of a post-mortem: looking back, with the knowledge of now we would have done it all differently
Check for loss aversion
Is the proposal perhaps too cautious? Sometimes teams are not creative or ambitious enough. Change the rewards so that risk is shared

Derived from: Before You Make That Big Decision, Kahneman, Lovello, and Sibony (2011)

10.4 Evaluating the Best Options (Evaluate)

In the third Evaluation phase, the focus narrows to comparing the most viable two or three options. This book introduces a 'Moral Considerations Matrix', a tool designed to delve deeper into the ethical implications of each option. The Moral Considerations Matrix emphasises the deontological (principles) and utilitarian (consequences) moral responsibilities of directors, so that directors can ensure that their actions are not only morally sound but also socially responsible, leading to outcomes that are ethically justifiable and broadly supported. This entails a careful balancing of the interests of various stakeholders, offering a more nuanced understanding of the ethical landscape surrounding the decision-making process.

This dual approach facilitates a deeper understanding of the moral landscape, enabling a more nuanced and informed decision-making process that respects ethical principles while striving for fairness and equity among all stakeholders.

10.4.1 Moral Consideration Matrix

The Moral Considerations Matrix serves to differentiate between utilitarian and deontological aspects within a moral dilemma (See Table 10.3). It offers directors a framework to organise their thoughts, compare them, and balance them out. This matrix not only clarifies the moral principles at risk but also outlines the impact of their decisions on the well-being and prosperity of various stakeholders. The matrix of moral considerations doesn't

Table 10.3 Moral consideration matrix

	Utilitarian consequences	Deontological moral norms
For +		
Against −		

give a straightforward, mathematical solution to the moral dilemma but rather provides a structured approach to navigating through it. Additionally, after the decision-making process, the matrix proves to be useful in communicating the decisions that are made.

Before the matrix is utilised, it should be preceded with a single question:

> Would it be morally appropriate to …

Followed by the potential option(s) that resulted from the previous, 'Explore all options'-phase. Each option should be analysed in a separate matrix to prevent misunderstanding or contamination.

The Moral Considerations Matrix lists as many arguments as possible for and against a potential decision in a moral dilemma, both the consequences of a potential decision (utilitarian) and the universal moral principles (deontological, right).

Bear in mind that utilitarian considerations, stemming from the ethics of consequences, also encompass moral aspects: directors have the duty to enhance a specific 'utility' for (a portion of) the stakeholders, ensuring fairness to all stakeholders and, through responsible citizenship, to avoid harming the well-being of as many individuals as possible. The repercussions of decisions can often be indirect: for instance, the potential dismissal of a CEO due to unethical behaviour not only impacts the CEO but might also significantly affect the strategic position of the company. This could threaten the company's continuity and, consequently, the interests of shareholders, consumers, employees, clients, and potentially a broader segment of society. Moreover, the company could face reputational harm, both from the CEO's actions and the subsequent decisions made by the board. This might have profound effects on the company's culture, customer perception, and ongoing viability. Thus, not all outcomes, whether direct or indirect, are straightforward to predict.

An Example: Controversy CEO Remuneration-Proposal

(see full description of this case in Part II of this book).

This scenario is drawn from the 2017 controversy over the CEO's pay at ING Bank. The core issue revolves around the moral justifiability of the Supervisory Board's decision to increase the compensation of the very successful CEO by 50 per cent. This increase was in line with a remuneration policy agreed upon several years prior and was still notably less than that of peers in similar positions. Concurrently, the broader workforce received a mere 1.7 per cent raise, resulting in the CEO's salary being thirty times higher than that of the average employee. Furthermore, ING was the recipient of a government bailout during the 2008 financial crisis, which the bank managed to repay by 2014. However, in 2017, public opinion still maintained that the bank was saved by public funds, and the salary increase occurred against the backdrop of an already delicate trust in the financial sector.

So, the matrix (Table 10.4) shows that proponents of the remuneration proposal will argue that the CEO plays a crucial role in the company's success, which benefits all stakeholders, justifies his remuneration due to responsibility. Additionally, they maintain that the agreed-upon reward aligns with previous commitments, showcasing integrity, and remains below the industry median, reflecting fairness. However, opponents highlight the negative impact of the reward debate on the company's image and the broader financial sector's credibility, citing a breach of responsibility and citizenship. They also point out the disparity between the CEO's reward increase and the modest 1.7% raise given to other employees, leading to an employee-CEO pay ratio of 1:30, which challenges the principle of fairness.

Table 10.4 Moral consideration matrix for ING's CEO salary Increase

	Utilitarian, consequences	Deontological, moral norms
For +	- Retaining CEO is crucial due to strategic vision and leadership capabilities - A competitive compensation package is essential for attracting (international) talent - Risk of a dissatisfied CEO stemming from unfulfilled compensation promises	- Honouring commitments and promises in compensation plan - Ensuring remuneration policy is in full compliance with legal and regulatory standards (citizenship) - CEO's salary is lower than peers raise concerns about fairness and justice
Against –	- Negative publicity causing harm and reputational damage to company, its individuals, and the broader banking sector - The CEO's salary is 30 times the average employee's salary raises concerns about fairness and equity - Trust in the financial sector has not yet been restored	- A salary increase amidst an ongoing investigation, with risks of legal actions and fines, reflects poorly on organisation's societal duties and ethical stance

It's evident that various moral principles could influence the situation, with the significance of these considerations varying from person to person. A director with a labour union background might prioritise addressing the disparity in wage distribution more than a director with experience in private equity, who may place greater emphasis on financial outcomes and strategic objectives. Similarly, a director who has observed a consistent breach in adhering to the (promised) remuneration policy over the past years might view this as a breach of integrity and unfair to the CEO, leading to a different decision compared to a director who, not having witnessed such precedents, may approach the proposal with more objectivity.

10.5 Refining the Choice (Refine)

During the fourth Refine phase, the aim is to pinpoint and address the vulnerabilities in the decision being considered. This phase also includes conducting final evaluations, considering the dilemma both from personal and external viewpoints, such as those of a role model, stakeholders, or the broader society (See Table 10.5). This phase underscores the importance of a comprehensive review, ensuring that the decision withstands scrutiny from both personal and public ethical standards.

Table 10.5 Final ethical tests

From your own perspective	From the other's perspective
Mirror test Can I still look at myself in the mirror after this?	**Shoe test** What would my role models do if they were in my shoes?
Slippery slope test If everyone did what we planned to do, what would the consequences be? When are we on thin ice?	**Front page test** What if this is on the front page of a major newspaper tomorrow?
Balance test When are values and interests in balance?	**Glasses test** How do others view this dilemma? Who are the stakeholders?
Generation test Can I tell this to my grandchildren later?	**Shoulder test** What if someone is looking over my shoulder?
	Grandma test Would my grandma understand this if I explained it to her?

In the context of corporate governance, ethical tests serve as essential tools for directors and board members to ensure their decisions align with personal integrity and broader stakeholder expectations, especially in situations where there is no clear right or wrong.

For example, the Mirror Test may help directors assess whether they can maintain their self-respect after disapproving of a controversial policy, such as implementing strict environmental standards that could limit production. Although this move may lead to preventing revenue losses, it might not align with a director's values and vision for the company's future. The Slippery Slope Test might be applied when considering aggressive tax avoidance strategies, prompting the board to consider the repercussions if every company followed this path and the risks of regulatory backlash. The Balance Test can be applied when directors must weigh the immediate need for layoffs to remain competitive against the moral responsibility to minimise social harm and support employees. This test ensures that the decision balances the company's financial stability and continuity with the dignity of negatively affected workers, as well as future workers who can keep their jobs due to financial stability. The Generation Test could be applied to determine whether museum trustees would be proud to share their decision with future generations if, for instance, they accept sponsorship of a polluting company to obtain short-term benefits, knowing that the polluting company reduces environmental health for years to come. Or, when adopting new technologies that might impact privacy, directors might ponder whether they'd want their future generations to live in a world shaped by these decisions.

From an external perspective, the Shoe Test might involve a director considering how an admired leader would handle the dilemma of sourcing raw materials from a region facing human rights issues while trying to support economic development. A specific version of the Shoe Test is the acronym 'WWJD' (*What Would Jesus Do?*). Directors, particularly those who with a Christian background, consider how Jesus would approach the situation, using his values of kindness and compassion as guidance, helping align decisions with Christian teachings on empathy and justice. The Front Page Test could guide directors when deciding on culturally or socially sensitive decisions or campaigns, helping them foresee the consequences if the decision or campaign's implications made the headlines. The Glasses Test encourages directors to examine their decisions from the perspectives of various stakeholders, such as employees, customers, and local communities. For example, when deciding whether to pay dividends to shareholders during the COVID-19 pandemic, while employees are being laid off or facing salary cuts, directors should consider both the economic and social impacts. The Shoulder Test can help directors assess the ethics of a decision, such as secretly using a cheaper but more polluting manufacturing process. If someone were watching over your shoulder, you would most likely feel ashamed of your actions. Finally, the Grandma Test could simplify complex decisions like adopting a new code of ethics or a charitable initiative; if a director can explain their rationale in straightforward terms that their grandmother would understand and approve of, it likely aligns with a clear sense of right and wrong.

These ethical frameworks not only guide directors towards morally sound decisions but also help maintain public trust and organisational legitimacy in the boardroom.

10.6 Implementing and Communicating the Decision (Act)

In the final step, the Action phase, directors not only implement the decision but also need to explain and disseminate it, even when facing opposition from society. This involves more than just action; it necessitates a thorough evaluation of the decision's impact: Did it achieve the anticipated outcomes? Reflecting on the decision, the process leading up to it, and the feedback received is essential. Such reflection raises questions about the decision's efficacy and the lessons that can be learned for future decisions. Might the feedback received necessitate a re-evaluation or revision of the original decision?

Once the action has been taken, the importance of communication comes to the forefront. In dealing with moral dilemmas, corporate directors often fail to prioritise communicating their decisions effectively. Rather than explaining how they reached their decisions, they may jump to defending them, which can lead to greater public outcry than understanding. The aim of communication at this stage is not to persuade the public that the decision was correct but to illuminate the various perspectives that were considered during the decision-making process. Here, the Moral Consideration Matrix proves invaluable in detailing the steps taken and highlighting the considerations deemed most critical by the directors.

Moreover, the public, politicians, and media are encouraged to adopt a more empathetic stance before levelling criticism such as 'Where was the moral compass?'. Understanding the sometimes-difficult position directors are in, balancing stakeholder interests and conflicting moral norms, is crucial. Transforming communication into a real dialogue could significantly narrow the gap between directors' decisions and public reactions, fostering a more understanding and less contentious environment.

Appendix

Table 10.6 Summary of ethical decision-making in the boardroom

Phase	Goal	Questions to ask (selection and supplemented)
Frame	Define and understand the precise nature of the issue to be discussed	• What are the facts? • What are the different perspectives or values at play in this dilemma? • How are these facts connected to the core values of the organisation? • What is the most important principle at stake here (individually and collectively)? • What assumptions (check for biases) are being made about the context within which this issue is being decided? • Are there *non-negotiables*, including relevant laws and regulations that must be complied with? • Who has a legitimate interest in this matter? What is the nature of each legitimate interest? Are the interests aligned or do they diverge? • What are the consequences of different choices we can make? What alternative solutions are there?
Shape	Think of options to solve the problem	• Is the dilemma possibly an 'amoral temptation', for example, the possibility of gaining an advantage from doing something dubious? • Is it a real dilemma in which competing values and principles seem to require incompatible results?

(continued)

Table 10.6 (continued)

Phase	Goal	Questions to ask (selection and supplemented)
Evaluate	Evaluate the options based on a Moral Considerations Matrix* in which both utilitarian and deontological considerations are set out and weighed * not in AICD	• Take the best options and apply the Moral Considerations Matrix. Indicate for all considerations whether this is an argument for or against the option • This moral considerations matrix reflects both the consequences and the six universal moral norms • The purpose of the table is to make clear what the consequences of the option are and to set the proposal against general and organisation-specific moral norms and core values
Refine	Identify and eliminate the weak points in the proposed decision	• Play the devil's advocate by identifying the main weak points of the obvious option • Adjust the proposal to eliminate the weak points without affecting the overall integrity and the necessity of the proposal • Subject the proposal to a few final tests (see the overview above), such as the mirror test, the glasses test, or the shoe test

(continued)

Table 10.6 (continued)

Phase	Goal	Questions to ask (selection and supplemented)
Act	Every ethical decision-making is practical; it ultimately requires that a decision has an effect	• Implement the decision • Check the result. Is it as expected? • Communicate and justify the decision, even if it is challenged • Reflect on the decision. And possibly: should the decision be adjusted? • What can we learn from this moral dilemma for our organisation and for our decision-making in the future? • How can we ensure that we are better prepared for similar moral dilemmas in the future?

Adapted from 'Ethics in the Boardroom: A decision-making guide for directors' AICD (2019)

Notes

1. Versteegt, J. (2023). Analysis, moral and ethical decision-making models, version 0.2.xlsx, ResearchGate.
2. Australian Institute of Company Directors (AICD). (2019). Ethics in the Boardroom. A decision-making guide for directors.
3. Blanchard, K., & Peale, N. (1988). The power of ethical management. New York, NY: William Morrow and Company, Inc.
4. Kem, J.D. (2016), "Ethical Decision Making: Using the 'Ethical Triangle,'" Command and General Staff College, Fort Leavenworth, https://www.cgscfoundation.org/wp-content/uploads/2016/04/Kem-UseoftheEthicalTriangle.pdf
5. Kahneman, D., Lovallo, D., & Sibony, O. (2011). Before You Make That Big Decision. Harvard Business Review, June 2011.

Part II

Moresprudence: Ten Cases of Moral Judgement in the Boardroom

Part II is all about 'moresprudence', a concept that explores the ethical and moral underpinnings of decision-making processes in the boardroom and how they align with wider societal values and norms. It seeks to assess the defensibility of the choice made by directors in moral dilemmas and examine the implications of these decisions taken in corporate settings. Like 'jurisprudence', which comes from the Latin 'juris prudentia', which is essentially providing a framework for understanding legal reasoning, morespurdence emphasises the importance of moral reasoning in navigating moral dilemmas. It encourages a reflection on the moral bases of decisions and their implications for stakeholders and the wider community. It also serves as a guidance for other dilemmas that may arise in the boardroom.

The moresprudence in this book comes from ten in-depth cases where directors faced different moral dilemmas. All cases involve legally defensible decisions, though some were later scrutinised in courts or by disciplinary panels. These cases, which have often garnered significant media or political attention, are used to illustrate the complex moral decisions directors must navigate. Following each case, over twenty shorter cases showcase similar or differing decisions by directors who were confronted with a comparable dilemma, to illustrate that the ultimate decision is not that black or white.

The detailed cases are described using public information, aiming to outline all possible considerations in a 'moral considerations-matrix' without judging the decisions made. It acknowledges the potential conflict between moral considerations and invites readers to reflect on what they might have done differently. The objective isn't to provide definitive answers but to encourage readers to consider alternative perspectives and the subjective nature of moral reasoning.

Each case is rounded off with an epilogue that offers insights into the decisions' aftermath, enhancing understanding of the real-world implications of boardroom choices.

11

The Case of Yahoo and the CEO Who Lied on His Resume

11.1 The Case

In January 2012, Scott Thompson was appointed as CEO of IT-company and search engine Yahoo. Coming from PayPal, he replaced interim CEO Tim Morse, who had taken over from Carol Bartz since September 2011. Bartz had been CEO from 2009 to 2011 but was dismissed in September, to her shock over the phone, by a lawyer of the board of directors.[1] Yahoo had thus gone through a turbulent time, but things seemed to improve with Thompson's arrival.

11.1.1 The Activists' Letter

On May 3, 2012, activist shareholder Daniel Loeb, on behalf of Third Point, sent a letter to Yahoo's board and simultaneously published it online.[2] Third Point was a group of shareholders owning 5.8% of Yahoo's shares.

The letter referred to two Yahoo documents, the annual report 'Form 10-K/A' and the proxy statement for shareholders, sent to the Securities and Exchange Commission (SEC) on April 27, 2012. These documents stated that Thompson had a bachelor's degree in both Accounting and Computer Science from Stonehill College. Third Point's investigation, including a Google search and checks with Stonehill College alumni, revealed that Thompson only had a degree in accounting, not computer science. This was confirmed by Stonehill College. Moreover, at the time Thompson graduated in 1979, Stonehill College did not offer a computer science program, which only began four years later. In 1979, Stonehill only offered one related course,

'Intro to Computer Science', of which Third Point suggested Thompson might have taken.

Third Point concluded that Thompson's embellishment of his academic credentials undermined his credibility as a technology expert and negatively reflected on his character as the CEO leading Yahoo at a critical moment. 'Now more than ever Yahoo! investors need a trustworthy CEO', they argued.

Third Point also noted inaccuracies in the resume of Yahoo board member Patti Hart, chair of the Selection and Nomination Committee and the Governance Committee. The 'Form 10-K/A' stated she had a bachelor's degree in marketing and economics from Illinois State University, but Third Point claimed she received a degree in neither marketing nor economics but held a degree in Business Administration. Yahoo later confirmed Hart had a bachelor's in business administration, with specialisations in marketing and economics.

Third Point demanded an explanation for these misrepresentations, arguing that if none was forthcoming, it confirmed that 'Yahoo is in dire need of a complete corporate governance overhaul'. Yahoo needed 'fresh, outside perspectives' from individuals not linked to the failed governance structure, with the appropriate expertise and highest integrity. Interestingly, Third Point had four such individuals in mind, including Loeb himself, and had publicised their qualifications on a special website: www.valueyahoo.com.

11.1.2 Ethical Code

Third Point also referred to Yahoo's ethical code, which applies to all Yahoo employees, including directors. The code states that disclosures in reports and documents filed with the SEC and other public communications must 'be full, fair, accurate, timely and understandable', and that information disclosed about the company must be 'clear, truthful, and accurate'.

11.1.3 The Process

On May 3, the successive events follow each other quickly. Around midday Yahoo admits in a first statement an error about the resume but at that time still praised his leadership qualities: 'there was an inadvertent error that stated Mr. Thompson also holds a degree in computer science. This, in no way, alters the fact that Mr. Thompson is a highly qualified executive with a successful track record leading large consumer technology companies. Under Mr. Thompson's leadership, Yahoo! is moving forward to grow the company and drive shareholder value'.³ On the same day, one of the directors declared that Thompson was 'a forthright, no-nonsense, straightforward personality and a likeable guy'.⁴ The stock price fell by 3.4 per cent.

However, at the end of the day, Yahoo released a statement, that its board would review the revelation that the bio of its CEO Scott Thompson contained an error and would make an appropriate disclosure about what happened.⁵ Later that night, an old radio interview with Thompson from his PayPal days resurfaced (TechNation radio show, 2009). The host, Moira Gunn asked him a direct question about his college degrees, specifically noting they were in accounting and computer science. Thompson didn't correct her and instead praised his early technical education at Stonehill College, even calling himself an engineer. 'Yeah. And that's really the background that I have, and it started back in my college days, and I think that's really the wonderful part of being an engineer is you think that way', he responded.⁶

Third Point also requested the paper trail that led to the hiring of Thomson. It appeared that Thompson was not selected by the executive search firm the company had retained to find a new CEO, Heidrick & Struggles. The due diligence on Thomson's credentials was also not conducted by Heidrick & Struggles, because the search firm had placed him at his job at the time at PayPal.⁷

On May 8, Thompson sent a memo to employees apologising about the disruption caused by his doctored resume, but 'he's not going anywhere'. He wrote that he was 'hopeful that this matter will be concluded promptly'. And in the meantime, 'we have a lot of work to do. We need to continue to act as one team to fulfil the potential of this great company and keep moving forward'.⁸ On the same day, board member Patti Hart resigned.⁹ She was also CEO of publicly traded International Game Technology (IGT), and IGT's board chairman, Philip Satre, stated that the Yahoo situation was too distracting from her main role. Finally, on this day, Yahoo's board appointed a three-person special committee to conduct a thorough review of CEO Scott Thompson's 'academic credentials, as well as the facts and circumstances related to the review and disclosure of those credentials in connection with Thompson's appointment as CEO'.¹⁰ The three independent directors in the committee were relatively new in the board and were all appointed after Thomson became CEO, the committee is advised by and an independent counsel Terry Bird of the law firm Bird.

The New York Times, drawing on information from insiders, provides a detailed account of the events that transpired in the week after May 3.¹¹ The chairman of the one-tier board, Roy Bostock, apparently discussed the situation with Thompson, still hoping it was a misunderstanding. Chairman Bostock urged Thompson to tell the truth, whatever it was, and make it public. If the allegations were true, Thompson should admit them publicly, apologise, and offer to resign. This would give the board a chance to respond to the situation and disapprove, but also an opportunity to support him. However, Thompson showed little reflection or remorse and reacted angrily to Daniel Loeb and Third Point and their tactics. He also blamed head-hunter Heidrick & Struggles, claiming they had prepared this resume when he was appointed at PayPal. The firm denied Thompson's claim in an internal memo to its employees: 'based on information in our possession, this allegation is verifiably not true, and we have notified Yahoo to that effect'.[12] This second lie 'was the final straw', according to one of the directors.

Also, in the meantime, several top executives and engineers approached the board calling for Thompson's firing.[13] A Yahoo employee in 2012 said, 'I can't work here if that's true', reflecting the sentiments of many at Yahoo's Silicon Valley headquarters. The situation was highly emotional for employees, with one saying, 'How can I work for a company that has a CEO who claims to be a computer scientist when he's not?'.

> I can't work here if that's true
> —Employee Yahoo, 2012

11.1.4 The Final Inevitable Step

The conclusion came on Friday, May 11, when the board convened to decide. During the meeting, Thompson called one of the directors and asked him to step out of the meeting. Thompson revealed that he had undergone thyroid surgery some time ago and had underestimated the symptoms. He now wanted to resign to focus on his health.

This allowed the board to handle Thompson's departure 'gracefully'. However, they decided that this medical issue should not affect the terms of his departure. The board planned to fire Thompson for 'cause' meaning he would not receive a severance package worth $16 million. This was formally ratified the next day. Yahoo's press release only stated that Thompson had left the company.[14]

11.2 Considerations

Would It Be Morally Appropriate to Keep the CEO in Position?

In evaluating Thompson's situation of course the board initially investigated the seriousness of the discrepancy on the resume and its origins. Questions as to whether the CEO never actually enrolled in the claimed education or was merely a course short of completing his degree might have influenced their assessment. Additionally, the board might have discussed the significance of the fact that an activist shareholder brought the issue to light, effectively putting pressure on the company or the potential oversight of the selection committee or head-hunter in this matter. While acknowledging these parties' roles and errors, the core issue remained the CEO's dishonesty.

Deciding whether the CEO should remain in his position after lying on his resume involves weighing different pros and cons. (see Table 11.1) On the one hand, the CEO's exceptional performance argued for his retention; his achievements suggested that the specifics of his resume may be less relevant. Moreover, providing the CEO with an opportunity to explain his actions and apologise could serve as a remedial step, and the company's stance against what could be perceived as shareholder blackmail underlines a commitment to autonomy and principled decision-making. On the other hand, the CEO's actions have led to substantial reputational damage for both him and the company, evoking outrage, and anger among employees, especially engineers. Misrepresenting the resume undermined trust and shifting blame to the recruitment agency by the CEO only deepened the deceit. Such actions not only set a potentially dangerous precedent but also contravened Yahoo's 'Code of Ethics', signalling a disregard for ethical standards and legal requirements in official documents. Compounded by the CEO's apparent lack of remorse and unwillingness to engage in self-reflection or apologise, these factors raised serious concerns about the integrity of leadership and the ethical climate within the company. Directors thus needed to balance the need for strong performance against the imperative for ethical leadership and trust within the organisation and its wider community.

The CEO's continued dishonesty regarding his resume (including statements on the radio, on his resume, and shifting blame to the head-hunter), coupled with a lack of introspection, rendered his position indefensible.

Table 11.1 The moral consideration matrix for Yahoo's board

	Utilitarian consequences	Deontological moral norms
For +	- It's essential for the company to keep the CEO due to his exceptional performance; is resume seems irrelevant for this	- The CEO should be given the chance to explain his actions and offer an apology - Company should refuse to succumb to shareholder blackmail
Against -	- The situation has led to reputational damage for the company, the CEO, and its employees - Employees, mainly engineers, are experiencing feelings of outrage and anger	- Misrepresenting a resume is lying and unacceptable - Blaming the recruitment agency exacerbates the deceit - If the CEO can falsify his resume details, it sets a precedent that others might follow - This behaviour is in direct violation of Yahoo's 'Code of Ethics' - The CEO shows little remorse, lacks self-reflection, and makes no apologies - There has been a failure to adhere to laws and regulations in official documents

11.3 Epilogue

11.3.1 Yahoo

After the departure of CEO Thompson and board member Hart, activist shareholder Daniel Loeb and two of his allies, Michael Wolf and Harry Wilson, were appointed to the board in May 2012. They also nominated the new CEO Marissa Mayer, who came from Google and was appointed in July 2012, staying until 2017. Loeb and his friends left at the end of 2013 after cashing in significantly on shares.

In July 2016, Verizon announced its intention to acquire Yahoo's internet activities for USD 4.83 billion. The deal was finalised in June 2017, marking the end of Yahoo as an independent company. During the sale process, two massive data breaches from 2013 and 2014 affecting all three billion user accounts were revealed, leading to a USD 350 million reduction in the sale price.

11.3.2 Thomson

Thompson's thyroid issues turned out to be less severe, and by the end of July 2012, he had already taken a new job at Shoprunners, a company he had previously collaborated with during his time at PayPal.[15] Co-founder Mike Golden said in a statement that he felt Thompson would be 'the perfect long-term CEO'. He stayed there until 2016 and is now active as CEO at Tuition. On LinkedIn, he now only mentions earning a bachelor's degree from Stonehill College without specifying the field.

11.4 Comparable Cases

11.4.1 Bausch and Lomb: CEO Stayed but Bonus was Revoked

On October 17, 2002, news came out that the resume of Ronald Zarrella, CEO of Bausch & Lomb, contained false information about his education. Bausch and Lomb published documentation including a master's degree in business administration from New York University. Although he did attend the NYU Business School, he left before graduating. At that time, he was almost a year the CEO of Bausch & Lomb. The next day Zarrella said he was 'embarrassed' about the false information in Bausch and Lomb's documentation and acknowledged that it was his 'obligation to proofread such things carefully and ensure their accuracy'. However, he had no plans to resign. At first instance, the board expressed to have 'every confidence in him' and expected that 'his continued contributions will generate sustained improvements in the company's operating performance'.[16]

Nevertheless, ten days later, the false resume did have consequences for Zarrella. On the 28th, he offered to resign which the board did not accept. They send Zarrella a letter in which they wrote that 'his lapse in judgment with regard to your biography is a serious matter and cannot pass without consequence'. However, while 'there is no other issue of trust or veracity about which we need to be concerned', the board also continued to believe that Zarrella was 'the right person to carry on the resurgence of the company'. The board did revoke an incentive bonus of around USD 1.1 million, which was agreed at the time of the hiring eleven months ago.[17]

Zarrella stayed at Bausch & Lomb until 2008, when the company was sold to private equity firm Warburg Pincus.

Notes

1. Carol Bartz lashes out at Yahoo board, Hayley Tsukaya, The Washington Post, September 8, 2011.
2. Third Point LLC Letter to Yahoo Board of Directors regarding discovery of discrepancies in educational records of CEO Scott Thompson and Director Patti Hart, via PR Newswire, May 3, 2012.
3. Yahoo's Response on CEO's Computer Science ResumeGate: "Inadvertent Error", Kara Swisher, AllThingsD, May 3, 2012.
4. In the Undoing of a C.E.O., A Puzzle, James B. Stewart, The New York Times, May 18, 2012.
5. Yahoo's Board Will "Review" Resume Discrepancy of CEO, Kara Swisher, All ThingsD, May 3, 2012.
6. In 2009 Interview, Yahoo CEO does not deny he has a CS Degree, and calls himself an 'engineer', Kara Swisher, AllThingsD, May 3, 2012.
7. Third Point Demands Records from Yahoo's C.E.O. Search, Michael J. De La Merced, The New York Times, May 7, 2012.
8. Yahoo CEO apologises for resume scandal but refuses to leave, Abram Brown, Forbes, May 8, 2012.
9. Patti Hart Will Not Seek Re-Election to Yahoo Board, press release Yahoo, May 8, 2012.
10. Yahoo! Board of Directors Forms Special Committee to Review CEO Academic Credentials, press release Yahoo, May 8, 2012.
11. In the Undoing of a C.E.O., A Puzzle, James B. Stewart, The New York Times, May 18, 2012.
12. Yahoo's Chief to Leave as Company Strikes Deal With Loeb, Michael J. De La Merced & Evelyn M. Rusli, The New York Times, May 13, 2012.
13. Yahoo's Thompson Out; Levinsohn In; Board Settlement With Loeb Nears Completion, Kara Swisher, AllThingsD, May 12, 2012.
14. Yahoo's Thompson Out; Levinsohn In; Board Settlement With Loeb Nears Completion, Kara Swisher, AllThingsD, May 12, 2012.
15. Ousted Yahoo CEO Thompson takes job at ShopRunner, Erin Kim, CNN, July 23, 2012.
16. Bausch & Lomb Executive Admits to Falsified Résumé, Leslie Wayne, The New York Times, October 12, 2002.
17. Bausch & Lomb Withholds CEO Zarrella's Bonus, Kevin Burke, The Street, October 30, 2002.

12

The Case of Maastricht University Paying Ransom After a Cyber Attack

12.1 The Case

On October 15, 2019, criminal hackers sent a phishing email to several individuals within Maastricht University. One of the employees clicks on the link in this email, resulting in the installation of malware from an external server on this employee's workstation. A second phishing email is clicked by another employee the following day. From that moment, the hackers have access to the university's network.[1]

The hackers remained under the radar for two months, but on December 23, 2019, over 200 servers were locked with malware, after which the crisis management plan, led by Vice Chairman Nick Bos, was activated. The hackers demanded 200,000 euros in bitcoins. With the involvement of experienced parties like the National Cyber Security Center, the police, and Fox-IT, the Board must decide whether to pay the ransom. The progress of education and research was the highest priority in this situation. The decision to pay or not to pay the ransom was a heavy moral assessment for the university's board and a 'devil's dilemma', 'with very significant moral objections' towards paying the ransom.[2]

> Very significant moral objections
> —Maastricht University, 2020

Bos later explained that the main question in the initial days around Christmas 2019 was, 'Are we going to pay the cybercriminals? What does it mean if we don't?' The options were developed by the crisis team, substantiated, and presented to the Board of Trustees and other stakeholders. Not paying would mean that the university would be out of commission for three to four months, with estimated monthly damages of 20 to 25 million euros. Thousands of students would face study delays with all the consequent effects. Researchers would experience delays in the work.[3] The Education Inspection later confirmed this: without payment, the recovery and rebuilding would have taken months, with no guarantee of full recovery, the progress of education and research would have been seriously compromised, and the costs of self-recovery would have been many times the ransom amount.[4]

12.1.1 Paying Ransom to Hackers is Undesirable

Paying ransom is considered undesirable as it sustains the hackers' business model and is illegitimate for government-funded organisations because it involves payment of (community) funds to criminals.[5] Paying ransom and thereby receiving the criminals' key does not guarantee success. The obtained key might not function properly, preventing recovery. Often, the entire IT infrastructure must still be rebuilt or replaced because the integrity of the IT infrastructure can no longer be guaranteed, and an organisation can no longer trust its systems. Finally, the criminals may retain any stolen data and can demand a new ransom to prevent its publication.[6]

12.1.2 Yet, Paying

ICT Director Bart van de Heuvel said they 'didn't make a hasty decision, and all interests were thoroughly weighed'. But in the interest of the continuity of education and research, it was decided on December 29 to pay the ransom: 'the scale tipped to the other side: we pay the ransom'. The university received the key to unlock the servers. On January 6, education could start again.

> We didn't make a hasty decision, and all interests were thoroughly weighed.
> —ICT Director Maastricht University

The university didn't immediately make the payment of the ransom public. Only a few days later, after reports from the university newspaper Observant on January 2, was it confirmed by the university. The university feared they were still at risk during the recovery process and did not want to give other hackers the idea that there was still something to gain.

12.2 Considerations

Would It Be Morally Appropriate to Pay Ransom After a Ransomware Attack?

The decision to pay ransomware might seem practical from a utilitarian perspective, aiming to minimise immediate harm to stakeholders, but it raises significant ethical concerns regarding the broader implications and indirect consequences of such actions. See Table 12.1 for the Moral Consideration Matrix for Maastricht University's Board. Paying ransomware demands after a cyberattack is a poignant example of the utilitarian perspective while the decision to pay the ransom is typically made after weighing the potential consequences of either action, paying or not paying. The decision to pay the ransom is often made under the belief that the negative consequences of not paying, like loss of sensitive data, disruption of services, financial losses from operational downtime, and reputational damage, outweigh the immediate financial cost of the ransom and the ethical dilemma of funding criminal activity.

> **Core Values: MAASTRICHT UNIVERSITY**
> Diversity and inclusion, sustainability, mutual respect, integrity, democratic principles and transparency.

However, this approach inherently involves several moral principles too. Paying the ransom may solve the immediate crisis by potentially securing the return of stolen data and restoration of services. However, it also encourages future cybercrimes, not just against the same entity but against others as well, by financially incentivising the perpetrators. By paying ransomware demands, an organisation indirectly supports the cybercrime ecosystem, thereby expanding the cycle of harm. Furthermore, the decision to pay focuses primarily on minimising harm to direct stakeholders. However, it neglects broader societal consequences, including contributing to the overall increase in cybercrime. Despite financial considerations, the university placed the well-being of its internal stakeholders (employees and students) above its wider societal duties, concentrating the impact analysis on internal effects. Upcoming laws that ban paying ransom to cybercriminals could shield administrators from the dilemma of balancing internal priorities against external societal interests.

Paying the ransom does not guarantee that the attackers will honour their word. There is always a risk that the data will not be decrypted or returned,

Table 12.1 The moral consideration matrix for Maastricht University's Board

	Utilitarian consequences	Deontological, moral norms
For +	- Enables employees to resume their work and ensures the preservation of valuable research, minimising disruption - Prevents study delays, ensuring educational timelines are maintained - Avoids the potentially higher costs associated with self-recovery efforts, considering the ransom amount to be comparatively lower	- Aligns with the university's ethical duty to shield its community from harm
Against −	- An ongoing threat of compromised files and systems, which could lead to future vulnerabilities - Utilising community funds for ransom payments raises concerns about the allocation of public resources - Fulfilling ransom demands perpetuates the profitability of the criminals' business model, potentially encouraging further criminal activities that harms society	- Upholding the integrity of the university and respecting moral standards against supporting unlawful activities - Contributing to the broader protection of society

or that the attackers may leave behind hidden malware for potential future exploitation. The university has consistently been transparent about its deliberations, sharing insights into the factors influencing its decisions. While this openness wasn't a direct factor in the decision-making process, there was considerable empathy for the decision to comply with the ransom demand.

12.3 Epilogue

12.3.1 Recovered Ransom Proves Financially Beneficial

Maastricht University discovered an unexpected financial upside when a portion of the ransom they paid was seized in 2022 after its recovery in 2020. Due to the significant appreciation in the value of these cryptocurrencies, the university benefited from a return of 500,000 euros on the original 200,000 euros paid in bitcoins. ICT Director Michiel Borgers announced that these funds would be allocated not to the university's general budget but to support students facing financial hardships.[7]

12.3.2 Considering a Ban on Ransom Payments

In 2021, the Ministry of Justice explored the idea of forbidding insurance companies from covering ransom payments for ransomware attack victims. Justice Minister Ferdinand Grapperhaus emphasised the government's strong recommendation against paying ransoms, 'the urgent advice from the cabinet remains not to pay ransom after a ransomware attack, as this sustains the criminal business model'. He also cited a report from the Cybersecurity Overview Netherlands, which indicated that ransoms paid by victims often finance further cyberattacks. Nonetheless, Grapperhaus acknowledged the financial dilemma for organisations, pointing out that the immediate costs of a ransomware attack, including potential data loss and other indirect damages, can far exceed the ransom itself, making payment seem like the more cost-effective option in the short term.[8]

12.4 Comparable Cases

12.4.1 Ferrari: Ransom Not Paid

At the end of 2022, Italian car manufacturer Ferrari denied being the victim of a cyberattack after ransomware gang RansomEXX. The hackers claimed it had stolen 7 GB of the company's data and posted it online. However, in March 2023, Ferrari did confirm they were attacked, although not sure it was the same attack, and customer names, addresses, email addresses, and telephone numbers were exposed. In an online statement Ferrari stated that 'as a policy, Ferrari will not be held to ransom as paying such demands funds criminal activity and enables threat actors to perpetuate their attacks'. They believed that 'the best course of action was to inform our clients'.[9]

12.4.2 Ashley Madison: Hackers' Demands Not Granted

The Ashley Madison website, founded in 2002 and known for facilitating extramarital affairs, was hacked on July 15, 2015. However, in this case, there was no demand for ransom, but hackers requested the shutdown of the complete website of Ashley Madison.

Ashley Madison is part of a Canadian firm called Avid Life Media (ALM). The slogan of Ashley Madisons website is: 'Life is short. Have an affair'. The hacking group named 'Impact Team' initially released a limited amount of user data, demanding the site's shutdown: 'We've got the complete set of profiles in our DB dumps, and we'll release them soon if Ashley Madison stays online'. By demanding a shutdown, this seems a hack with a moral message, also implied by the first statement of Impact Team: 'Too bad for those men, they're cheating dirtbags and deserve no such discretion. Too bad for ALM, you promised secrecy but didn't deliver'.[10] The promised secrecy refers to the promise of ALM to delete user accounts after customers paid an additional USD 19. So, in this case no ransom was demanded.

Ashley Madison did not give in so when their demands were not met, Impact Team indeed released a more extensive file, 60 gigabytes, on August 18 revealing the personal information of 32 million users. Their message, titled 'Time's up!', read: 'Avid Life Media has failed to take down Ashley Madison. We have explained the fraud, deceit, and stupidity of ALM and their members. Now everyone gets to see their data'. And: 'Find yourself in here? It was ALM that failed you and lied to you. Prosecute them and claim damages. Then move on with your life. Learn your lesson and make amends. Embarrassing now, but you'll get over it'.[11]

On the same day, Ashley Madison published a statement[12] in which they strongly criticised the moral message of the hackers, who 'have appointed themselves as the moral judge, juror, and executioner, seeing fit to impose a personal notion of virtue on all of society. We will not sit idly by and allow these thieves to force their personal ideology on citizens around the world'. Also, they argued that the website is not illegal but for freethinking people, and that the hackers are criminals. 'This event is not an act of hacktivism; it is an act of criminality. It is an illegal action against the individual members of Ashley Madison, as well as any freethinking people who choose to engage in fully lawful online activities'.

> It is an act of criminality.
> —Ashley Madison in 2015

However, the data leak resulted in public shaming and extortion of many users, among which politicians, priests, celebrities, and other public figures were found among the listed membership. Additionally, numerous users faced personal and professional repercussions, including job losses and broken marriages. The leak was linked to at least two suicides.[13] The CEO Noel Biderman stepped down on August 28. Despite the severity of the hack, no one has been charged in relation to it.

In a class action Avid Life Media was held responsible for the data leak due to 'inadequate data security practices and misrepresentations' and in 2017 they settled for USD 11.2 million. Although at first, Ashley Madison lost more than a quarter of its revenues, in 2023 it continues to operate successfully and still advocates discreet relationships of all kinds: 'married, attached, looking to explore, or just curious to discover what's out there'. In 2023 a 3-episode documentary on the matter, called The Ashley Madison Affair, aired on Disney +.

12.4.3 MGM Resorts: Ransom Not Paid, Ceasars Entertainment: Ransom Paid

MGM Resorts, the largest owner of hotels and casinos on the Las Vegas Strip, announced that they were hacked in September 2023.[14] The hackers were able to access personal information, including names, contact information, gender, date of birth, and driver's license, passport, and even some Social Security numbers. Hotel room digital keys and slot machines weren't working, websites went offline for a while, and guests waited in hours-long lines to check in.

MGM did not pay the ransom; however, according to CEO Hornbuckle this was not a decision based on the moral principle of not paying criminals. In fact, before hackers asked for the ransom, MGM was already rebuilding its systems. Hornbuckle stated 'I'd love to tell you there was this, you know, "a jump on a white horse moment and devil be damned, we're not paying these bastards", but the reality is because we caught this so early and we were on them'.[15]

> We're not paying these bastards
> —MGM CEO Hornbuckle

The incident reduced MGM's third-quarter earnings by about USD 100 million.

One of MGM's competitors, Ceasars Entertainment, was hacked in the same period. According to their filing to the SEC, physical properties and online and mobile gaming applications were not disrupted, but hackers did acquire access to their loyalty program database which includes driver's license numbers and/or social security numbers for a significant number of members. Ceasars did pay ransomware of around USD 15 million, about half of the amount that was requested.[16]

12.4.4 Royal Dutch Football Association: Ransom Paid

On April 4, 2023, the Royal Dutch Football Association (KNVB) disclosed a cybersecurity breach. They assured that key operations remained secure, email systems were unaffected, and football matches would proceed as scheduled. Yet, they reported the theft of KNVB staff personal information, with ongoing efforts to identify the full extent of the breach.[17] Tech journalist Daniël Verlaan reported the internal concerns, highlighting the hackers' access to sensitive documents, including passport copies and contracts of Dutch national team members.[18] To prevent the release of the stolen data, cybercriminal group Lockbit demanded a ransom exceeding one million euros, that had to be paid by April 29 at 19:42. Online, screenshots showcasing the names of folders such as 'Confidential Zeist' and 'Disciplinary Cases' were shared, indicating the nature of data at risk.

Ten days before the deadline, on April 19, Daniël Verlaan wrote on his Twitter account @danielverlaan, 'Remarkable. The countdown clock of Lockbit for the KNVB has stopped'. And that this 'normally means that a victim has paid or has bought more time'.

> Ultimately outweighed the principle of not giving in to extortion
> —The Royal Dutch Football Association

This was only months later, in September, confirmed by the KNVB. They stated that an expert investigation failed to precisely identify the stolen or accessed data and 'this presented us with a dilemma without an option that felt comfortable for us'. For the KNVB, preventing the dissemination of personal data that could affect personal lives 'ultimately outweighed the principle of not giving in to extortion'.[19]

Notes

1. The description of this case is largely based on the analyses of 1. Education Inspection: Cyberattack Maastricht University (BRIN: 21PJ), May 2020, 2. University Magazine Observant: Als ik een beroep doe op mensen om te werken met kerst, dan moet ik er zelf ook zijn, ('If I call on people to work at Christmas, then I must also be there myself',) Riki Janssen, Observant, December 11, 2020, and 3. SURF, the ICT collaboration organization of educational and research institutions in the Netherlands, Wat Universiteit Maastricht leerde van de ransomwareaanval (deel 1) en (deel2) ('What Maastricht University

learned from the ransomwareattack (part 1) and (part 2), Surf.nl. Also, the quotes from Nick Bos, vice-chairman of the board and head of the crisis management team, and Bart van den Heuvel, ICT director, come from these sources.
2. 'Zeer grote morele bezwaren' tegen betaling losgeld ('"Very strong moral objections" to the payment of ransom'), *Observant*, February 5, 2020.
3. Als ik een beroep doe op mensen om te werken met kerst, dan moet ik er zelf ook zijn, ('If I call on people to work at Christmas, then I must also be there myself',) Riki Janssen, *Observant*, December 11, 2020.
4. Als ik een beroep doe op mensen om te werken met kerst, dan moet ik er zelf ook zijn, ('If I call on people to work at Christmas, then I must also be there myself',) Riki Janssen, *Observant*, December 11, 2020.
5. Binnen zonder kloppen  Digitale weerbaarheid in het hoger onderwijs ('Enter without knocking – Digital resilience in higher education'), Inspectie van het Onderwijs, ministerie van OCW, July 2021.
6. Parliamentary questions, October 7, 2021, Appendix to the Proceedings, ah-tk-20212022–225.
7. Universiteit Maastricht krijgt deel losgeld na hack terug, door gelukkige timing crypto fors meer waard ('Maastricht University recovers part of the ransom after hack, due to fortunate timing crypto significantly more valuable'), Huib Modderkolk, *de Volkskrant*, July 2, 2022.
8. Cybersecuritybeeld Nederland ('Cybersecurity Netherlands'), (CSBN), 2021, p. 29.
9. Cyber incident in Ferrari, press release Ferrari, March 2023,
10. 'Discreet' cheating website Ashley Madison suffers data breach, Charlie Osborne, ZDNET.com, July 20, 2015.
11. Hackers Finally Post Stolen Ashley Madison Data, Kim Zetter, Wired.com, August 18, 2023.
12. Statement from Avid Life Media Inc., August 18, 2015.
13. Life after the Ashley Madison affair, Tom Lamont, The Guardian, February 26, 2016.
14. MGM Resorts international statement on cybersecurity issue, official statement MGM, September 12, 2023.
15. MGM Hackers Waited for Days Before Issuing Their Ransom Demands, Margi Murphy, Bloomberg, October 12, 2023.
16. Caesars paid millions in ransom to cybercrime group prior to MGM hack, CNBC, September 14, 2023, and Casino giant MGM expects

$100 million hit from hack that led to data breach, Zeba Siddiqui, Reuters, October 6, 2023.
17. KNVB-servers getroffen door cyberinbraak ('KNVB servers hit by cyber intrusion'), KNVB statement, April 4, 2023, KNVB website.
18. Cybercriminelen eisen meer dan miljoen euro van KNVB na ransomware-aanval ('Cybercriminals demand more than a million euros from KNVB after ransomware attack'), Daniel Verlaan, RTL News, April 19, 2023.
19. Informatie cyberinbraak KNVB ('Information on KNVB cyber intrusion'), KNVB statement, September 12, 2023.

13

The Case of the British Museum and Its Long-Time Partnership with BP

13.1 The Case

The partnership between the British Museum and British Petroleum (BP) heads back to 1996. For over 25 years BP have been a reliable and loyal partner for the Museum and 'one of the British Museum's longest standing corporate supporters'. BP has supported numerous special exhibitions and special public events at the British Museum, and in 2000 funded the 'BP Lecture Theatre'. This theatre seats more than 300 people, with a raised stage and cinema-style screen, and is available for hire for events like conferences and AGMs.

13.1.1 Long-standing Relationship Reconfirmed in 2016

In 2016 the long-standing relationship was reconfirmed for five years but was later prolonged with one year due to COVID-19 and was supposed to end in February 2023. In 2016, Hartwig Fischer, Director of the British Museum, was grateful for the support. 'BP has supported the British Museum for the past 20 years which has enabled the Museum to host magnificent exhibitions and events with a great public benefit'.[1] At the same time, BP continued to support the National Portrait Gallery, the Royal Opera House, and the Royal Shakespeare Company. Before this renewal of the sponsorship British-Egyptian novelist and member of the Board of Trustees since 2012 Ahdaf Soueif raised internally the issue of 'BP's very high-profile sponsorship of public exhibitions with the museum's board, the chair of trustees and the director'. According to Soueif she was surprised by 'how little it seems to trouble anyone'.[2]

> The museum needs to take a clear ethical position
> —Ahdaf Soueif in 2019

13.1.2 Trustee Resigns

Three years later, in 2019, Ahdaf Soueif announced that she resigned from the British Museum's board of trustees in protest at the institution's position on issues such as sponsorship, outsourcing, and repatriation.[3] She wrote that her 'resignation was not in protest at a single issue; it was a cumulative response to the museum's immovability on issues of critical concern to the people who should be its core constituency: the young and the less privileged'.[4] She added that 'the world is caught up in battles over climate change, vicious and widening inequality, the residual heritage of colonialism, questions of democracy, citizenship and human rights. On all these issues the museum needs to take a clear ethical position'.

Workers at the British Museum in London, all members of the Public and Commercial Services (PCS) Union Culture Group issued a public statement expressing their solidarity with Soueif.[5] They argued that the sponsor deal allows BP 'to propagate the myth that, without its existence, we would not have access to the collections of our publicly funded museums and galleries'. And that the museum is being used 'to greenwash the activities of a company whose actions threaten lives the world over, both now and in the future'.[6]

In 2019 BP expressed their worries on their website about 'the increasing polarisation of debate and attempts to exclude companies committed to making real progress, is exactly what is not needed'.[7]

13.1.3 Open Letters

The debate continued and on February 14, 2022, an open letter was sent to the directors and trustees, accusing BP of using its sponsorship to 'greenwash' its public image, given the company's environmental impact. It was signed by more than 302 museum-, heritage- and archaeology-professionals, calling on the British Museum to cut ties with the oil giant BP.[8] They see the sponsorship 'as part of a strategy of reputational management' while 'BP is taking advantage of the British Museum's status as a highly respected institution'. With the sponsorship BP associate its brand 'with values of high culture, art, education, sophistication, reason, and knowledge'. Also, they argued that BP's funding makes up less than 1% of the museum's overall income, and can be missed, which was also mentioned in 2019 by Soueif. The letter emphasised that the British Museum's leadership on this issue would have far-reaching consequences while it would send a strong signal that fossil fuel corporations are no longer welcome in cultural life.

13.1.4 BP and the National Portrait Gallery

A few years later, by the end of 2022, a similar relationship between BP and the National Portrait Gallery ended. After 30 years of sponsorship for which the Gallery was 'hugely grateful'.[9] By then, a new contract between BP and the British Museum has not yet been announced. The Chair of the Board of Trustees George Osborne gave a speech in November 2022, in which he stated 'Our goal is to be a net zero carbon museum – no longer a destination for climate protest but instead an example of climate solution'.[10] Culture Unstained, member of the Art Not Oil coalition and part of the international movement for #FossilFreeCulture, reacted to this statement: 'Well, George, if that's true, there's no way the Museum can sign a new sponsorship deal with BP. Is this the end?'.[11]

13.1.5 Rumours About the End of the Partnership

On June 2, 2023, the Guardian announced the end of the partnership between the British Museum and BP,[12] but this was denied on the same day by the British Museum.[13] A spokesperson said that 'in times of reduced public funding, corporate sponsors like BP allow us to fulfil our mission to deliver unique learning experiences to our visitors. We have not ended our partnership with BP. BP is a valued long-term supporter of the Museum and our current partnership runs until this year'. The museum said that certain terms of the deal remain in effect because it has verbally agreed to let BP exercise its supporter benefits that it was not able to utilise during the pandemic until at least the end of 2023.[14]

13.2 Considerations

Would it be Morally Appropriate to Continue with the Sponsor Deal with BP?

In the debate over whether museums should accept sponsorship from oil companies, the utilitarian viewpoint of sponsorships can be defended on the grounds that they bring substantial, non-financial benefits. Financial support from oil companies can enable museums to reduce entry fees, expand educational offerings, and enhance exhibits. The increased accessibility promotes cultural enrichment and educational opportunities for a wider audience, arguably contributing to societal well-being. However, the utilitarian approach also acknowledges potential drawbacks. The environmental damage associated with oil companies and the public's adverse reaction to such sponsorships could decrease museum attendance and tarnish the institution's reputation, suggesting that the negative consequences might outweigh the positive. See Table 13.1 for the Moral Consideration Matrix for the British Museum Board of Trustees.

> **Mission British Museum**
> "The Museum is driven by an insatiable curiosity for the world, a deep belief in objects as reliable witnesses and documents of human history, sound research, as well as the desire to expand and share knowledge."[15]

Conversely, accepting oil company sponsorships from the deontological perspective can be justifiable if it aligns with the museum's duty to promote culture and education without compromising its ethical principles. However, deontological ethics also raises concerns about the implications of accepting funding from sources that are at odds with societal well-being. If an oil company's operations contribute to environmental degradation or conflict with the museum's mission to foster social responsibility, then the sponsorship could be viewed as an ethical compromise, potentially eroding public trust and integrity.

The decision is not merely a financial one but a reflection of the institution's values and its commitment to both its immediate community and global ethical standards.

Table 13.1 The moral consideration matrix for the British Museum Board of Trustees

	Utilitarian consequences	Deontological, moral norms
For +	- Sponsorship enables lower entrance fees, widening access to the museum and its educational value	- Adhere to core value of promoting culture and education - Showing commitment, gratitude, and loyalty for years of support by long-term partner BP
Against -	- Protests against the sponsorship could endanger the museum's collection and staff safety, potentially affecting visitor numbers - The funding from BP is not essential because other sources might also be available - A decrease in visitor numbers because of those against the sponsorship choosing not to visit	- Sponsorship may be seen as endorsing 'greenwashing', undermining the museum's role in promoting environmental awareness - Exploiting the museum's prestige for corporate image enhancement and risk of damaging reputation by supporting a company with environmentally harmful practices

13.3 Epilogue

13.3.1 December 2023

On December 19, 2023, the British Museum announced a new multi-year partnership deal with 'long-term supporter BP'.[16] BP will provide GB 50 million over 10 years to help deliver the Museum's Masterplan. 'The partnership will also help deliver on plans to maintain public access for generations to come. The Museum is very grateful for BP's support at this early stage of the Masterplan'. The agreement was announced alongside its masterplan of which they said that 'it will be one of the most significant cultural redevelopment projects ever undertaken' and includes phasing out of the use of fossil fuels.

It appeared that in its November-meeting the board discussed 'additional risks to the security of the collection that may follow the announcement of sponsorship' and seems to anticipate on the significant public disapproval of the agreement. The Chair reminded the trustees that, when 'they accepted the corporate sponsorship, the security of the collection was one fundamental consideration not only in reaching the decision but also in the timing and handling of any announcement'. They also expressed their concerns for 'the personal safety of staff and Trustees'.[17]

13.3.2 Consensus, Agree to Disagree, Stepping Down

The agreement to proceed with the sponsorship deal was not reached by consensus. Instead, it was settled through an acceptance of differing opinions: agreeing to disagree. This becomes evident from the minutes of the meeting on June 29, which stated that 'some Trustees expressed significant personal objections to accepting funds from companies in the sponsor's industry'.[18] However, it was determined that these objections were not substantial enough to necessitate their withdrawal from participating as trustees in the decision-making process. Furthermore, the minutes read that the board of trustees expressed a 'desire to operate as a united board on this matter' and 'it was unanimously agreed that accepting the sponsorship was on balance in the best interests of the Museum and the protection, display and use of its collection'.

However, a few months later, in the meeting of November 27th deputy-chair of the board, Muriel Gray decided to step down due to the upcoming announcement, just before the final discussion about the deal started.[19] She informed the Board of Trustees at the beginning of the meeting that she had made 'a personal decision' to submit her resignation as a Trustee to the government. She 'would continue to support the Museum and wished her colleagues on the board all the best' after which she left the meeting. Yet another trustee, Mary Beard, confirmed later in an email to The Times that she also had personally opposed the sponsorship deal but had accepted the view of the majority. 'I only have this to say. I accepted as a Board member the view of the majority of the Trustees (who I know looked long and hard at this). But it was not my view and speaking personally, this would not have been my decision'.[20] So far for the desire to operate as a united board.

> Speaking personally, this would not have been my decision
> —Trustee Mary Bear.

13.3.3 Support

Not everybody was against the new deal, Lord Ed Vaizey, a former Conservative culture minister said on BBC radio 'We tend to treat BP as a pariah - BP has put a huge amount into the arts and has been treated very badly by some of the beneficiaries of that funding'.[21]

13.4 Comparable Cases

13.4.1 Tate Museum, National Portrait Gallery and Royal Shakespeare Company

Several UK cultural institutions did conclude their partnerships with BP.

In 2017, the Tate Museums ended a 26-year relationship that was hailed as an outstanding example of patronage' and 'one of the most significant long-term corporate investments in UK arts and culture'.[22]

The relationship between Royal Shakespeare Company and BP was ended by the end of 2019. Since 2013, BP sponsored the youth tickets (16–25 years) with 5 GBP. However, these young people expressed their concern about the BP sponsorship which was 'putting a barrier between them and their wish to engage with the Royal Shakespeare Company'. It was a difficult decision, and 'there are many fine balances and complex issues involved, and the decision has not been taken lightly or swiftly'.[23]

> There are many fine balances and complex issues involved
> —Royal Shakespeare Company in 2018.

13.4.2 Van Gogh Museum and Shell

In 2018, the Van Gogh Museum in Amsterdam concluded its partnership with Shell. This collaboration enabled research into the condition of Van Gogh's paintings for 18 years, with Shell providing high-tech equipment in their laboratory to analyse the paint in detail. A museum spokesperson emphasised that this was the only feasible method for such research during that period. However, this association faced criticism from Fossil Free Culture activists, who argued that 'Shell is exploiting cultural institutions to enhance its image, which is something a cultural institution should never support'. The museum clarified that the end of this collaboration was not a response to these protests but a natural conclusion of the research project. They acknowledged considering the implications of working with an oil company, but maintaining the material-technical understanding of pigments, ageing, and fading remained a paramount objective for the preservation of the paintings.[24]

13.4.3 Oxycontin and the Opioid Crisis

It's not only oil money that activists are fighting against at museums. A recent prominent controversy involves the Sackler family, known for their pharmaceutical company Purdue Pharma, which produces the heavily addictive Oxycontin and is responsible for the Opioid Crisis. Since 2017, the pressure group Sackler P.A.I.N has been staging protests at museums across the U.S. and Europe calling for the removal of the Sackler's family name. Among others, the Victoria and Albert Museum, the Guggenheim Museum and the National Gallery in London faced protests and 'die-ins' due to the Sackler family's links to the opioid crisis. This led to these museums cancelling sponsorships and donations from the Sackler family. The protests were a significant example of ethics-driven activism, pushing museums to reassess their funding sources and consider the impact of accepting money from controversial figures or industries.

In 2019, the director of the Victoria and Albert Museum still publicly expressed support for the Sackler sponsorship. During a radio interview, he stated that he was proud that the museum was supported by the Sackler family and that 'we are not going to be taking names down or denying the past'. He mentioned that private funding had become crucial, with a 30% reduction in public funding in recent years. The museum does consider ethical matters seriously but also respects the Sackler family's vision for the future. At that time, Theresa Sackler was serving as one of the trustees of the Victoria and Albert Museum.[25] In May 2022, both the National Gallery in London as the Guggenheim in New York announced that the Sackler name will be removed from respectively Room 34 and the Art Education Center. The Guggenheim believes this is 'in the best interest of the museum and the vital work it does'. Protest group Sackler P.A.I.N called the sponsorships 'blood money' and warned other billionaires for these kinds of actions; they hope that 'billionaires who shower institutions with their blood money watch the Sacklers' cultural reckoning and take note that they can be next'.[26]

A few months later, in October 2022, also the Victoria and Albert Museum now dropped financial ties with the Sackler family and the name Sackler was removed from the Sackler Centre for Arts Education and the Sackler Courtyard.[27]

Notes

1. BP and leading UK cultural institutions extend partnerships for a further five years, Press release website BP, July 28, 2016.
2. On Resigning from the British Museum's Board of Trustees, Ahdaf Soueif, July 15, 2019.
3. On Resigning from the British Museum's Board of Trustees, Ahdaf Soueif, July 15, 2019.
4. Trustee resigns from British Museum over its stance on sponsorship and repatriation, Geraldine Kendall Adams, website Museums Associations, July 16, 2019.
5. The PCS union Culture Group represents 4,000 museums & heritage workers across England, Scotland, and Wales, including at the British Museum, Tate, and National Gallery.
6. British Museum Workers Issue Statement in Support of Trustee Who Resigned, Hakim Bishara, Hyperallergic, July 22, 2019.
7. We're disappointed and dismayed that the RSC has decided to end our partnership early, Press release website BP.com October 2, 2019.
8. An open letter to the British Museum concerning BP sponsorship, Natasha Reynolds, February 16, 2022.
9. BP and the National Portrait Gallery announce end of partnership, Press release website BP.com, April 21, 2022.
10. Speech by George Osborne Chair, Annual Trustees Dinner, British Museum, November 2, 2022.
11. Will the British Museum finally break it off with BP? Culture Unstained, December 12, 2022.
12. British Museum ends BP sponsorship deal after 27 years, Esther Addley, The Guardian, June 2, 2023.
13. The British Museum and BP's sponsorship deal will end after 27 years, Benjamin Sutton, The Art Newspaper, June 2, 2023.
14. British Museum ends BP sponsorship deal after 27 years, Esther Addley, The Guardian, June 2, 2023.
15. https://www.britishmuseum.org/about-us/british-museum-story
16. British Museum sets out next steps for the Masterplan, Press release British Museum, December 19, 2023.
17. The British Museum Board Meeting November 27, 2023, website The British Museum.
18. The British Museum Board Meeting June 29, 2023, website The British Museum.

19. British Museum signs £50 m funding deal with BP, Sean Seddon, BBC News, December 20, 2023.
20. Trustee quits British Museum over record £50 m sponsorship deal with BP, David Sanderson, The Times, December 19, 2023.
21. British Museum signs £50 m funding deal with BP, Sean Seddon, BBC News, December 20, 2023.
22. BP to end Tate sponsorship after 26 years, Nadia Khomami, The Guardian, March 11, 2016.
23. We are to conclude our partnership with BP, press release Royal Shakespeare Company, October 2, 2019.
24. Van Gogh Museum stopt met samenwerking Shell ('Van Gogh Museum ends collaboration with Shell'), Jorien van der Keijl, Het Parool, August 28, 2018.
25. V&A boss proud of funding from US family linked to opioid crisis, Mark Brown and Amy Walker, July 10, 2019, The Guardian.
26. Guggenheim Removes Sackler Name Over Ties to Opioid Crisis, Zachary Small, May 10, 2022, The New York Times. The Guggenheim Museum, Which Long Resisted Calls to Drop the Sackler Name, Has Finally Quietly Removed It, Sarah Cascone, May 9, 2022, News.artnet.com.
27. V&A drops financial ties with Sackler family over links with opioids, Vanessa Thorpe and Joanna Walters, October 1, 2022, The Guardian.

14

The Case of Bud Light and the Partnership with a Transgender Influencer

14.1 The Case

14.1.1 Bud Light

Bud Light, is an iconic American light lager beer, brewed by Anheuser-Busch, part of AB InBev. Introduced in 1982, it quickly rose to become one of the best-selling beers in the United States. Its light body and lower calorie content compared to regular beers make it a favoured choice among beer drinkers looking for a lighter option.

14.1.2 Dylan Mulvaney

Dylan Mulvaney is a transgender influencer with more than 2 million followers on Instagram and 10 million followers on TikTok. In the US, Mulvaney has gained considerable attention by her journey of transition which was widely followed in 2022 through her 'Days of Girlhood' series. The series got mixed reactions, and these highlight the polarised nature of discussions surrounding gender identity today. Supporters see the series as a positive step towards inclusivity and understanding. Critics, however, raise concerns about potential mockery, representation issues, and its role in broader cultural debates.

14.1.3 Instagram Post

On April 1, 2023, Mulvaney shared a post including a cheerful video on Instagram @dylanmulvaney. She is dressed as Holly Golightly (Audrey Hepburn) from Breakfast at Tiffany's and promotes a Bud Light contest around March Madness. 'Happy March Madness!! Just found out this had to do with sports and not just saying it's a crazy month! In celebration of this sports thing @budlight is giving you the chance to win $15,000! Share a video with #EasyCarryContest for a chance to win!! Good luck! #budlightpartner'. The video showed that Bud Light sent her a personalised beer can with her face on it, to celebrate a full year of her 'Days of Girlhood' series and included a USD 15,000 giveaway, sponsored by Bud Light.

14.1.4 Boycott

A significant backlash erupted on Twitter as users criticised the advertising campaign, labelling it an attempt to disseminate gender-related propaganda. On April 2, John Cardillo, a conservative commentator, and former NYPD officer, expressed his disapproval on Twitter (@JohnCardillo): 'Who the hell at @budlight thought it was a good idea to make a grown man who dresses like little girls their new spokesperson? Brands must stop listening to their woke creative teams and get in touch with their consumer demographics'. His tweet was widely shared and discussed.

Subsequently, on April 4, Kid Rock, an American singer-songwriter, escalated the situation by posting a video on Twitter (@KidRock) where he was seen shooting at dozens of Bud Light canes. The video culminated with Kid Rock extending his middle finger and voicing a defiant 'F*ck Bud Light. F*ck Anheuser-Busch'. The video went viral and spawned imitators. Before Instagram-influencer Bri Teresi aimed at the cans of Bud Light, she warned 'Go woke, go broke'. Country singer Travis Tritt announced a ban on the brand for his tours.

> Go Woke. Go Broke.
> —Influencer Bri Teresi on Instagram

Vox, an online platform, disclosed on April 13 that it had received several emails, allegedly also dispatched to Anheuser-Busch, alleging the placement of explosives at multiple company sites. This development escalated the tensions surrounding the campaign.[1]

14.1.5 Bud Light

Initially, an Anheuser-Busch spokesperson told Fox News that Anheuser-Busch 'works with hundreds of influencers across our brands as one of many ways to authentically connect with audiences across various demographics. From time to time, we produce unique commemorative cans for fans and for brand influencers, like Dylan Mulvaney. This commemorative can was a gift to celebrate a personal milestone and is not for sale to the general public'.[2]

Ten days afterwards, following Vox's revelation of emails mentioning explosives placed at stores, a spokesperson from Anheuser-Busch declared in a statement that 'the safety of our employees is always our top priority. We are working with local law enforcement to ensure the security of our people and our facilities'.

Then, on April 14, Anheuser-Busch published a rather vague press release on their website and on social media, with the title 'Our Responsibility To America'.[3] CEO Brendan Whitworth emphasised that their intention was never to become entangled in divisive debates, stating the company was 'never intended to be part of a discussion that divides people. We are in the business of bringing people together over a beer'. He underscored the significance of accountability and 'the values upon which America was founded: freedom, hard work and respect for one another'. Concurrently, Whitworth highlighted his commitment as CEO to 'building and protecting our remarkable history and heritage'. However, he did not address the boycott, nor did he mention the threats and derogatory remarks associated with it.

Whitworth's statement seemed to seek understanding for his attempts to limit brand damage, while also subtly yielding to the boycott. This was inferred from his comments about spending a significant amount of time travelling across America, 'listening to and learning from our customers, distributors and others'. There was a noticeable lack of overt support for Mulvaney or the LGBTQ + community, as well as an absence of efforts to promote reconciliation.

On April 22, two marketing executives took a leave of absence, both Alissa Heinerscheid, responsible for Bud Light marketing, and her boss Daniel Blake who oversees marketing for Anheuser-Busch's mainstream brands, were placed on leave.[4] Just days before the release of the Mulvaney video, at the end of March, she mentioned in a podcast the necessity for Bud Light to embrace inclusivity to expand its consumer base, critiquing past ads for their 'fratty, sort of out-of-touch humour'. After the Mulvaney post, Heinerscheid also faced intimidation, harassment, and death threats. Additionally, photographs from a 2006 Harvard party featuring Heinerscheid, where there was an abundance of alcohol and she was seen inflating balloons from condoms, were released and circulated across digital platforms. This led to accusations of hypocrisy, whereas the party at Harvard seemed to exemplify a 'fratty' atmosphere.

14.1.6 Donald Trump (1)

The boycott of Bud Light came from conservative activists, but former president Donald Trump remained relatively silent on the matter. He did refer to the boycott in a message on May 7, 2023, on Truth Social (he was banned from Twitter at that time) 'It's time to beat the Radical Left at their own game. Money does talk—Anheuser-Busch now understands that'. His son, Donald jr. defended the brand a few days before 'So here's the deal. Anheuser-Busch totally sh*t the bed with this Dylan Mulvaney thing. I'm not, though, for destroying an American, an iconic company for something like this'.[5] Trump Jr. also said that the company refrains from engaging in the 'woke nonsense' prevalent among others in the beer industry, asserting that their competitors are 'far more guilty' of such practices. However, The Independent suggested that the Trump family's reluctance to criticise the company stems from their personal financial interests. Trump's financial disclosures showed that he holds a significant financial interest in Anheuser-Busch, between 1 and 5 million USD.[6]

14.1.7 Standing with the LGBTQ+ Community

Singer Garth Brooks, also a bar owner in Nashville, did take another view and explicitly stated that 'we're going to serve every brand of beer' and directs people to other bars if you cannot be inclusive 'if you [are let] into this house, love one another. If you're an a** hole, there are plenty of other places on lower Broadway'. He also adds that he wants his bar to 'be a place you feel safe in'. He was intimidated himself and on Twitter people said they would burn their merchandise.[7]

TV-host John Oliver, host of the show 'Last Week Tonight', critiqued Anheuser-Busch's April 14 response and mentioned a recent advert featuring a horse traversing various US landscape, with the narrator invoking the 'story of the American spirit'. Oliver observed that the company, eager to avoid alienating anyone, produced a commercial that, in essence, vaguely celebrates America: 'they are clearly so afraid of offending anyone, they put out an ad essentially saying America, something something'. He also pointed out that

Anheuser-Busch missed a crucial opportunity to publicly disavow the intimidation tactics used against them: 'When bigots are loudly announcing, they don't like your beer because they are bigots, that is an opportunity for you to say, "Then our beer is not for you"'.[8]

Also, due to the rather vague statement, the company leadership was accused of distancing themselves from this whole situation. In turn this led to a boycott of the brand by LGBTQ + venues. On NBC News, Mark Robertson, co-owner of four Chicago-based LGBTQ + bars, said, 'They have chosen to side with a group of people who are being very hateful, who do not value, you know, the human rights or the lives of the LGBTQ + community'. Robertson expressed that this whole situation is not about economic prosperity, but about human rights, 'You can't, on the one hand, say we're going to continue to put rainbows on our cans, and we're going to continue to sponsor parades, while on the other hand, basically bending over to what is a lot of hate and vitriol'.[9]

14.1.8 'Radical' Feminists' Perspective on Women's Rights and Safe Spaces

Bud Light's advertisement sparked outrage not just among conservatives but also drew criticism from some more radical feminist groups, often referred to as: TERFS (trans-exclusionary radical feminists). Their concern relate to the implications of transgender women's inclusion in areas traditionally reserved for cisgender women, and they adhere to another moral principle: to protect women's rights and spaces. Transgender women's participation in various societal domains, including sports games, safe spaces for women, and representation of women in positions of power and in media and advertising, raise concerns about fairness, safety and integrity, and representation of cisgender women. Transgender women may take opportunities that would have otherwise gone to cisgender women, in industries where women have historically been underrepresented or marginalised.

Critics of these views argue that this excludes and delegitimises the experiences and identities of transgender women, framing them as oppositional to the interests of cisgender women. Advocates for transgender inclusion emphasise the importance of solidarity among all women and argue for approaches that ensure fairness, safety, and equality without compromising the dignity and rights of transgender individuals.

The description of this case is not meant as an attempt to solve this discussion, but rather focus on de business decision Bud Light had to make, after the backlash already occurred.

14.2 Considerations

Would it be Morally Defensible to Capitulate to the Boycott and Stop Supporting the Transgender Influencer?

The Bud Light case is an example of moral values that are not general principles as sometimes assumed. The conversation around this case is highly nuanced and contentious, reflecting broader societal debates about gender identity, inclusivity, and women's rights. Research of the Pew Research Center revealed the American public is divided over the extent to which our society has accepted people who are transgender: 38% say society has gone too far in accepting them, while a roughly equal share (36%) say society hasn't gone far enough.[10]

In the description of this case, therefore, we do not aim to solve this multifaceted view on this societal debate but we will only illustrate the dilemma of Bud Light, between, on the one hand, capitulating to the boycott and giving in to harassment but also listening to concerns being made by different stakeholders, or at the other hand holding on to their decision to be a showcase of an inclusive company, standing with the harassed trans woman too, and taking public responsibility in a heated debate for which they are accountable too. See Table 14.1 for the Moral Consideration Matrix for Bud Lights' Board of Directors.

> **DEI Statement of Anheuser-Busch[11]**
>
> Our purpose is to create a future with more cheers. To achieve this, our company must be an inclusive and diverse workplace. Here, we all feel we belong whatever our personal characteristics or social identities, such as race, nationality, gender identity, sexual orientation, age, abilities, socioeconomic status, religion, and others.
>
> An Inclusive Future: A Future With More Cheers is one where everyone belongs—where we can all be our true, authentic selves at home, at work, or in our communities.

The ongoing boycott of the brand poses significant risks, not only endangering safety in workplace and retail environments but also threatening a decline in market share, sales, shareholder value, and employment opportunities. This boycott has also surfaced in the context of honouring the rights of cisgender women, a viewpoint endorsed by a section of the employees, consumers, business partners, and societal groups who believe the brand's collaboration fails to reflect their perspectives.

Table 14.1 The moral consideration matrix for Bud Lights' Board of Directors

	Utilitarian consequences	Deontological, moral norms
For +	- The ongoing boycott of the brand could significantly impact safety in the workplace and retail environments - The continuation of the boycott could lead to a decrease in market share, sales, shareholder value, and employment opportunities	- Honouring the principle of protecting the rights of cisgender women, a stance advocated by part of the employees, consumers, business partners, and segments of society who felt the collaboration did not represent their views
Against -	- LGBTQ + employees may feel neglected and unsupported, potentially leading to their departure and a reduction in workforce diversity - Without public support for Mulvaney, she continues to face intimidation and bullying	- Honouring the values of a LGBTQ + -inclusive society, which is supported by part of the employees, consumers, business partners, and societal groups in favour of the collaboration - Refuse to engage with forms of activism deemed unacceptable, such as boycotts and blackmail, and stand firm against intimidation - Adhere to the DEI statement of the company, 'we all feel we belong', explicitly referring to gender identity - Take responsibility and accountability by continuing to support Mulvaney, who has also been subjected to harassment too because of a prior marketing decision by the company ('Hiring a trans person and then not publicly standing by them is worse, than not hiring a trans person at all', see Epilogue)

Concurrently, LGBTQ + employees might feel marginalised and unsupported, risking their departure and diminishing workforce diversity. Amidst these tensions, Mulvaney faces continued intimidation and bullying without public backing, highlighting the necessity of standing against such coercion. Upholding the values of an LGBTQ + -inclusive society, advocated by another segment of stakeholders in support of the collaboration, demands rejecting unacceptable forms of activism like boycotts, bullying and blackmail. It's crucial to adhere to the company's DEI statement, 'we all feel we belong', which explicitly acknowledges gender identity. This scenario underscores the importance of taking responsibility and accountability by steadfastly supporting Mulvaney, who has endured harassment because of a previous marketing choice by the company.

14.3 Epilogue

14.3.1 Mulvaney

On June 29, 2023, Mulvaney reacted for the first time on Instagram 'Trans people like beer too!' and shared a video starting with drinking a glass of beer and then explaining she has something on her chest. In the 4-minute video, she does not mention Bud Light but explained that 'I took a brand deal with a company that I loved and posted a sponsored video on my page'. She expressed that she had faced an unimaginable level of bullying and transphobia, leading to her being stalked and feeling too frightened to leave her house. She revealed her expectation for the brand to show support, which never came. In her opinion, hiring a trans person and then not publicly standing by them is worse, than not hiring a trans person at all. She ended the video with that no matter 'how many thousands of horrible messages, news anchors misgendering her, or companies going silent', she can look in the mirror and see the woman that she is and loves being.

> Hiring a trans person and then not publicly standing by them is worse, than not hiring a trans person at all
> —Dylan Mulvaney in 2023

The lack of support for Mulvaney was also regretted by some of the employees of Anheuser-Busch.[12] Employees were assured by their managers not to worry, with claims of ongoing conversations with her. Managers also expressed their doubts on the completeness of the narrative in her June post, suggesting that the actual level of communication was more extensive than she indicated. An employee wished they had firmly maintained that their actions were inclusive, underlining the message, 'We did this; beer is for everyone; get over it'.

Mulvaney did not delete her post for Bud Light, it got more than 195 K likes and 10,000 comments, of which many hate comments as well as supportive messages. In November 2023 she was on the cover of Forbes Magazine in a special on businesswomen '30 under 30'. Mulvaney responded in Instagram: 'This was my dream; I couldn't be more grateful. And buckle up, we're just getting started @forbes' @dylanmulvaney, November 28, 2023.

14.3.2 Bud Light

Anheuser-Busch reacted on the statement of Mulvaney that the company never reached out to her.[13] A spokesperson stated their ongoing commitment to long-standing partnerships, including those with the LGBTQ + community, but emphasised the paramount importance of employee and partner privacy and safety. Moving forward, their focus will be on brewing exceptional beer for all and playing a significant role in important moments for their consumers.

In July, Anheuser-Busch announced that it would lay off 350 employees due to the declines of sales and in August, Anheuser-Busch presented the results for the second quarter of 2023.[14] The presentation showed a decline in revenue of 10.5% due to the 'volume decline of BudLight' (slide 7). On the next slide (8), the company did not explicitly refer to the controversy regarding the post of Mulvaney but implicitly stated that in the future Bud Light will focus on topics for which they expect no criticism: they will 'concentrate on platforms that *all* our consumers love'. The company hide their choices behind the wish of 'most consumers' who apparently agree they want 'their beer without a debate, Bud Light to focus on beer and Bud Light to concentrate on platforms that all our consumers love – e.g., NFL, Folds of Honor, Music'. In November 2023, the chief marketing officer, Benoit Garbe, announced that he was resigning at the end of the year.

Bud Light sales fell by 20%-30% in 2023 and lost its 20 years status as the top-selling beer in the US. The Human Rights Campaign Foundation removed Anheuser-Busch, Bud Light's parent company, from its list of LGBTQ + equality top-rated companies. This action followed the company's handling of backlash against a sponsored post by transgender woman Dylan Mulvaney. Initially, the collaboration was viewed positively as a sign of inclusion. However, the company's response to the subsequent criticism showed a lack of support for Dylan and the trans community, failing to uphold its values of diversity, equity, and inclusion, according to Jay Brown from The Human Rights Campaign Foundation.[15]

14.3.3 Kid Rock

In November 2023, Kid Rock expressed his desire to move past the controversy. He firmly stated that he wasn't offering apologies but instead highlighted the boycott's effect on Bud Light's employees rather than on Mulvaney. Identifying as 'a conservative, a patriot', he shared his preference to steer clear of 'cancel cultures and boycotts' which, in his view, predominantly harm the working class. Additionally, he noted his Christian faith underpins his belief in forgiveness, specifying that his stance on forgiveness pertains to Bud Light's actions, not his own. Kid Rock acknowledged that Bud Light 'made a mistake', but he questioned the fairness of relentlessly punishing the company to the extent of jeopardising employment, asking, 'you wanna hold their head under water and drown them and kill people's jobs?'.[16]

14.3.4 Donald Trump (2)

On February 7, 2024, Donald Trump tried again to restore the value of his financial interest in Anheuser-Busch. On Truth Social he wrote 'The Bud Light ad was a mistake of epic proportions, and for that a very big price was paid, but Anheuser-Busch is not a Woke company'. Also, he referred to the significant contribution of the company to its employees 'Anheuser-Busch spends $700 million a year with our great farmers, employ 65 thousand Americans, of which 1,500 are Veterans'. He concludes by writing that 'Anheuser-Busch is a Great American Brand that perhaps deserves a Second Chance? What do you think?'.

On the same day, well-known transgender and former Olympic Swimmer Caitlyn Jenner backed the message of Trump on X (former Twitter): 'As someone that worked for this incredible American company, and got to know them very well, I raced for @AnheuserBusch in the 80's I agree with @realDonaldTrump'. Jenner did not express any support for the LGBTQ + community or Mulvaney but stated that Anheuser-Busch 'made a huge mistake and has paid a large price. I think it is time to move forward'. On the same day, the stock price increased by approximately 3%.

14.4 Comparable Cases

14.4.1 Nike

Mulvaney also has a paid partnership with Nike, and just a few days later than the Bud Light post, she posted a photo of her working out in a Zenvy legging and Alate Bra, and tagged @nikewomen. On TikTok a user started a 'burn bra challenge' and recorded herself lighting her Nike bra on fire, saying that Nike should be 'ashamed of itself'.[17]

Nike reacted not directly to this post of Mulvaney but on April 6, the company did post a statement on Instagram with a call out for 'comments that contribute to a positive and constructive discussion'. Nike directly addressed people on Instagram, 'You are an essential component to the success of your community', and they urge commenters to 'Be kind ♡ Be inclusive ♡ encourage each other ♡ Hate speech, bullying, or other behaviours that are not in the spirit of a diverse and inclusive community will be deleted'. @Nike, April 6, 2023.

14.4.2 Target

Retailer Target introduced a pride collection in the Spring of 2023, to celebrate Pride month. It included for example swimwear made for those who identify as transgender with 'tuck-friendly' crotches. Angry customers began to call for a boycott and Target removed some of the products off the shelves.

In return, on June 15, 2023, Target CEO Brian Cornell received a public letter from a group of 15 attorneys general.[18] The letter started with stating the strong commitment of the AGs 'to protecting the civil rights of LGBTQIA + individuals' and the 'resolute and unequivocal support for the LGBTQIA + community'. The AGs were concerned about the recent events in Target stores, including intimidation and destruction of certain Pride-related merchandise and Target's resulting decision to remove some Pride merchandise from its stores. The AGs pointed out to the importance of the Pride merchandise at Target. It 'helps LGBTQIA + people see that they enjoy considerable support and that loud and intimidating fringe voices and bullies do not represent the views of society at large'. They were also concerned 'it sends a message that those who engage in hateful and disruptive conduct can cause even large corporations to succumb to their bullying and that they have the power to determine when LGBTQIA + consumers will feel comfortable in Target stores—or anywhere in society'. They expressed their concern about the chain's removal of some of its Pride products while this is 'a message that those who engage in hateful and disruptive conduct can cause even large corporations to succumb to their bullying'.[19]

Notes

1. The Bud Light boycott, explained as much as is possible, Emily Stewart, June 30, 2023, VOX.
2. Bud Light says pact with trans activist Dylan Mulvaney helps 'authentically connect with audiences', Brian Flood and Lindsay Kornick, FOX News, April 3, 2023.

3. Our responsibility to America, press release Anheuser-Busch, April 14,, 2023, www.anheuser-busch.com/newsroom/our-responsibility-to-america
4. 2 Executives Are on Leave After Bud Light Promotion With Transgender Influencer, Amanda Holpuch and Julie Creswell, April 25, 2023, The New York Times.
5. Donald Trump Jr. opposes Bud Light boycott, citing company's donations to Republicans, Timothy H.J. Nerozzi April 15, 2023, FOX New.
6. Trump kept quiet on the Bud Light boycott. It turns out he owns Anheuser-Busch stock, Andrew Feinberg, Independent, April 26, 2023.
7. Garth Brooks addresses 'stir' over saying his bar will serve Bud Light, NBC News, June 13, 2023.
8. John Oliver Blasts Budweiser's Response to Backlash Over Trans Influencer Partnership, Carly Thomas, April 23, 2023, Hollywoord Reporter.
9. Chicago gay bars boycott Anheuser-Busch for distancing itself from Dylan Mulvaney, NBC News, May 10, 2023.
10. Americans' Complex Views on Gender Identity and Transgender Issues, Kim Parker, Juliana Menasce Horowitz And Anna Brown, June 28, 2022, PEW Research Center.
11. https://www.ab-inbev.com/who-we-are/diversity-equity-inclusion/
12. 'Panic and rash decision-making': ex-Bud Light staff on one of the biggest boycotts in US history, Owen Myers, September 19, 2023, The Guardian.
13. Dylan Mulvaney says Bud Light's backlash response was 'worse than not hiring a trans person at all', Clare Duffy, June 30, 2023, CNN Business.
14. Anheuser-Busch presentation, 2Q23 Results August 3, 2023, https://www.ab-inbev.com/investors/
15. Anheuser-Busch loses top LGBTQ + rating over its Bud Light response, Danielle Wiener-Bronner, May 19, 2023, CNN.
16. Kid Rock says it's time to move past Bud Light boycott: 'Let the thing go', Victor Morton, The Washington Times, November 17, 2023.
17. Nike critics launch a 'burn bra challenge' and rail against its treatment of female athletes amid growing backlash for its work with a transgender influencer, Matthew Kish, Business Insider.

18. Letter of 15 Attorney Generals, June 16, 2023. Target Pride Letter at https://illinoisattorneygeneral.gov/Page-Attachments/Target%20Pride%20Letter%202023.06.16.pdf
19. Analysts: Pride flap likely hurt Target - Despite gains in traffic to its stores and website, retailer found "there is no easy way to satisfy everybody.", Nicole Norfleet, August 15, 2023, Star Tribune.

15

The Case of a Modern Art Museum and Conflict of Interests

15.1 The Case

15.1.1 Beatrix Ruf

Beatrix Ruf, a German-born curator, is highly regarded in the international art world and is 'known as one of the most influential figures in the world of international contemporary art'.[1] She became the director of the Stedelijk Museum in Amsterdam in 2014, following an impressive tenure at the Kunsthalle Zurich. Her biography includes collaborations with, among others, the Centre Pompidou in Paris, Tate Liverpool, the Irish Museum of Modern Art in Dublin, the Museum of Contemporary Art in Chicago, the Berkeley Art Museum in San Francisco, and the Moderna Museet in Stockholm.[2]

In 2017, the Board of Trustees, Beatrix Ruf and the Stedelijk Museum in Amsterdam were embroiled in controversy due to various forms of alleged conflicts of interest, including a substantial bonus from Ruf's former employer, art agreements with a member of the Board of Trustees, and reciprocated donations.

15.1.2 Bonus

Ruf apparently received a bonus of one million Swiss francs from publisher Michael Ringier and his company Ringier AG, for whom she had curated the art collection for twenty years. After joining the Stedelijk Museum, Ruf was no longer employed by Ringier AG but remained involved as an expert, for which she received this substantial 'bonus'.³ Both her role and the amount were verbally communicated to the chairman but not shared with the entire Board of Trustees, nor was it reported in the annual report. Ringier AG had also become a lender and benefactor of the museum. In the New York Times, the director of Culture + Entrepreneurship said that side activities that benefit an individual rather than the institution are not consistent with the Cultural Code 2014, and this is even more true for a museum that heavily depends on public money. However, he added that if the board allowed these side activities, and 'it turns out to be not a good choice, then the board may have to resign'.⁴ Ringier said in the same article that 'the money that I think everybody talks about in this company is the money she got for the 20 years of work for us, and had nothing to do with an ongoing advisorship'.

15.1.3 Purchase/Donations from Board of Trustees

Furthermore, there were loan agreements and combined purchases/donations with one of the Trustees. No improper advantage was gained, but again, there was no reporting. The then-chairman of the Board of Trustees, Ferdinand Grapperhaus, responded in October 2017 that loans from Trustees only need to be explained in annual reports if the board deems there to be a conflict of interest, and according to Grapperhaus, 'it had not been judged that there was a conflict of interest'.⁵ On the other hand, 'collectors, dealers, and artists all know that the purchase of a work by a public collection, or even just its temporary display, will increase its and the artist's value'.⁶

15.1.4 Donation Not Free of Charge

Finally, there was a donation from German art collector Thomas Borgmann that was not entirely 'for nothing'; he wanted to receive 1.5 million euros in the form of purchases from his collection. The museum bought works by Michael Krebber and Matt Mullican at a relatively high price, contributing to a price-inflating effect for these artists.

15.1.5 Cultural Governance Code 2014⁷

Following the worldwide development of Corporate Governance Codes, a Cultural Governance Code was established in The Netherlands in 2004. In 2017, the Code 2014 was applicable. The Code emphasises transparency and accountability. Transparency should create trust and confidence, helping to maintain public support for the cultural sector. Accountability should assist the different stakeholders active in the cultural sector, such as funding agencies, the general public, sponsors, supporters, and other stakeholders to ascertain whether an organisation is efficient and effective. The Code 2014 comprises nine principles, which are further elaborated on in practical recommendations.

Principle 8 focuses on managing conflicts of interest, requiring board and supervisory board members to avoid any real or perceived conflicts. Key recommendations include: transactions with potential conflicts must get prior approval from the supervisory board (8.2), board members should not engage in activities conflicting with the organisation's interests (8.4), members must not exploit commercial opportunities meant for the organisation for personal or familial gain (8.5), and any possible conflicts should be immediately reported to the supervisory board's chairman, with full disclosure for discussion in the absentia of the involved member (8.6). Additionally, decisions perceived to have a conflict of interest need to be detailed in the Annual Report (8.8).

15.2 Considerations

Would a (Potential) Conflict of Interests Be Morally Acceptable?

Allegations of conflicts of interest and transparency deficiencies might diminish public trust in the museum, possibly leading to a decline in support and funding. (See Table 15.1 for the Moral Consideration Matrix for the Stedelijk Museums' Board of Trustees) Involvements in transactions suspected of art price inflation could distort the broader market, undermining the accessibility and fairness that are pivotal to the art community. Furthermore, the controversy linked to these activities could tarnish the museum's reputation and hinder its ability to achieve its public mission. Such behaviours could breach the Cultural Governance Code 2014, particularly in terms of managing conflicts of interest and maintaining transparency. Not reporting significant financial transactions and conflicts of interest in the annual reports violates principles of transparency and accountability, potentially prioritising personal gain over the institution's interests and compromising the integrity of the museum and its leadership.

On the other hand, the bonuses and donations received by Ruf, along with her international recognition, bring financial advantages not only for herself but also for the museum. These benefits could help further the museum's mission, improve its public offerings, and enhance its collection with artworks

Table 15.1 The moral consideration matrix for the Stedelijk Museums' Board of Trustees

	Utilitarian consequences	Deontological, moral norms
For +	- The bonuses and donations bring financial benefits to both Ruf and potentially the museum, which can be used to further its mission and enhance its offerings to the public - Ruf's international stature enhances the museum's profile, attracting more visitors and increasing its educational impact - The acquisition of artworks from connected parties enriches the museum's collection, offering greater cultural value to its audience	- The involved parties adhere to agreements made, fulfilling obligations to one another based on mutual consent - If the board approved Ruf's side activities, it adheres to organisational governance structures, provided the board was fully informed
Against −	- The alleged conflicts of interest and lack of transparency erodes public trust in the museum, potentially leading to decreased public support and funding - The involvement in transactions that inflate art prices contributes to broader market distortions, affecting the accessibility and fairness of the art market - The controversy detracts from the museum's reputation and integrity, impacting its ability to serve its public mission effectively	- The actions appear to contravene the Cultural Governance Code 2014, especially regarding managing conflicts of interest and ensuring transparency - Failing to report significant financial transactions and conflicts of interest in the annual report goes against principles of transparency and accountability - Engaging in activities that potentially put personal gain over the institution's interests, compromises the integrity of the museum and its leadership

from connected parties. Such contributions have the potential to elevate the museum's profile, attract more visitors, and amplify its educational impact, assuming these activities receive approval from an informed board, thus aligning with organisational governance and mutual consent agreements.

15.3 Epilogue

The City of Amsterdam initiated an inquiry, leading to the publication of a 127-page report on governance.[8] While the integrity of those involved was not questioned by the researchers, the infringements of the Code 2014 were deemed 'reproachable', albeit 'not seriously so', affirming that the integrity of the individuals concerned should remain unquestioned. Notably, the researchers described the Board's decision to accept Ruf's resignation amidst controversy and prior to the conclusion of an external investigation as 'particularly regrettable'. The report includes several key findings and suggestions.

The Board of Trustees failed to adhere to four aspects of the Code 2014, contrary to claims on the Stedelijk Museum's website which incorrectly stated compliance. Among these four aspects, two pertained to potential conflicts of interest: the Board did not adequately disclose in its annual reports any decisions potentially affected by conflicting interests, including details on loans from trustees and the intricate dynamics of acquisitions and donations. Furthermore, the Board neglected the stipulation that any decisions involving a Trustee with a possible conflict of interest should be made in that Trustee's absence. The remaining issues concerned the deficient procedure in the selection and review of the external auditor, and the lack of an opportunity to interrogate the external auditor about the annual financial statements, as they were absent from the relevant meeting.

Concerning the bonus issue, the researchers highlighted that Beatrix Ruf's mere verbal notification to the Board's then-chairman about receiving a bonus from her previous employer, Ringier, was inadequate. This was irrespective of the bonus's intention, its non-inclusion in her employment terms, its irrelevance to her role at the museum, and its failure to provoke undue conflicts of interest as per Sect. 7.1.3of their report.

Additionally, one of the ten recommendations offered by the researchers was the advisement against accepting donations and loans from the museum's management and Trustees for the foreseeable future, emphasising the need for transparency in such matters. Although these actions might not inherently violate any laws or be ill-intended towards the museum's welfare, regaining public trust is deemed crucial, underlining the importance of ensuring the integrity of decision-making remains unquestionable.

> Win–win situations are permissible.
> —Report on conflicts of interest at the Stedelijk Museum

Another recommendation focuses on agreements regarding loans from external parties, and it seems that the researchers are also addressing the media. The researchers recommend everyone 'to pay less attention to whether the counterparty benefits from the funding or loan' and that 'win–win situations are permissible'. The question of whether the counterparty has an interest in the donation or loan is 'no longer relevant and often also speculative' if it has been determined in a pure manner that the museum's interest—taking all relevant circumstances into account—is served by the donation or loan. 'Conflict of interest is not necessarily reprehensible; it can also be fruitful: the art is to avoid the negative aspects and stimulate the positive'.

In the wake of the report's publication, three Board of Trustees members, including the acting chairman, resigned, representing nearly half of the Board's composition.

15.3.1 Beatrix Ruf

Beatrix Ruf gave an interview to the New York Times,[9] three weeks after she resigned. She stated that she resigned because 'she felt the ongoing negative publicity surrounding her side activities was harmful to the museum' and the private consulting work had been approved by the Board of Trustees, and that claims of a conflict of interest were 'baseless'. 'She hoped to clarify her role in what she called a "misunderstanding"', and explained that the payments she received were primarily a severance package from the Ringier Collection, unrelated to any concurrent roles during her tenure.

This raises the question of whether a clear justification initially could have changed the outcome, an early admission of the lack of transparency, followed by a commitment to full disclosure, might have allowed Ruf to retain her position. The failure to provide such clarifications, created suspicions among observers, that all may not be as it seems. The key issue here seems to be transparency, especially critical when public funds are involved.

From 2019 till 2022, Beatrix Ruf joined the team of the Garage Museum of Contemporary Art in Moscow.[10] In 2020 she also became the director of the privately funded Hartwig Art Foundation aiming to promote young artists in contemporary art. The Hartwig Art Foundation will be renting a former courthouse in Amsterdam and will renovate and extend this monumental building. It should lead to a permanent space dedicated to the research, production, and presentation of contemporary visual art, time-based art, and future art forms in Amsterdam.[11]

15.3.2 Cultural Governance Code 2019[12]

In 2019, the Cultural Governance Code was updated. The committee describes four developments that have led to new themes in the revised Code, of which the fourth one refers to errors that were 'occasionally made in the area of integrity and overlapping interests'. To prevent unwanted overlapping interests, it was necessary to agree on rules on how to contain them and solve them as quickly as possible. The Code 2019 describes overlapping interests as multiple concurrent interests or roles held by an individual, such as a manager or supervisor. It acknowledges that in certain contexts, overlapping interests can be advantageous, or even essential, for cultural organisations. For example, fundraising initiatives led by managers or the leveraging of a supervisor's network. However, overlapping interests may be considered undesirable, particularly when they interfere with each other to the extent that a manager's or supervisor's independence is compromised. Such situations pose a risk to the organisation, potentially eroding its credibility and trustworthiness. A conflict of interest occurs when a manager or supervisor has a personal interest, whether direct or indirect, that compromises their capacity to advocate for the cultural organisation's interests impartially and objectively with integrity.

15.4 Comparable Cases

15.4.1 Victoria and Albert Museum

In 2022, Nicholas Coleridge and Ben Elliot, respectively chair and member of the Board of Trustees of the Victoria & Albert Museum, were involved in activities that seemed to mingle with their personal interests with those of the museum. Coleridge auctioned a private tour to benefit the Conservative Party without the trustee board's formal consent, while Elliot himself also co-chair for the Conservative Party used the museum for events linked to his business, Quintessentially, potentially gaining personal benefits from his trustee position. These incidents have led to criticism for blurring the lines between personal and charity interests, raising concerns about conflicts of interest. Labour Party said, 'selling assess to the museum to fundraise for a political party breaches the museum's commitment to political impartiality'.[13]

15.4.2 UK Code of Conduct for Board Members of Public Bodies 2019

The board of trustees of the Victoria and Albert Museum in London is appointed by the UK Prime Minister and the museum is a non-departmental public body sponsored by the Department for Digital, Culture, Media, &

Sport. Therefore, it should adhere to the Code of Conduct for Board Members of Public Bodies.[14] This Code includes principles about the use of resources: 'You must not misuse official resources, including facilities and equipment, for personal gain or for political purposes' (3.8). Also, it includes principles on political activities, such as 'in your public role, you should be, and be seen to be, politically impartial. You should not occupy a paid party-political post or hold a particularly sensitive or high-profile role in a political party' (3.11) and 'on matters directly related to the work of the body, you should not make political statements or engage in any other political activity' (3.12). Members of the House of Lords are exempt from these requirements (3.14), however, they 'must exercise proper discretion on matters directly related to the work of the body and recognise that certain political activities may be incompatible with your role as a board member' (3.14). Also, they also should 'not use, or attempt to use, the opportunity of public service to promote your personal interests or those of any connected person, firm, business or other organisation' (5.7).

15.4.3 Response of the Museum

On June 20, the Director of the V&A, Tristram Hunt clarified on Twitter that private venue hire is a significant source of income, which helps keep the museum free and open to the public, as well as supporting the care of its collections. He added that political parties are welcome to rent spaces on commercial terms, explicitly stating their openness to such arrangements as long as they are on commercial terms, and finished with a personal note: 'Personally, I hope the Labour Party might one day be in a position to do so…' @TristramHuntVA.

Furthermore, a spokesperson of the Victoria and Albert Museum explained that the contentious event was simply a typical corporate hire, with no trustees involved in its booking and all fees aligned with their standard public rates, ensuring fairness and transparency. The spokesperson further highlighted the V&A's reliance on diverse revenue streams, including venue hires, memberships, exhibitions, retail, and sponsorships, to support its wide range of programs, maintain its collections, and keep the museum accessible to the public. This approach underpins the museum's financial strategy to sustain its operations and educational initiatives. Also, the Department for Media, Culture and Sport defended the events, noting that Elliot's' company Quintessentially paid for the venue use, with the transactions documented in the V&A's accounts.[15]

Notes

1. Museum Leader Who Resigned Calls Controversy a 'Misunderstanding', Nina Siegal, New York Times, November 7, 2017.
2. Contemporary art museums can't avoid conflicts of interest—but we need to trust their directors, Robert Hewison, Apollo. The International Arts Magazine, November 1, 2017.
3. Gratis kunst die stiekem toch 1,5 miljoen kost ('Free art that secretly costs 1.5 million'), Daan van Lent en Arjen Ribbens, NRC, October 7, 2017.
4. Museum Leader Who Resigned Calls Controversy a 'Misunderstanding', Nina Siegal, New York Times, November 7, 2017.
5. Gratis kunst die stiekem toch 1,5 miljoen kost ('Free art that secretly costs 1.5 million'), Daan van Lent en Arjen Ribbens, NRC, October 7, 2017.
6. Contemporary art museums can't avoid conflicts of interest—but we need to trust their directors, Robert Hewison, Apollo. The International Arts Magazine, November 1d, 2017.
7. Cultural Governance Code 2014, Cultuur + Ondernemen.
8. Report 'Governance en de WNT bij het Stedelijk Museum Amsterdam' ('Governance and the WNT at the Stedelijk Museum Amsterdam'), Jan Peeters en Sjoerd Eisma, June 4, 2018, and, Ruf en het Stedelijk: de conclusies van de onderzoekers, met toelichting van NRC ('uf at the Stedelijk: the conclusions of the researchers, with explanation from NRC'), Paul Steenhuis, NRC, June 21, 2018.
9. Museum Leader Who Resigned Calls Controversy a 'Misunderstanding', Nina Siegal, New York Times, November 7, 2017.
10. Former Stedelijk Museum director Beatrix Ruf to join Moscow's Garage Museum, ArtForum.com, November 5, 2019.
11. https://www.hartwigartfoundation.nl/en/museum/
12. Cultural Governance Code 2019, Cultuur + Ondernemen.
13. Row over private tour of Victoria and Albert Museum for wealthy Tory donor, David Wilcock, MailOnline, May 17, 2022.
14. Code of Conduct for Board Members of Public Bodies, June 2019.
15. Activist group's film projection on Victoria and Albert Museum façade raises concerns about trustees' politics, Gareth Harris, June 21, 2022, The Art Newspaper.

16

The Case of G-Star and the Legal and Moral Obligations Towards a Vietnamese Supplier

16.1 The Case[1]

16.1.1 G-Star

G-Star Raw C.V. (G-Star) was founded in 1989 and was initially well-known as a trendy denim brand that later expanded to include shoes, jackets, and accessories. In 2011, G-Star became a limited partnership with a statutory seat in Curacao, claiming to do so to maintain a competitive edge in the market and facilitate further growth as a private enterprise.[2] However, this move also resulted in undisclosed revenue figures. G-Star frequently collaborates with influential figures in various fields, such as chess player Magnus Carlsen, F1 driver Max Verstappen, and rapper Snoop Dogg. To boost G-Star's recognition in the United States, in 2016 the fashion label brought in American pop star Pharrell Williams as a shareholder.[3] This partnership comes after two years of collaboration between G-Star and Pharrell Williams' company Bionic Yarn.

16.1.2 Vert Fashion

Vert Fashion Company Ltd. (Vert) is a Vietnamese clothing factory that has been producing jackets, swim trunks, and shirts for G-Star for many years.

16.1.3 The Framework Agreement

In June 2016, Vert and G-Star entered into a framework agreement outlining the terms of their collaboration. This framework agreement explicitly states that nothing in this agreement shall be interpreted as a minimum ordering obligation for G-Star or a sales obligation for Vert. Each order is to be negotiated separately: Article 2.3 of the agreement states: 'Framework only. Nothing in this Agreement shall be interpreted or construed as an obligation of G-Star or G-Star Affiliate to issue any Purchase Order or as any minimum order commitment for either of them. Nor shall this Agreement obligate Supplier to sell any Products to G-Star or any G-Star Affiliate'.[4]

The agreement also referenced the corporate social and environmental responsibility policy (CSR policy) of G-Star, incorporating it as an annex. G-Star's CSR policy includes provisions related to working conditions, health and safety, prohibition of child labour, wages, and the prevention of excessive working hours. Additionally, G-Star was a member of Better Buying, a platform that encourages the production of products under safe working conditions.

16.1.4 Additional Agreement: Whistler Jackets

Separate from the framework agreement, in December 2018, Vert and G-Star entered into a separate agreement to produce winter jackets called 'Whistler' for the years 2019 through 2021. This agreement imposed an obligation on Vert to produce and deliver 100,000 Whistler jackets each year from March to May, with deliveries starting in June, allowing the jackets to be available in stores in the fall. In the remaining months, Vert produced summer jackets, swimwear, and overshirts for G-Star under the framework agreement. During these years, Vert's factory operated almost entirely on orders from G-Star.

16.1.5 Impact of COVID-19

In October 2019, G-Star announced plans to further expand its presence in the United States, China, and the Netherlands. However, in July 2020, it became known that G-Star was facing financial difficulties, primarily attributed to the COVID-19 pandemic. Many countries experienced the closure of physical stores. In May, the Australian division of G-Star, with 57 retail locations including two flagship stores in Sydney and Melbourne, applied for creditor protection. The company announced its intention to investigate what the 'right investments and focus regions are, to manage this crisis as effectively as possible. In the coming period, we will increasingly focus on our largest markets, such as the Netherlands and Germany'.[5] In July, the American (31 retail locations) and Swedish (12 retail locations) divisions filed for bankruptcy.[6]

16.1.6 Termination of Both Contracts

In April 2020, G-Star informed Vert that, due to global measures related to COVID-19, orders for the third quarter of 2020 needed to be scaled back. A portion of the orders was cancelled, and another part was reduced. In August 2020, G-Star notified Vert that certain orders placed in previous years would not be fulfilled in 2021, and shortly afterwards, this decision extended to the Whistler jackets as well. On August 26, Vert's director informed G-Star that Vert couldn't absorb the impact of G-Star's last-minute decision not to place certain orders, posing significant risks to Vert's continuity. Vert would be forced to send employees home due to insufficient work.

On August 28, G-Star e-mailed to Vert: 'We are concerned to hear about your intention to send staff home during October/November and are surprised about the high volumes you anticipated without our confirmation'. Also, G-Star stated that 'the drop in demand for the padded outerwear products as well as a reduced sourcing team here at HQ (due to recent restructurings caused by COVID-19), forces us to consolidate production with less vendors in order to optimize efficiency'. They announced the termination of all collaborations, stating, 'we herewith share our formal notice that we will not be placing any outerwear or bulk production orders with Vert, nor any other outerwear vendor in Vietnam', and 'We have always appreciated our partnership and the way that we have worked together'.

Three days later, Vert's director inquired whether G-Star was aware that their lack of timely preparation for this decision would force him to let people go. A significant portion of Vert's employees worked on piece rate, and without a constant flow of work, employees would earn insufficiently, prompting them to seek other employment. On September 1, 2020, an online meeting took place, involving G-Star's Head of CSR. The Head of CSR referred to responsibility according to the CSR policy and expressed a desire to prevent layoffs among workers at the factory in Vietnam. She aimed to explore the possibility of placing cancelled orders.

Despite this discussion, the relationship hardened thereafter, exacerbated by G-Star's lack of response to the above commitment, even after insistence from Vert. In October, Vert held G-Star liable for incurred damages.

Now, the CEO of G-Star personally joined the discussion, stating in an email (October 16) that 'although our position is that we are not obligated to make payment or place an order, we are keen, out of gratitude for the relationship and collaboration over the past years, to part ways in a mutually acceptable manner'. G-Star proposed accepting certain already-produced items and those for which materials had been purchased, with a total value of approximately USD 900 k.

On November 16, 2020, the CEO terminated the framework agreement, which inherently had no obligations, effective July 31, 2021. In February 2021, G-Star placed an order for 56,000 Whistler jackets with SnowTex Outerwear Ltd. in Bangladesh, to be delivered in the fall of 2021.

Vert claimed damages amounting to over USD 17 million, including lost revenue from the Whistler jacket (USD 2.4 million), other G-Star orders (USD 4.1 million), other clients (USD 8.2 million), and the depreciation of the factory (USD 2.7 million).

16.2 Considerations

Would it be morally appropriate to unilaterally terminate agreements with Vert?

See Table 16.1 for the Moral Consideration Matrix for G-Stars' Board of Directors. In 2020, G-Star is undeniably going through a challenging time, but the company is not on the brink of collapse. In this case, G-Star attempts to restructure the production of, among other things, winter jackets to make it more cost-effective and better navigate through the financial and COVID-19 crisis. Consequently, a portion of the negative financial consequences falls on the supplier, Vert. The termination of production at Vert by G-Star involves both legal and several moral components. For the Whistler jackets, there was a contractual obligation, and if G-Star no longer needed the jackets, it might have been (morally) justifiable for G-Star not to acquire products for which there was no demand. In that case, G-Star could have provided financial compensation. However, because G-Star did place the order for the jackets in Bangladesh, indicating a demand, there was also a moral consideration. In this decision, G-Star did not consider its long-standing relationship with Vert and the financial repercussions this had for the supplier.

Under the framework agreement, there was no contractual obligation: simply ceasing to place orders would naturally dissolve the relationship with the supplier. However, at the time of terminating the production of the jackets (end of August), it would take another half year (until March) before

Table 16.1 The moral consideration matrix for G-Stars' Board of Directors

	Utilitarian, consequences	Deontological moral norms
For +	- G-Star's financial measures, including the cancellation of orders and partnering with a supplier in Bangladesh, could be seen as necessary steps to manage financial difficulties effectively, aiming to minimise losses and secure the company's future - Continuing 'framework' orders mitigates risk of a worker shortage by March, which is critical for maintaining the factory's ability to fulfil Whistler and other orders, ensuring stability for both G-Star and Vert	- Actions were in line with agreement's terms, hence adhering to the agreed contractual terms - Partially mitigating the situation by proposing to accept some already-produced items shows an attempt to honour their corporate social responsibility, even if not legally required
Against −	- Vert's dependence on G-Star orders risks bankruptcy and employee departure - The abrupt end to orders in September leaves no time for Vert to find new clients - Workers paid per piece lose income without orders	- Cancelling orders, despite the existing relationship and dependency created, fail to fulfil ethical obligations to a long-term partner - Communication and execution of decisions lacks transparency and consideration, undermining trust, and fairness towards Vert - Actions contradict with CSR policy, especially if the policy's intention is to prevent layoffs and ensure the welfare of workers in their supply chain - Whistlers' jackets still needed, ordering them Bangladesh is an 'immoral temptation*'

* Succumbing to a moral temptation compromises one's ethical principles for material gain

the production would restart. While this termination seems to have no immediate consequences, the intervening period (August to March) was always filled with other products. Vert had relied on these orders and could not find new buyers for this gap in production on short notice. This meant that workers were left jobless, and the factory would go bankrupt. This was also a risk for G-Star; the production of the jackets in March could be jeopardised if the factory went bankrupt or had no workers in the meantime. The alternative production in Bangladesh could accommodate this.

> **BrandValues G-STAR**[7]
> We are RAW: We are real, honest and authentic. We dare to stand out while keeping our feet on the ground. And always with a sense of humor.
> We are INNOVATIVE (..) We are EAGER (..)

16.3 Epilogue

G-Star's Sustainability Reports 2020 and 2021 do not mention this case, nor similar dilemmas. CEO Rob Schilder writes in the foreword to the 2020 Sustainability Report[8] that in this year 'that was heavily marked by COVID-19, the importance of sustainability has become even more evident. These unprecedented times make us extra aware of our responsibilities. We intentionally work with a small and durable supplier base, enabling us to establish long-term relationships. We are in close contact with all our partners to try to limit disruptions in our supply chain wherever we can'. In the 2021 Sustainability Report, he re-emphasised G-Star's responsibilities: 'Dealing with a continuing pandemic with several lockdowns and a volatile demand and retail landscape, has emphasised our responsibilities even more. On the one hand close communication and collaboration with our partners in the supply chain has never been more important to ensure our social responsibility'.[9]

16.3.1 Court Decisions

In March 2023, the Amsterdam court ruled on the case, with two different perspectives on the Whistler order and the Framework orders.

16.3.2 Whistler Jackets

The court found that G-Star's announcement in 2021 not to purchase Whistler jackets constituted an 'evident and severe violation' of the agreement to procure all Whistler jackets from Vert until 2021. Unlike the framework agreement, the three-year commitment specifically addressed the delivery of Whistler jackets between the parties, with exclusivity, and G-Star should not have ordered 56,000 jackets from SnowTex in Bangladesh.

16.3.3 Framework Agreement

The court addressed the framework agreement, stating that even if it hadn't been terminated, the relationship between the parties could still effectively end if no further orders were placed. In fact, there was no legal obligation to continue the partnership. Therefore, from this perspective, the court deemed the termination of the framework agreement and its deadline as essentially irrelevant. However, Vert argued that it was entitled to expect regular orders from G-Star under the agreement. This expectation was partly based on G-Star's Corporate Social Responsibility (CSR) policy, which promotes ethical business practices. Vert contended that G-Star's actions contradicted this policy.

On this matter, the court ruled that the parties' rights and obligations towards each other are determined not only by their explicit agreement but also by reasonableness and fairness. This standard requires that each party consider the legitimate interests of the other. Although G-Star was not obligated under the framework agreement to place orders, the court found it particularly harsh that in August 2020, G-Star suddenly announced it would place virtually no orders in the following year. This decision was significant because, for years, G-Star had been the primary occupant of Vert's production capacity. The court concluded that G-Star had failed to take Vert's interests into account.

Furthermore, the court criticised G-Star for not honouring its commitment, stated in September 2021, to seek ways to prevent sudden layoffs in the factory. G-Star was aware that many Vert employees were paid on a piecework basis. This payment method meant that without consistent work, employees would not earn enough, leading to a high turnover rate.

16.3.4 Final Judgment

In a provisional ruling, in March 2023, the court determined that G-Star's obligations extended beyond merely placing the 2021 Whistler jacket order with Vert. G-Star was also required to issue additional orders sufficient to fill the quiet period before the Whistler order's execution. This decision was influenced by several factors, including the necessity for G-Star to consider Vert's interests, stemming from their long and intensive partnership, and to align with G-Star's Corporate Social Responsibility (CSR) policy. The court highlighted this obligation considering the substantial commitment made for the expected production of Whistler jackets in 2021. G-Star's obligation to

Vert would persist only until the completion of this order, with the possibility of terminating the collaboration around May 2021.

In this provisional ruling, the court declared that G-Star must provide compensation to Vert for the losses incurred. The court's judgment is provisional, allowing the parties an opportunity to address certain points related to the damages; the final decision is deferred until then.

On November 23, 2023, the court arrived at the composition of a total sum of USD 2.5 million in damages.[10] The major part came from the value of the enterprise, assessed at USD 1.9 million, based on two different scenarios, a 'closure scenario' (45% probability; 1.2 million enterprise value) and a 'restart scenario' (55% probability; 2.5 million enterprise value). Furthermore, the remaining lost profits of around 600 K, resulted from the abrupt cessation of orders, the cancellation of 56,000 Whistler jackets, the cancellation of regular orders, and the inability to serve other customers.

16.3.5 Acquired by WHP

On September 5, 2023, it was announced that WHP Global, a New York-based global brands company will acquire a majority interest in the G-Star, setting the stage for further global growth and expansion.[11] The existing G-Star shareholders, including founder Jos van Tilburg, will retain a stake in the brand and CEO Rob Schilder and his team will continue to operate the brand's marketing and product development functions as well as the wholesale, retail, and e-commerce distribution out of the Amsterdam headquarters. WHP owns among others Anne Klein, Joe's Jeans, Isaac Mizrahi, Lotto, Toys "R" Us. The transaction is expected to close in before the end of 2023. It is unknown whether Pharrell Williams is still a shareholder in G-Star.

16.4 Comparable Cases

During the early stages of the COVID-19 pandemic in March 2020, businesses exhibited varied initial responses, some of which were hastily made, possibly out of panic. A distinct contrast became evident among companies: while some hastily cancelled all orders, disregarding the impact on their suppliers, others approached the situation more responsibly, considering the repercussions of their decisions. As time progressed, these differences began to diminish. This shift was largely due to increasing public outcry over abrupt cancellations and the establishment of global agreements, including those led by the United Nations, which encouraged more unified and considerate business practices. The website Workers Rights monitored the status of companies regarding the extent to which they fulfil their obligations.[12]

16.4.1 Primark

On March 20, 2020, amidst the escalating COVID-19 crisis, Primark made a pivotal decision. In a move citing the 'force majeure' clause, synonymous with unforeseeable circumstances, they chose to cancel and withhold payment for all orders not shipped from factories by March 18. CEO Paul Marchant candidly expressed the company's position, stating, 'we have large quantities of existing stock in our stores, our depots and in transit that is paid for and if we do not take this action now, we will be taking delivery of stock that we simply can't sell. This is an unprecedented action for unprecedented and frankly unimaginable times'.[13] This move, however, was met with substantial backlash. A month later, following discussions with their suppliers, Primark revised its decision. On April 17, they committed to also compensate for the orders already in production, adding a supplementary sum of GBP 440 million to their pay-out.

In a significant alignment with global efforts, on April 22, 2020, Primark echoed the sentiments of the International Labour Organization of the UN. This announcement called for urgent collaboration among various stakeholders to provide crucial support to workers in the global garment industry, who were deeply affected by the ramifications of the COVID-19 pandemic.[14]

Notes

1. The description of this case is largely drawn from the ruling of the Amsterdam District Court in this matter: ECLI:NL: RBAMS: 2023:1913, dated March 22, 2023.
2. G-Star wordt G-Star Raw C.V., website Fashion United, April 7, 2011.
3. Pharrell co-owner G-Star! February, 2016, press release G-Star.
4. Ruling of the Amsterdam District Court: ECLI:NL: RBAMS: 2023:1913, dated March 22, 2023.
5. Australische dochter jeansmerk G-star staat op omvallen ('Australian daughter jeans brand G-star is on the verge of collapse'), Maarten van Dun, *het FD*, May 18, 2020 and Nederlands modemerk G-Star in zwaar weer in het buitenland ('Dutch fashion brand G-Star in heavy

weather abroad'), Michou Basu & Jan Braaksma, *het FD*, July 10, 2020.
6. Na jaren van buitenlandse groei laat G-Star zich weer zien in Nederland ('After years of foreign growth, G-Star shows itself again in the Netherlands'), Jan Braaksma, *het FD*, October 17, 2019.
7. https://careers.g-star.com/about-gstar/
8. RAW Responsibility G-Star Raw Sustainability Report 2020.
9. RAW Responsibility G-Star Raw Sustainability Report 2021.
10. Amsterdam District Court, ECLI:NL: RBAMS:2023:7299, dated November 22, 2023.
11. WHP Global to Acquire Global Denim Brand G-Star RAW, press release, September 5, 2023, https://www.whp-global.com/2023/09/05/3175/
12. Covid-19 Tracker: Which Brands Acted Responsibly toward Suppliers and Workers? website Workers Rights Consortium, last updated in April 2021.
13. Coronavirus shutdown ravages high street as retailers take emergency action, Zoe Wood & Mark Sweney, The Guardian, March 20, 2020.
14. Primark Endorses Ilo Covid-19 Global Garment Industry Action Announced Today, website Primark, April 2020.

17

The Case of Heineken and Leaving Russia During the Ukrainian War

17.1 The Case

On February 24, 2022, Russia invaded Ukraine and began a horrible war with over 200,000 deaths, including many civilian casualties, eight million people fleeing and many human rights violations.[1] When the war broke out in February 2022, about fifty Dutch companies were active in Russia.[2]

17.1.1 Moral Calls to Leave Russia

Across the globe, the conflict swiftly prompted official actions, including the imposition of sanctions and ethical appeals for corporations to withdraw from the involved nation. This led to many firms exiting the country: many businesses were getting tougher on Russia than sanctions required. Josh Lipsky, head of the GeoEconomics Center, noted this as a novel and intriguing trend. Usually, he explains to CNN, businesses keep investing in a market if profitable. Yet, a common understanding emerged that it was inappropriate to market certain goods.[3] Companies were opposed to supporting, in any manner, a state and government guilty of infringing another nation's sovereignty, responsible for war casualties, or seen as benefiting from the Ukraine conflict.

This call to leave the country is not equally simple for every company. Governance experts call it 'ethical tightrope walking' in the *Financial Times*. Companies need to come up with a very clear statement about what their priorities are and what actions they are taking because otherwise, they can expect a lot of criticism from employees, investors, and customers.[4]

> Ethical tightrope walking.
> —Financial Times, March 2022

The article particularly refers to the moral obligation to patients of pharmaceutical companies. They are partly allowed to remain active in Russia because pharma is simply different from, for example, McDonald's, 'people can live without hamburgers, but they can't live without essential medicines'. The production and sale of beer fall more into the McDonald's category than into the medicines category. However, like many other food products, beer is not subject to the sanction legislation.

17.1.2 Gradual Withdrawal of Heineken from March 2022

Heineken announced on March 9, 2022, that it 'will stop the production, advertising and sale of the Heineken-brand in Russia'.[5] The Russian division of the company will be isolated from the broader organisation (ringfenced), to stop the 'flow of monies, royalties and dividends out of Russia'. No longer will it accept 'any net financial benefit' derived from the Russian operations. In deciding its next steps, it is considering the significance of its 1800 employees, who have been integral to the company for over twenty years.

According to the Dutch Investors' Association (VEB), Heineken still has sixteen other local and nine international brands in Russia at that time, including Amstel and Affligem, which they continue to sell.[6] This was followed by internal criticism and on March 28, the company sent a new press release in which they indicated to leave the country completely.[7] According to their statement these activities are 'no longer sustainable nor viable'. The company is targeting an orderly transition to a new owner, ensuring full adherence to both international and local laws. During this transition, the foremost priority is the safety and well-being of the employees. Additionally, to lower the risk of nationalisation, they will maintain the recently scaled-down operations throughout this period. Heineken commits to paying the wages of its 1800 employees until the end of 2022 and pledges to do everything possible to secure their future employment. The company reiterates that it will not benefit financially from any transfer of ownership, with an estimated financial loss amounting to EUR 400 million.

The associations for private and institutional investors (VEB and Eumedion) support this proposal: 'It is the right thing to do. You do not want to support this regime directly or indirectly. It is simply war now', says the chief economist of the VEB Jasper Jansen.[8] Director Rients Abma of

Eumedion refers explicitly to the (moral) decision that Heineken must make between indirectly contributing to human rights violations and the interests of employees (and Russian customers). The VEB calls, in general terms, also for transparency at the AGMs 'and then we want the honest story. If you only write off activities, you remain the owner'.

17.1.3 One Year Later, February 2023

During the year, Yale has created a system where companies receive a report letter from A to F, depending on their position in Russia, where an A '*Withdrawal*' means a complete departure and F '*Digging In*' means no adjustment in the company's operations.[9] Early February 2023, Heineken received an A-grade ('completely withdraws'), just like Boskalis and Fugro. Unilever and Philips receive a D 'buying time' and coffee brewery JDE Peet's is the only company to receive an F because they according to the researchers have not made any adjustments in their operations.[10] (See the response from JDE Peet's at the hearing of the House of Representatives in the epilogue.)

In mid-February 2023, Heineken releases the annual figures for 2022. The revenue and profit in 2022 were significantly higher than in 2021: 34.7 billion euros revenue and 4.2 billion euros operating profit. Following the annual figures, CEO Dolf van den Brink is interviewed for *de Volkskrant* of February 15.[11] When asked whether the departure from Russia has been completed, Van den Brink indicates that he is working hard to find a reliable buyer and that the 'remaining core business' is still functioning, so the salaries of the 1800 employees can be paid. The plan is to be able to transfer the company in the first half of 2023. Van den Brink also says in the interview that 'if you say something, you have to do it'. He says in that interview also, in the context of the business climate in the Netherlands, not in the context of the war in Ukraine: 'We note that the Netherlands used to be both merchant and preacher, and now is becoming very much only a preacher'.

17.1.4 Follow the Money

At the time, Heineken's ongoing efforts to sell its Russian operations didn't attract much attention. However, less than a week later, on February 21, the investigative journalism platform Follow the Money published an article titled 'Heineken breaks promise and still invests in Russia', sparking widespread public indignation.[12] The piece revealed that far from winding down, Heineken was actively expanding by launching 61 new brands, capitalising on the exit of competitors. An episode of Arjen Lubach's late-night TV show, akin to Jimmy Fallon's Tonight Show, highlighted how one of Heineken's new offerings, the black Irish stout Black Sheep, filled the void left by Guinness's departure from Russia. The show also featured a statement from Heineken's Russian division: 'After Coca-Cola and Pepsi withdrew, Heineken decided to enter the market for non-alcoholic carbonated products'.[13]

A newspaper article refers to a text on the website of the Russian subsidiary, which has since been offline due to technical problems: '2022 was a turbulent year for all market players, but at the same time offered plenty of opportunities and opened up new possibilities for the development and growth of our business. We are proud to announce that we have reached record heights in several segments'.[14]

> This is morally indefensible
> —Minister Foreign Affairs Hoekstra

Minister of Foreign Affairs Hoekstra, discussing the Heineken situation on a radio show, found it 'difficult' and chose not to comment on the specifics, stating it was not his place but the responsibility of the directors. However, he broadly remarked 'that companies should think twice before pretending that you can just continue here' and that this 'is morally indefensible'.[15] The Minister of Finance, speaking on TV, admitted to being unaware of the details and therefore wanted to stay away from 'tough words' but expressed surprise and a desire to understand how it can be 'that on the one hand a company says it is withdrawing and you read then another story, then we all want to know how that can be'..[16]

17.1.5 Heineken Statements

On February 21, Heineken issued a response expressing that they 'are greatly concerned about recent publications that incorrectly state, "Heineken has broken its promise to leave Russia." This is absolutely untrue and misleading'.[17] The company clarified that its Russian operations were entirely separate, with no financial benefits, including dividends, corporate fees, or royalties, flowing back to Heineken. It emphasised that the Russian branch was autonomously operated by local staff to avert nationalisation and sustain their livelihoods under challenging conditions that hampered the search for a trustworthy purchaser, projecting a financial loss of €300 million. The statement reiterated Heineken's dedication to terminate their activities in Russia 'in the right way': 'The war in Ukraine is a terrible tragedy. As we terminate our activities in Russia, we aim to do so in the right way. This means that we fulfil our commitments for a proper settlement with care for our people'.

> We aim to do so in the right way
> —Heineken, February 2023

However, by March 6, the initial statement was retracted, replaced by a new announcement aimed at articulating the dilemmas Heineken faced, the ethical guidelines driving their decisions, and the measures undertaken.[18] Heineken underscored three core tenets: the well-being and safety of its employees in Russia, ensuring the company's operation until its sale without yielding any financial profit to the Heineken Group, and steadfastly upholding the decision to leave Russia.

Furthermore, Heineken unveiled a document comprised of nineteen questions aimed at illuminating the intricacies involved in their Russian market exit strategy. The company conceded that its approach to rolling out new products could have been communicated more clearly, acknowledging that this bred doubts about their dedication to withdrawing from Russia and apologising for any resultant perplexity. The primary reasons for introducing new products and continuing Amstel sales were to dodge insolvency, thereby keeping the business viable for a potential sale and protecting the jobs of the 1,800 employees involved.

17.2 Considerations

Was it morally appropriate to keep the brewery running in Russia?

Heineken was not the only company that had not exited Russia at that time. In March 2023, research indicated that only 9 per cent of companies had successfully done so. Heineken faced significant criticism, one reason being that some observers perceived the company's dilemma as an 'amoral temptation'—benefiting from questionable actions—rather than a genuine dilemma involving conflicting values and principles.

This view was exacerbated by Heineken profiting from its competitors' withdrawal, introducing new brands, and venturing into new markets (like soft drinks), despite having pledged to withdraw. The company's euphoric and somewhat proud communication on its Russian website about these developments was deemed inappropriate and failed to reflect the complex balance of interests at play. On March 6, 2023, Heineken had not offered any other communication, such as explaining the importance of keeping the company viable for sale to employees and management. However, with a subsequent Q&A release, they attempted to articulate the board's considerations more clearly. The somewhat inappropriate announcements regarding revenue in Russia were subsequently removed from their online platforms.

> The only question is: do you think it's worth it?
> —Journalists Persson and Dekker, 2023

The importance of the employees was paramount for Heineken. (See Table 17.1 for the Moral Consideration Matrix for Heinekens' Board of Directors) The majority of the nineteen questions that Heineken posted on its website on March 6, 2023, referred to this importance. That other companies had made different considerations and perhaps cared for their employees in a different way was not explained. They, too, faced criminal prosecution in the event of intentional bankruptcy. According to journalists Michael Persson and Wilco Dekker, the key question was: 'do you act according to the letter of the law or the spirit of the law?' Relying solely on legal arguments was not a justification, according to them: 'Every company that withdrew from Russia had to break contracts to do so, with partners, suppliers, staff. That costs money. The only question is: do you think it's worth it?' Russia expert Helga Salemon from the Dutch foreign institute HCSS commented on this: 'Directly or indirectly, you keep the regime in place by staying. You keep filling the treasury'. And the Ukrainian Minister of Foreign Affairs, Dmytro Kuleba, referred to it as 'blood money'.[19]

In March 2023, the question arose whether many companies were still active in Russia out of opportunism or whether it was genuinely difficult to leave the country quickly and decently. Journalist Jan Braaksma described how complicated it was to exit the country, noting that the Russian government required financial discounts on the selling price, there were few potential buyers, also because some potential buyers were on the sanctions list. One option mentioned was a sale to local management, for a symbolic amount.[20]

Table 17.1 The moral consideration matrix for Heinekens' Board of Directors

	Utilitarian, consequences	Deontological moral norms
For +	- A stable turnover and the introduction of new products, and to ensure the company remains viable for sale is crucial for the well-being of 1,800 Russian employees - Avert nationalisation to prevent financial benefits accruing to Russia - A gradual withdrawal, costing €300 million, instead of a hasty exit, might be less expensive	- Remaining loyal to, and bearing responsibility for, the welfare of 1,800 Russian employees - Remaining loyal to- and bearing responsibility to Russian management by preventing the criminal prosecution - Avoiding nationalisation as a moral principle and responsibility - Still fulfil promise to withdraw from Russia, although not immediately - Condition: no financial gain from the war and accept the financial loss of €300 million - Condition: Honest and timely communication regarding the withdrawal from Russia
Against -	- Potential reputational harm for Heineken, including dissatisfaction among employees outside of Russia - Even if not intended, indirect support for a regime and a country involved in human rights abuses	- Heineken Russia might still unintended and indirectly benefit from the conflict - Failing to fulfil the promise to withdraw immediately from Russia - Might suggest absence of support for Ukraine

17.3 Epilogue

In early March 2023, following an investigation by Follow the Money, Yale University downgraded Heineken's rating to a grade E: 'Buying Time', from its previous grade A: 'Withdrawal' awarded in February.[21]

On April 20, 2023, Heineken disclosed at the AGM that a buyer for their Russian brewery had been secured. To ensure the sale proceeded smoothly, they refrained from revealing the buyer's identity. Gerben Evers, the chairman of the Association of Securities Owners (VEB), responded critically to the prolonged process, suggesting it was a strategy to bide time, and viewed the introduction of new products as an attempt to 'dress up the bride for the marriage'.[22]

The VEB insists that the sale must not generate any profit and that Heineken should not derive any benefit from Russia. It urges that the company fully incorporate the financial impact of its exit in its financial statements. Evers emphasised that taking a complete loss on the departure is 'a moral obligation'.

In August 2023, the deal is closed. Heineken sold its Russia business for €1, transferring all assets, including seven breweries, to Arnest Group. Arnest Group owns a major can packaging business and is the largest Russian manufacturer of cosmetics, household goods and metal packaging. Arnest Group has committed to maintaining employment for the 1,800 employees in Russia for the next three years. The sale includes phasing out Amstel production within six months and discontinuing the licensing of international brands in Russia, except for a 3-year license for some regional brands needed for business continuity. Heineken will not provide brand support or receive any proceeds, royalties, or fees from Russia, and there is no option for Heineken to return to the Russian market.[23]

In March 2024, Yale again rated Heineken A, 'Withdrawal'.[24]

17.4 Comparable Cases

The downgrade in the Yale list of Heineken in March 2023 prompted discussions about the fairness of the list and the actual progress of companies, previously rated A, in withdrawing from Russia as of March 2023. The Yale ranking appears to be primarily based on self-reported information from the companies. Research by IMD revealed that, out of over 1,400 EU and G-7 companies tracked, only 9 per cent had exited Russia by the end of December 2022.[25] These Western companies faced various challenges in terminating their operations, like those encountered by Heineken. Reasons included a reluctance to leave behind Russian employees, customers, or suppliers who were not involved in the decision to invade Ukraine, the societal importance of certain products and services such as the provision of life-saving medicines, the lack of willing buyers at an adequate price, or obstacles erected by the Russian government that hamper or delay sales.

17.4.1 Carlsberg

The Danish beer brewer Carlsberg had announced to leave Russia simultaneously with Heineken in 2022. The (Dutch) CEO Cees 't Hart gave an extensive interview to *the FD* in July 2022.[26] Through this interview, 't Hart gave an insight into the difficult dilemma they were dealing with. 't Hart referred to the lack of sanctions for the beer market and the influence of societal pressure to leave: 'We have always assumed that we could do business somewhere unless there were sanctions and governments banned countries. This is the first time that social media so vehemently insisted on a departure, even though we were not violating any sanctions'. He noted that more is being asked of companies are now being asked more than politics sets requirements, and 'if this is the new reality, it feels like rewriting the rules of the chess game, then we must henceforth take even broader account of the countries in which we are active'.

The considerations to keep the breweries running are for Carlsberg like the considerations of Heineken. When asked by *FD*-journalist Pieter Couwenbergh whether the breweries in Russia are currently just running, 't Hart confirms: 'Yes. Because what happens if we close the business? What happens to the stuff? They could fall into the wrong hands or be nationalised. More than eight thousand people and families would then be without work and income, not to mention businesses that supply our breweries. That is a high price for ordinary people. Don't forget that it's about beer goes, a regular product. They brew the local brands, not Carlsberg. And the profit is donated to charities. But the breweries in Russia are legally and financially completely set separate'.

> It's a Catch-22.
> —Cees 't Hart in *FT*, February 2023

A year later, in February 2023, he called this in the *Financial Times* a 'Catch-22': 'If we take out the international brands, it cannot be sold. Then it would be nationalised. But if we do the licenses, we might get some criticism from the outside world'.[27] At that time, Carlsberg also foresees that it can only be completely out of Russia by the end of the second quarter of 2023. 't Hart indicated that 'the reverse integration, the process of decoupling the Russian operations from the rest of Carlsberg, was more complex than he had assumed'. The company will also include a buyback option in the sale, although 't Hart expected that this will not be possible within 10–15 years. Like Heineken, Carlsberg was also rated as 'E' on the Yale list in early April.

However, in July 2023, the Russian government temporarily assumed management of the shares belonging to Baltika, the local brewery owned by Carlsberg and Danone's Russian subsidiary, according to a decree signed by President Vladimir Putin. Previously, the Russian branches of Germany's Uniper and Finland's Fortum were already under government management. Carlsberg noted in a statement that following the presidential decree, the future of the earlier announced sale was now significantly uncertain.[28]

On September 1, CEO 't Hart was succeeded by Jacob Aarup-Andersen. In October 2023, Aarup-Andersen announced that the company had severed all connections with its Russian operations and would not engage in any agreement with the Russian government that could legitimise the seizure of its assets. He added, 'There is no way around the fact that they have stolen our business in Russia, and we are not going to help them make that look legitimate'.[29]

Notes

1. Ukraine war: US estimates 200,000 military casualties on all sides, BBC, 10 November 2022.
2. Over 1,000 companies have curtailed operations in Russia—But some remain, Yale School of Management, CELI, March 6, 2023.
3. Why many businesses are getting tougher on Russia than sanctions require, Chris Isidore, CNN Business, March 3, 2022.
4. Western drugmakers walk ethical tightrope over Russian ties, Jamie Smith & Hannah Kuchler, Financial Times, March 18, 2022.
5. Heineken stops production and sale of Heineken® beer in Russia, Press release, March 9, 2022.
6. Russische pijn is ongelijk verdeeld bij de drie grote bierbrouwers ('Russian pain is unevenly distributed among the three major brewers'), VEB, March 10, 2022.
7. Heineken N.V. announces decision to leave Russia, Press release, March 28, 2022.
8. Heineken en Carlsberg weg uit Rusland ('Heineken and Carlsberg leave Russia') Richard Smit, *het FD*, March 28, 2022.
9. Yale CELI List of Companies Leaving and Staying in Russia, March 7, 2023.
10. Nog steeds te koop in Rusland: Magnum-ijsjes, scheerapparaten van Philips en koffie van Douwe Egberts ('Still available for sale in Russia: Magnum ice creams, Philips shavers, and Douwe Egberts coffee'), Michael Persson & Wilco Dekker, *de Volkskrant*, 10 februari 2023.
11. Heineken-topman: de koopman en dominee Nederland wordt nu wel heel erg alleen dominee ('Heineken CEO: the merchant and the preacher—The Netherlands is now becoming too much of a preacher'), Wilco Dekker, *de Volkskrant*, February 15, 2023.

12. Heineken breekt belofte en investeert toch in Rusland ('Heineken breaks promise and invests in Russia anyway'), Olivier van Beemen, *Follow the Money*, February 21, 2023.
13. De Avondshow ('The Tonightshow') wthArjen Lubach, *VPRO*, February 22, 2023.
14. Heineken onder vuur om activiteiten Russische tak na 'zwabberende communicatie' ('Heineken under fire for Russian branch activities after 'wavering communication'), Wilco Dekker, *de Volkskrant*, February 23, 2023.
15. Hoekstra: Investeringen in Rusland moreel niet uit te leggen ('Hoekstra: Investments in Russia are morally indefensible'), *BNR*, February 21, 2023.
16. Kaag is 'heel verbaasd' over investeringen Heineken in Rusland ('Kaag is 'very surprised' about Heineken's investments in Russia'), *RTL-Z*, February 21, 2023.
17. Heineken's reactie op onjuiste berichtgeving over Rusland ('Heineken's response to incorrect reporting about Russia'), Press release, February 21, 2023.
18. Heineken's commitment and approach to leaving Russia, Questions & Answers, March 6, 2023.
19. Nog steeds te koop in Rusland: Magnum-ijsjes, scheerapparaten van Philips en koffie van Douwe Egberts ('Still available for sale in Russia: Magnum ice creams, Philips shavers, and Douwe Egberts coffee'), Michael Persson & Wilco Dekker, *de Volkskrant*, February 10, 2023.
20. Weggaan uit Rusland: Wees dan bereid je verlies te nemen ('Leaving Russia: Be prepared to take your loss'), Jan Braaksma, *het FD*, March 4, 2023.
21. Less than Nine Percent of Western Firms Have Divested from Russia, Simon Evenett (University St Gallen en Niccolò Pisani (IMD), 20 December 2022, SSRN-ID = 4,322,502.
22. VEB verwijt Heineken gebrek aan leiderschap bij vertrek uit Rusland ('VEB criticizes Heineken for lack of leadership in leaving Russia'), Jan Braaksma, *het FD*, April 21, 2023.
23. Heineken completes exit from Russia, Press release, August 23, 2023.
24. Yale CELI List of Companies Leaving and Staying in Russia, March 23, 2024.
25. Less than Nine Percent of Western Firms Have Divested from Russia, Simon Evenett (University St Gallen en Niccolò Pisani (IMD), December 20, 2022.

26. Carlsberg-ceo Cees't Hart over vertrek uit Rusland. 'Alsof de regels van het schaakspel werden herschreven' ('Carlsberg CEO Cees't Hart on leaving Russia. 'As if the rules of the game of chess were being rewritten'), Pieter Couwenbergh, *het FD*, July 14, 2022.
27. Carlsberg seeks buyback clause as it nears exit from Russia, *Financial Times*, February 7, 2023.
28. Russia seizes control of shares in Danone and Carlsberg subsidiaries, The Guardian, July 17, 2023.
29. Carlsberg CEO: Russia has 'stolen our business', Jacob Gronholt-Pedersen, Reuters, November 1, 2023.

18

The Case of ADIDAS and Kanye West (Ye)

18.1 The Case

18.1.1 Kanye West, Ye

Kanye West, addressed as Ye since 2016, is a well-known American rapper, singer, songwriter, record producer, fashion designer, and influencer. A celebrity indeed. In addition to his music and fashion designs, Kanye has been involved in various other projects, including directing films and politics. In 2015, West launched his own highly successful streetwear clothing line called Yeezy.

Adidas has been working with Kanye since 2013, but this partnership gained more substance in 2016 when the Yeezy collection was brought under Adidas. This is announced grandly with terms like 'historic' and ' unprecedented' and 'the most significant partnership ever created between a non-athlete and an athletic brand'. [2] The estimated revenue of Yeezy is two billion dollars per year.

18.1.2 Controversy

Kanye often stirs controversy with his provocative remarks. In May 2018, for example, in an interview on TMZ Live, he said, 'When you hear about slavery for 400 years, for 400 years! That sounds like a choice'. A petition was then launched by Care2 asking Adidas to drop him: 'tell the world they do not want anything to do with anyone who believes that millions of Africans chose to toil the fields in bondage for 400 years'.[3]

Although Adidas initially did not respond, two days later, they issued a statement distancing themselves from Kanye's slavery remarks. CEO Kasper Rørsted stated on Bloomberg that he distanced himself from Kanye's comments but clarified that the company had not discussed dropping the rapper as a designer.[4] On CNBC, the CEO said, 'Kanye has helped us have a great comeback in the US' and 'There is no doubt the Yeezy brand has a fundamental impact on our overall brand'.[5]

In August 2022, it is announced that CEO Rørsted will step down but will stay on until a new CEO is found in 2023. The relationship between Kanye and Rørsted was already strained before, but after the announcement of Rørsted's departure, Kanye posted a fake front page of The New York Times on Instagram with the text 'Kasper Rørsted also dead at 60' (September 1, 2022). This was a variation of the inappropriate post he previously posted after the breakup of his ex-wife Kim Kardashian with her new boyfriend, Pete Davidson. 'Skete Davidson dead at age 28' (August 8, 2022).

18.1.3 The Limit is Reached

In early October 2022, things went awry again with Kanye. It started with him wearing a T-shirt to Paris Fashion Week with the text '*White Lives Matter*' on the back. He received a lot of criticism, including from fellow rapper Diddy on Instagram (October 5): 'Don't mess with Black Lives Matter' and 'Don't play with it. Don't wear the shirt. Don't buy the shirt. Don't play with the shirt. It's not a joke'.

Then, on October 8, Kanye sent multiple anti-Semitic texts via Twitter and Instagram, such as 'I'm a bit sleepy tonight but when I wake up, I'm going death con 3 On JEWISH PEOPLE' (referring to a military threat level, defcon 3). A week later, on October 16, he responded to the controversy and his role at Adidas in a 45-minute podcast Drink Champs: 'The thing about me and Adidas is like, I can literally say anti-Semitic shit, and they can't drop me. I can say anti-Semitic things, and Adidas can't drop me. Now what?'.

> I can say anti-Semitic shit, and Adidas can't drop me. Now what?
> —Kanye West on the Drink Champs podcast, October 16, 2022

This was most likely the last straw because almost two weeks later, on October 25, Adidas finally acted, the limit is reached. In the press release, they reject anti-Semitism and hate messages: 'Adidas does not tolerate antisemitism and any other sort of hate speech. Ye's recent comments and actions have been unacceptable, hateful, and dangerous, and they violate the company's values of diversity and inclusion, mutual respect, and fairness'.[6] Adidas decides to terminate the partnership, the production of Yeezy, and payments to Ye immediately. They expected a short-term negative impact of $250 million.

18.2 Considerations

Would an ongoing commercial relationship with Kanye West be morally appropriate?

See Table 18.1 for the Moral Consideration Matrix for Adidas' Board of Directors. On the one hand, terminating the partnership could lead to significant financial repercussions for Adidas, including potential job losses and the challenge of dealing with unsellable stock, which could worsen financial difficulties. Customers might also be disappointed by the loss of a preferred brand. Ethically, maintaining the collaboration could be seen as respecting freedom of speech by distinguishing between the brand and Kanye West's controversial statements, honouring contractual agreements, and demonstrating loyalty to West, thereby valuing steadfast partnerships.

Conversely, Adidas risks damaging its brand reputation, as a customer-signed petition indicates a loss of public trust. Ignoring or appearing to condone West's hate speech could inadvertently amplify antisemitic discourse, with harmful effects on the Jewish community and broader societal implications. Ending the partnership is crucial to uphold Adidas's ethical principles, aligning the brand's actions with its core values and demonstrating a commitment to high ethical standards and zero tolerance for discrimination. This decision reflects the importance of standing against discrimination, supporting community values, and advocating for universal rights, which are fundamental to Adidas's identity and ethical responsibilities.

It took a long time for Adidas to finally act against Kanye's provocative statements. Apparently, the contribution of Yeezy to Adidas' revenue still weighed the heaviest. Kanye was also aware of this when he stated that he could 'literally say anything' and Adidas would not drop him. Intervening would have significant consequences, not only for Kanye but would also lead to job losses. The weighing of the interests of employees and customers, who benefit from the survival of the Yeezy brand, against those of minorities constantly offended by Kanye, had previously tilted in favour of the former group.

Table 18.1 The moral consideration matrix for Adidas' Board of Directors

	Utilitarian, consequences	Deontological moral norms
For +	- Ending the collaboration will have a significant financial impact for Adidas, leading to potential job losses - Customers face the disappointment of losing a preferred brand - Adidas will be confronted with the challenge of holding unsellable stock, further exacerbating financial strains	- Maintaining a distinction between the brand and individual viewpoints, Adidas is not responsible for Kanye West's controversial statements - Allow freedom of speech, the autonomy of individuals to express their opinions, even if those expressions are widely condemned - Honour contractual agreements and stay loyal to Kanye West, emphasising the value of steadfast partnerships
Against -	- The brand's reputation is at stake, as evidenced by a customer-signed petition, indicating a loss of public trust and approval - By appearing to condone or overlook hate speech, there is a risk of amplifying antisemitic discourse with negative consequences for the Jewish community and society at large	- Taking a stand against Kanye West's comments is essential for upholding Adidas's ethical stance - Continuing the partnership highlights a misalignment with the core values - Upholding community values and advocating for universal rights such standing against discrimination - Reflect Adidas's commitment to high ethical standards and zero tolerance for discrimination

> **VALUES ADIDAS**[7]
> Courage, Ownership, Innovation, Teamplay, Integrity and Respect

However, upon parting ways, the company now refers to the overriding importance of adhering to core values of diversity and inclusion, mutual respect, and honesty and not tolerating anti-Semitism. These arguments could have been used earlier. Until 2022, Adidas consistently distanced itself from Kanye's statements but argued that they did not directly control him. However, this seems like avoiding taking responsibility. Until 2022.

18.3 Epilogue

18.3.1 New CEO

On November 8, the new CEO was announced, the Norwegian Bjørn Gulden from rival Puma. Although Gulden only starts on January 1, 2023, Rørsted leaves a few days after the announcement, on November 11.

18.3.2 Financial Impact

In February 2023, Adidas presented the outlook for 2023, revealing that the damage for Adidas could amount to a one-billion-dollar lower operating result. At that time, the company has not yet decided what to do with the existing Yeezy inventory. If they do not sell this inventory 'this would lower revenues by around € 1.2 billion and operating profit by around € 500 million this year'.[8]

During the Annual General Meeting on May 11, 2023, Gulden announced plans to sell the inventory valued at 1.2 billion dollars. A portion of the proceeds will go to advocacy groups affected by Kanye's statements. However, Kanye also benefits, reportedly receiving a 15 per cent commission. This decision disappointed some advocacy groups, as it seems to punish Adidas more than Kanye. Following this announcement, Adidas' stock price increased by 2 per cent. In 2023, the two Yeezy drops positively impacted net sales for around € 750 million in 2023 and the company announced it would sell the whole inventory at least at cost.[9]

18.3.3 More Problems for Adidas Due to Kanye

In November 2022, the music magazine Rolling Stone came with more allegations of Kanye's misconduct, including accusations of bullying, playing porn, and showing indecent, erotic photos to Adidas employees, including his ex-wife, Kim Kardashian. Rolling Stone interviewed over twenty (former) employees of Adidas and Yeezy and received a copy of an (anonymous) letter sent by several employees to Adidas executives, including the company's new CEO. The letter was titled 'The truth about Yeezy: A call to action for Adidas Leadership'. The employees described how Ye deliberately created a culture of fear and intimidation, leading to years of verbal abuse, vulgar tirades, and harassment. They claim that the top at Adidas was aware of these methods.'The board members and the executive team turned their moral compass off by ignoring both Kanye's inflammatory public behaviour and the Yeezy team's complaints regarding troubling partner dynamics'.[10]

> The board members and the executive team turned their moral compass off
> —Adidas employees

Adidas responded that it is unclear whether the reports are true. They did announce an immediate independent investigation into the matter but only do so after one of the major shareholders, Union Investment, asked for it in the Financial Times. Janne Werning, Head of ESG Capital Markets & Stewardship: 'Adidas needs to disclose when the management and the supervisory board was first informed about the internal allegations'.[11]

On April 28, 2023, a lawsuit was filed against Adidas on behalf of all shareholders who owned Adidas shares on May 3, 2018, the date he made the slavery remark on TMZ. The court documents stated that Adidas was aware of Kanye's problematic behaviour and that the company had not taken meaningful precautions to limit negative financial exposure if the partnership were to end. According to the shareholders, the CEO and CFO consciously misled the investor or at least 'acted with reckless disregard for the truth'.[12]

Adidas responded to the shareholder lawsuit in February 2024, dismissing it as an unfounded attempt to frame the end of its partnership with Kanye West as securities fraud, and calling the action opportunistic. The company argued it had made thorough disclosures about potential performance risks, including issues with partners and stakeholders. Adidas recounted its efforts to address concerns about West's controversial behaviour and statements since 2018, maintaining that the profitable partnership's termination in 2022 was unforeseeable. The company refuted the lawsuit's allegations, asserting that there was no evidence Adidas made false statements with intent or gross negligence, calling for the lawsuit's immediate dismissal for lacking merit.

18.4 Comparable Cases

18.4.1 Nike and Colin Kaepernick

The case of Nike and Colin Kaepernick shows that a company, risking the loss of revenue, can also choose to explicitly continue supporting a controversial celebrity. Nike took a position in a polarised discussion, making them a part of it.

Colin Kaepernick played as a quarterback for the San Francisco 49ers but was not fielded from 2016 onward due to his action of kneeling during the

American national anthem at NFL games. Kaepernick, born to an African American father, peacefully protests against racial injustices in his country. He is supported by players nationwide and sparked the 'Take a Knee' trend but is no longer contracted by an NFL team due to the controversy following this trend. Then-US President Donald Trump got involved, and the NFL established in 2018 a National Anthem Policy that kneeling during the anthem was prohibited, players could stay in the locker room.[13]

> Believe in something. Even if it means sacrificing everything.
> —Nike, 2018

In 2018, Nike announced that Kaepernick would be the new face of the 'Just Do It' campaign. The black-and-white image of the quarterback is accompanied by the message: 'Believe in something. Even if it means sacrificing everything'. Like Kaepernick's action, Nike received both compliments and severe criticism, including a widely shared call for a boycott and videos on social media of Nike clothing and shoes being set on fire. The stock initially dropped by 3 per cent but quickly recovered, and ultimately, revenue even increased.

Nike's CEO, John Donahoe, explained in 2020 that behind every decision of the company to comment on societal issues, there is indeed a strategy, and it is not taken impulsively. Donahoe is guided by 'what is good for our consumer, good for our athletes, good for our company'. However, if certain topics do not relate to the company's core focus, Nike is unlikely to issue a statement on them, according to Donahoe.[14]

In 2020 NFL-Commissioner Roger Goodell said in a new statement 'We, the National Football League, condemn racism and the systematic oppression of black people. We, the National Football League admit we were wrong for not listening to NFL players earlier and encourage all to speak out and peacefully protest'.[15] In 2018, Colin Kaepernick received Amnesty International's Ambassador of Conscience Award.

Notes

1. Yeezy—Adidas and Kanye West make history with transformative new partnership Adidas + Kanye West, press release Adidas, June 29, 2016.
2. Adidas, Drop Kanye West for Calling Slavery a 'Choice', Care2 Petitions, The Petition Site.
3. Adidas sticking with Kanye West after his slavery remarks, Bloomberg, May 3, 2018.

4. Adidas is standing by Kanye West, who said slavery 'sounds like a choice', CNBC, May 3, 2018.
5. Adidas terminates partnership with Ye immediately, pressrelease Adidas, October 25, 2022.
6. https://www.adidas-group.com/en/magazine/series/value-series
7. Adidas provides top- and bottom-line outlook for 2023, pressrelease Adidas, February 9, 2023.
8. Adidas full-year results exceed latest expectations; company decides not to write off most of its yeezy inventory, Press release Adidas, January 31, 2024.
9. Adidas launches probe into claims that Kanye West showed employees porn, Elisabeth Garber, *Rolling Stone*, November 24, 2022.
10. Adidas to launch probe into claims about Kanye West playing pornography to staff, Olaf Stobeck, *FT*, November 24, 2022.
11. Adidas shareholders launch class-action lawsuit over Ye fallout, Chantal Da Silva, *NBC News*, May 1, 2023.
12. NFL owners approve national anthem policy for 2018, Austin Knoblauch, NFL.com, May 23, 2018,
13. Nike's new CEO reveals how the company decides when to take a stand on social issues  and when to stay quiet, Shoshy Ciment, *Business Insider*, February 9, 2020.
14. Roger Goodell: NFL 'wrong' for not listening to protesting players earlier, June 5, 2002, NFL.com.

19

The Case of AJAX and the Inappropriate Behaviour of a Director

19.1 The Case

19.1.1 AFC Ajax

Amsterdamsche Football Club AFC Ajax NV is one of the three leading football clubs in the Netherlands. In April 2021, it was placed 20th in Forbes' list of the most valuable football clubs, with a valuation of approximately USD 413 million.[1] Since the inception of the Dutch Premier League ('Eredivisie') in 1956, Ajax has secured the title 36 times, along with four UEFA Champions League victories, notably achieving three consecutive wins (1971, 1972, 1973) under the star player Johan Cruyff. At the beginning of 2022 Ajax is second in the Dutch premier league.

Additionally, since 1998, Ajax has been publicly traded on the Euronext Stock Exchange. In 2021, the executive board of Ajax included two former internationally acclaimed footballers: Edwin van der Sar, a former goalkeeper for Ajax, Juventus, Fulham, and Manchester United, as well as a 130-time player for the Dutch national team, serves as the managing director. Marc Overmars, a former winger for Ajax, Arsenal, and FC Barcelona, with 86 appearances for the Dutch national team, holds the position of director of football affairs since 2012.

19.1.2 EGM

On December 17, 2021, the schedule for an extraordinary general meeting (EGM) set for January 28, 2022, was announced. The meeting's agenda included the nomination of Georgette Schlick as a new non-executive director, along with the proposed reappointments of three executive directors: Susan Lenderink as financial director, Menno Geelen as commercial director, and Marc Overmars as director of football affairs.

The reappointments of the three executive directors were not obligatory. Specifically, Overmars' current term was due to continue until November 2024, and that term was now effectively extended until June 30, 2026. The rationale provided in the meeting's agenda highlights 'his expertise and experience, as well as his performance in the role of director of football affairs' as key factors for this decision. Additionally, the proposal includes a one-off 'signing fee' of 1.25 million euros.[2]

On January 28, 2022, the EGM was held virtually due to COVID-19 restrictions. According to the report, Peter Mensing, chairman of the remuneration committee, presented the appointments. He highlighted that Marc Overmars had attracted international interest. Mensing noted that Overmars, alongside Van der Sar, forms a crucial foundation for sustained success, and an additional sum is being awarded 'is appropriate for the performance delivered' and to counteract foreign interest. The overarching goal mentioned was 'securing the long-term strategy and successes' of the club.[3]

Due to the virtual nature of the EGM, queries were submitted and addressed in writing. Notably, the issue of the signing fee wasn't debated during the EGM. When questioned about the timing of the reappointments, given that the current terms hadn't yet ended, the response indicated that the Board was keen on retaining the management team at Ajax for an extended period to maintain the club's current sporting, commercial, and organisational achievements. It is explicitly mentioned that Marc Overmars was approached by other clubs.[4]

19.1.3 Overmars' Resignation

Just nine days after the EGM and the reappointment of Overmars, on Sunday, February 6, Ajax sent out a press release that Overmars resigned with immediate effect due to 'a series of inappropriate messages sent to several female colleagues over an extended period of time'.[5] Overmars' reaction was included in this press release. He offered his apologies and among other things indicated that he was 'ashamed' and 'did not realise he was crossing the line this, but that was made clear to him in recent days'. He acknowledged that the behaviour was 'unacceptable' which he now realises. 'But it is too late'. And he sees no other option than to leave Ajax.

19.1.4 The Days In Between

The Dutch investors association VEB sent out a letter on February 14, 2022, with some questions and requests for clarification. In their response dated February 25, Ajax gave an overview of the timeline of events.[6] It seems that on January 25, Edwin van der Sar sent an email to all staff members, directing their attention to the availability of confidential counsellors. This action was taken in response to the scandal surrounding The Voice of Holland, to ensure employees knew where to report any instances of inappropriate behaviour.[7] On January 26, an employee notified Van der Sar about possible instances of misconduct by the director of football affairs. Subsequently, on January 27, 2022, a day prior to the EGM, this matter was brought to the attention of the chairman of the board. The information did not include specific details like facts, names, or dates, and the extent and seriousness of the allegations were not yet known.

19.1.5 Media

The details and severity of the misconduct were primarily revealed through the investigative work of NRC journalists Danielle Pinedo, Fabian van der Poll, and Steven Verseput.[8] They initiated an investigation into power abuse at Ajax in December 2021 following a tip-off about inappropriate conduct. The journalists interviewed eleven current and former Ajax employees and published their findings the day after the resignation, revealing a pattern of behaviour by Overmars. This included sending numerous inappropriate messages, including multiple *dick pics*, identifiable as being sent from Ajax's premises due to distinctive bathroom tiles in the background. The NRC article indicated that signals of this behaviour at Ajax were overlooked, and personal experiences were shared in limited circles and remained rumours.

A few days later, NRC also covered an internal online meeting held on February 9 for all Ajax employees, where the club provided some additional clarification. Van der Sar highlighted the importance of football, referencing that evening scheduled KNVB cup match with the remark 'Football always goes on'. However, the club's press chief also expressed regret that (former) employees had gone public without the media department's consent.[9] Later, in the Supervisory Board's report for the 2021/2022 financial year, the Board acknowledged and thanked the women who reported the inappropriate behaviour.

19.1.6 Van der Sar

On Sunday, February 13, before the premier league match against FC Twente, Van der Sar responded for the first time on national television.[10] He confirmed that the reports were already known before the EGM of January 28, but that further research had to be done. In one interview, he said that he received 'signals about eight or nine days' before the departure of Overmars 'that there might be something going on'. That you must investigate very carefully, which we did with an 'independent external agency'. Van der Sar also referred to the right of reply, and that 'signals are nice, but it's not like something is immediately on your desk'. Van der Sar: 'You can't act on rumours'.

> You can't act on rumours.
> —Edwin van der Sar on Dutch television, February 13, 2022

When it became clear around Wednesday, February 1, that the inappropriate behaviour was 'large-scale and long-term', the other directors took the next steps. In another interview, Van der Sar added that he has had a tough time due to disappointment and sadness and that he has also considered quitting. He also said that 'these kinds of situations can't be learned from books. What is the right thing to do. What steps should be taken?'.[11] Here too, he indicates that it has affected him personally 'I was inundated with questions. It was a rollercoaster. And personally, it affected me a lot'.

19.2 Considerations

Would it be morally appropriate, before rumours are confirmed, to reappoint Overmars as Executive Director? And, would it be morally appropriate, after rumours are confirmed, to keep Overmars as Executive Director?

In this scenario, at least two moral dilemmas present themselves: the decision to reappoint Overmars at the EGM despite serious signals of inappropriate behaviour and the debate over Overmars' continued role as Ajax's technical director. The Moral Consideration Matrix for Ajax's Board of Directors in Table 19.1 includes both moral dilemmas.

> **Core values Ajax**
> We want to be the best.
> We are Amsterdam's direct.
> We strengthen each other.
> We think offensive.
> We bring talent to bloom.
> We show leadership.

19.2.1 Reappointment at the EGM

The chairman of the Supervisory Board, Leen Meijaard, described the situation as 'dramatic and deeply affecting for the women subjected to such behaviour'. He noted that upon becoming aware of the issue, immediate actions were taken, and they carefully weighed, and considered what was best to do. According to Ajax, the option to delay the EGM was considered, but there was a lack of sufficient information to warrant such a decision. Delaying could have potentially caused considerable speculation and unrest, which were not addressable at that time. Additionally, postponing the EGM could have been perceived as unsafe by the affected employee, which might have compromised the process of establishing the truth.[12] At the AGM in November 2022, Ajax once again confirmed that they had let the EGM go ahead because at the time of the EGM 'there were no names, no facts, no data about the cross-border behaviour of the director of football affairs were known and no hearing and counter-hearing had been applied'.[13]

> Carefully weighed and considered what was best to do.
> —Chairman of the Supervisory Board of Ajax, Leen Meijaard

Additionally, in their annual report, the Supervisory Board detailed their approach to the situation. In addressing the complaints, the Supervisory Board opted to wait for a clearer understanding of their nature. Before making any public accusations, it was crucial to have concrete statements from potential victims. A concern was that a media frenzy might discourage these individuals from coming forward. Additionally, there was a risk of unfairly tarnishing Overmars' reputation if the allegations were later found to be baseless.

By proceeding with the reappointment, Ajax chose to shield Overmars' reputation and avoid potential disorder, prioritising these factors over immediate transparency with the shareholders until more information became available. The Association of Securities Owners (VEB) has repeatedly indicated, first with a letter on February 14 and later at the AGM in November 2022, having trouble with the continuation of the EGM. It involved price-sensitive information known to the directors, and investors were misled by not mentioning a word at the EGM about the signals already received.[14]

19.2.2 Resignation

After the EGM, when the indications of inappropriate behaviour were confirmed, Overmars' departure was seen as unavoidable 'he has unfortunately really crossed boundaries'. Chairman Meijaard expressed their regrets from a football perspective: 'Marc is probably the best football director Ajax has ever had'.

Overmars is clearly of great value to the sporting and thereby also financial performance of Ajax. Losing him as director of football affairs has a major impact on the prosperity and well-being of the club, the Ajax company, and thus for the players, supporters, and shareholders. However, his behaviour is unacceptable and there must be consequences attached to it. If not, this will have damaging consequences for the reputation of Ajax, sponsors may withdraw, and the victims may not feel supported. The consequences can range from offering apologies to dismissal. The Supervisory Board has chosen the latter. Later (see the epilogue), various stakeholders suggested whether there were other options for satisfaction and whether dismissal was necessary.

In essence, the decision to reappoint Overmars at the EGM, despite the emerging allegations and the subsequent consideration of his role as director, encapsulates the tension between maintaining strategic leadership for the club's success and upholding ethical standards.

Subsequently, a third moral dilemma could emerge, is it appropriate for Overmars to make a comeback to Ajax after a set period? See for some additional information in the epilogue to this case.

Table 19.1 The moral consideration matrix for Ajax's Board of Directors

	Utilitarian, consequences	Deontological, moral norms
For +	**Continuation of re-appointment at EGM** - Immediate action based on unsubstantiated allegations could harm the club's reputation if claims were later found to be unfounded, potentially leading to legal and financial repercussions **No resignation for Overmars?** - Overmars' strategic contributions to the club's success provides value to Ajax's sporting and financial performance	**Continuation of re-appointment at EGM** - Protecting Overmars' reputation if rumours turn out to be not substantive or false (loyalty) - Acting too quickly might discourage complainants from reporting about the rumours (integrity) **No resignation for Overmars?** - After Overmars' sincere apologies, retaining him could be an act of mercy, allowing for redemption and for loyalty - If victims' wish for acknowledgment over dismissal, emphasises the importance of addressing harm in a way that honours their preferences
Against -	**Continuation of appointment at EGM** - If allegations are later confirmed, the damage to the club's reputation can be more severely, leading to a loss of trust among fans, potential sponsorship withdrawals, and harm to the club's market value **No resignation for Overmars?** - Ajax: reputational damage and cancellation of sponsors - Complainants/female employees: complaints are not taken seriously enough (responsibility)	**Continuation of appointment at EGM** - Incorrect information at AGM against the regulations (citizenship) **No resignation for Overmars?** - Allowing Overmars to remain in his position would directly conflict with Ajax's core values and ethical standards, particularly those concerning respect, integrity, and responsibility towards employees and stakeholders

19.3 Epilogue

19.3.1 Financial and Sporting Performances

On January 28, 2022, Ajax's share price was around EURO 14.40. The day after the announcement of February 6, the share fell by almost 7 per cent to EURO 13.40 during the day and closed 3 per cent lower at EURO 14. Major sponsors, Ziggo of the men's team and ABN AMRO of the women's team demanded an independent investigation into the inappropriate behaviour. The CEO of ABN AMRO said in a reaction 'You can imagine what a dilemma this is. On one hand, we want to support the women of Ajax, and on the other hand, we see what is happening now', and 'management must conduct a thorough investigation into the extent of the problem. We are in daily discussions with Ajax's management to understand how they are going to respond. Then we will determine our stance'.[15] Ziggo extended their sponsorship in June 2022, ABN AMRO in September 2022.

19.3.2 Overmars and Royal Antwerp

A month after his dismissal, Overmars is presented as the new sporting director at Royal Antwerp FC. Overmars himself reacts to his appointment: 'I want to turn that page and start a new chapter. And I want to do that here'. And: 'It's been very unfortunate, and you have to get through that, and move on'.

The club, along with its owner Gheysens, faced significant criticism. Flemish football journalist Hans Vandeweghe commented on the disrupted moral compass of Belgian football, specifically pointing out that Paul Gheysens seemingly lacked a moral compass entirely.[16] Consequently, Royal Antwerp experienced the loss of several sponsors. The anticipated partnership with Nike, set to start in the 2022–2023 season as the shirt sponsor, fell through. Additionally, the HR company Select Group terminated their collaboration, stating, 'The decision to appoint Overmars is in direct conflict with our company's values and norms'.[17]

Regarding Overmars, arrangements were made for him to repay bonuses and the signing fee, totalling 1.5 million euros, with half due in 2022 and the remaining in 2023.[18] In November 2022, these payments had not yet been made. This was confirmed both at the AGM of November 2022 and in the annual report for 2021/2022 (published by the end of September 2022). The annual report (p.141) stated that 'the full prepaid signing fee of 1,250,000 euros has now been reclaimed but not yet received'. It also mentioned that 'a loan agreement has been executed for this claim'. The annual report for 2022/2023 (published September 2023) does no longer mention the fee, nor the payment or the outstanding amount of a loan.

At the end of December 2022, a quiz on national television titled 'You can't do anything anymore' featured twenty questions, including 'the willy of Marc Overmars'. The questions were: 'How quickly did Overmars get a new job?' and 'Is sending a dickpic punishable?'.[19]

19.3.3 Call for Overmars' Return

Ajax secured the championship title in the 2021–2022 season and was the runner-up in the KNVB Cup. However, the 2022–2023 season saw them finish third, a position last held in 2009, and they were defeated in the cup final by PSV. Ajax's stock value declined by about 23 per cent a year later (end of April 2023), trading at around 11 euros. Gerry Hamstra and Klaas-Jan Huntelaar temporarily stepped in as technical directors, though their transfer strategy faced criticism.[20] Alfred Schreuder, appointed as the new coach for the 2022–2023 season, was dismissed in January 2023 due to poor results, with John Heitinga taking over until the season's end.

Former footballer Keje Molenaar, a lawyer and ex-chairman of the members' council, suggested in January 2023 the potential return of Overmars, citing the importance of the technical director role in the club's success. He questioned the thoroughness of the investigation against Overmars, noting no formal charges or prosecution. Molenaar argued that Overmars was dismissed hastily and suggested consulting employees about continuing with him. He believed Overmars had learned from his mistakes and would not repeat them.[21] In March 2023, Ajax's hardcore fan group, the F-side, demanded Overmars' return, saying 'It has now lasted long enough! We want Marc Overmars back!' Football analyst Aad de Mos echoed this sentiment, acknowledging Overmars' errors but advocating for a second chance.[22]

19.3.4 The Internal Investigation

Following the inappropriate conduct by Overmars, the Supervisory Board appointed Bezemer & Schubad, a skilled and independent agency, to carry out a comprehensive investigation. Ajax's official website released a statement acknowledging the gravity of Overmars' actions. The investigation found that several women at Ajax had experienced 'unwanted behaviour, ranging from inappropriate jokes, derogatory or hurtful remarks, an unwanted arm around the shoulder, and other intrusive behaviour'.[23] Notably, none of the women had filed a formal complaint. The agency recommended the establishment of an independent oversight committee that would report directly to the Supervisory Board and provide guidance on enhancing a safer work and sports environment across all levels of the club. As per the annual report for the fiscal year 2021/2022, this advisory and oversight committee was set up in September 2022.

In September 2022, news came out that not only Ajax employees but also players from the Ajax women's team suffered from the inappropriate behaviour of Overmars. Ajax player Merel van Dongen (2015–2018) said she had no negative experiences with Overmars, but 'you heard things sometimes. He would sometimes make a remark that you thought: not so neat, not professional. He saw us not only as employees but also as flirting material'. Two other players talk about a situation where Overmars touched a player on the massage table in the physio room and dismissed it as a joke 'but it was not experienced that way'.[24]

19.3.5 The Disciplinary Investigation, Part 1

Ajax referred the case involving boundary-crossing behaviour on February 16, 2022, to the Institute for Sports Justice (ISR), as reporting such incidents has been compulsory for Dutch sports clubs since 2018. The ISR may impose sanctions ranging from a warning to expulsion from a sports federation. ISR Director stated that their investigation relied on voluntary statements, as they lack the authority to compel testimony under oath. Furthermore, the women involved appear hesitant to testify.[25] Contrary to reports by NOS, both Ajax and Overmars asserted they were cooperating with the investigation. In February 2023, Ajax inquired about the progress of the case and offered assistance for the investigation in September 2022 and January 2023. Overmars' spokesperson stated that they have responded to ISR's written questions in September 2022 and were committed to fully cooperating, although the details of these communications remain confidential.[26]

From the ruling of the disciplinary committee, more information about the complaint became public. Most of the messages from Overmars to the complainant were sexually explicit, both in text and photos, spanned over a period of more than 3.5 years and had a significant impact on her. Despite wishing to remain anonymous and continue her employment, the complainant's primary goal was to see an end to this behaviour. An external expert, upon reviewing extensive evidence including 75 zip files (300 pages) of WhatsApp conversations, confirmed the sexually explicit nature of the communications from the accused to the complainant.

When confronted, Overmars expressed remorse, admitting to the misconduct while claiming unawareness of the unwelcome nature of his actions, and expressed a desire to apologise personally. Despite his response, the disciplinary committee found him responsible for repeated violations of conduct over an extended period. Considering his leadership position and the resultant publicity and damage to his reputation, the committee decided on a sanction. They imposed a two-year ban from holding any position within the federation or its affiliated organisations, with one year suspended subject to a two-year probation, reflecting the gravity of the violations and the expectation of exemplary behaviour from someone in his role.

The KNVB announced the suspension of Overmars to FIFA, fulfilling an obligation under international guidelines. FIFA is set to conduct its own evaluation of the case.[27] According to FIFA's code, confederations and associations are required to immediately notify FIFA of any sanctions related to serious violations, which include, among others, sexual abuse, or harassment. Furthermore, in cases of severe infringements such as discrimination, match manipulation, misconduct against officials, forgery, and sexual misconduct, the relevant sports bodies must seek a global extension of the sanctions from FIFA's Disciplinary Committee, ensuring these sanctions have a worldwide impact.[28]

In January 2024, FIFA confirmed that Marc Overmars' national suspension would be enforced on a global scale. Consequently, he is temporarily unable to continue in his position as the technical director of Royal Antwerp FC in Belgium.[29] Overmars challenged the decision, with a spokesperson arguing that a worldwide work ban for a year was excessive for a single instance of inappropriate conduct, for which the ISR had already penalised him. However, the appeal was unsuccessful, and the global prohibition will remain in effect until November 2024.

19.4 Comparable Cases

19.4.1 Just Eat Takeaway: Temporary Suspension of Director

Just before the 2022 AGM, Just Eat Takeaway faced allegations against director Jörg Gerbig, concerning potential personal misconduct at a corporate event. Following these allegations, an investigation commenced, but the Board pre-emptively withdrew Gerbig's nomination for reappointment and informed stakeholders about the ongoing investigation. The decision to retract the nomination occurred swiftly, from when the allegations surfaced on May 1 to the AGM on May 4, while the investigation, still in its early stages, had yet to reach any conclusions.[30] Gerbig expressed confidence in a positive investigation outcome, and the press release clarified that the allegations did not relate to financial mismanagement or reporting failures. The suspension of his reappointment meant Gerbig ceased being a director post-AGM.

The minutes of the AGM showed that directors were only aware of the notification a few days in advance, that they were in a 'rollercoaster' during these days, but that they would not go into details further at this time.[31] The share fell by about 9 per cent that day.

On August 3, the company disclosed the completion of the investigation and re-nominated Gerbig for directorship, without detailing the investigation's nature or findings. Media wrote that a woman had filed a complaint about Gerbig after the annual ski trip for the staff. The annual ski trip was subsequently cancelled in 2023.[32] Also, reference was made to an internal message in which Gerbig apologised to employees, but without making clear for what exactly: 'As a member of the Board of Directors, I realise that I am held to the highest standards', he writes in response to the announcement of his return. 'I therefore apologise to all of you, as colleagues and friends, if I have given a different impression, which has led to a complaint. I can assure you that I will do better in the future and behave appropriately'.[33]

At the November EGM, a near-unanimous vote favoured his reappointment, without any detailed explanation of the allegations or the investigative findings provided.

19.4.2 Luis Rubiales Kissing Jenni Hermoso at Football Worldcup

On Sunday August 20, 2023, the Spanish Womens' Football team beated England in the World Cup final in Sydney. At the official post-match ceremony, the president of the Spanish football federation, Luis Rubiales, kissed the forward, Jenni Hermoso, on the lips.[34] In the next few days Rubiales is accused of more masculine inappropriate behaviour. A new video occurred where Rubiales made an obscene gesture by grabbing his scotch to express his joy about the game, where he was standing in the same area as where the Spanish queen and her 16-year-old daughter are watching the game. Another video shows he is tossing around one of the players over his shoulders, on the field.

In statements later released to the media by the Spanish football federation, Hermoso was quoted as saying, 'it was a totally spontaneous mutual gesture because of the immense joy that winning a World Cup brings. The president and I have a great relationship, his behaviour with all of us has been outstanding and it was a natural gesture of affection and gratitude'.[35]

The Spanish minister of equality, Irene Montero, described it as 'a form of sexual violence'.

On October 30, 2023, FIFA announced that the FIFA Disciplinary Committee banned Luis Rubiales from all football-related activities at national and international levels for three years, having found that he acted in breach of Article 13 of the FIFA Disciplinary Code. Article 13 addresses 'offensive behaviour and violations of the principles of fair play', specifying that individuals who breach norms of decent conduct or insult anyone, whether a natural or legal entity, particularly through offensive gestures, signs, or language, are liable to face disciplinary actions.[36] FIFA added their absolute commitment to respecting and protecting the integrity of all people and ensuring that the basic rules of decent conduct are upheld.[37]

On the same day Rubiales announced in a statement on X (@LuisRubiales17), that he would appeal the decision: 'I will go to the last instance to ensure justice is served and the truth shines through'.

In January 2024, he lost the appeal.[38] Rubiales is potentially heading to trial for a sexual assault charge, which could result in a prison sentence ranging from one to four years. Additionally, Rubiales, along with three soccer federation executives, including the former coach Jorge Vilda, could be charged with coercion. This follows allegations that they pressured Hermoso into publicly supporting Rubiales.[39]

Notes

1. The World's Most Valuable Soccer Teams: Barcelona Edges Real Madrid To Land At No. 1 For First Time, Mike Ozanian, April 12, 2021, Forbes.
2. Agenda and Explanation of the agenda extraordinary general meeting AFC Ajax NV published December 17, 2021.
3. Report of the Extraordinary General Meeting of Shareholders of AFC Ajax NV, January 28, 2022.

4. Questions posed in writing by shareholders in advance with answers, EGM AFC Ajax NV, January 28, 2022.
5. Marc Overmars leaves Ajax effective immediately, February 6, 2022, www.ajax.nl/artikelen/marc-overmars-vertrekt-per-direct-bij-ajax/
6. Letter of Ajax to the VEB, February 25, 2022, www.veb.net/media/616787/20220225-brief-ajax.pdf
7. In this talent show on TV, there were multiple instances of inappropriate behavior by the program's coaches towards the participating talents. See also: Wat is er aan de hand bij The Voice of Holland? (What's going on at The Voice of Holland?), NOS, January 15, 2022.
8. De appjes van Marc Overmars werden almaar dwingender (Marc Overmars' messages became increasingly insistent), Danielle Pinedo, Fabian van der Poll & Steven Verseput, NRC, February 7, 2022.
9. Wat gebeurde er bij Ajax in de week van de zaak-Overmars? (What happened at Ajax in the week of the Overmars case?), Danielle Pinedo, Fabian van der Poll & Steven Verseput, NRC, February 12, 2022.
10. Interviews with Joep Schreuder, aired on NOS Sport, February 13, 2022, and with Hans Kraay jr., on ESPN, February 13, 2022.
11. Ajax wist voor herbenoeming Overmars al van gedrag directeur (Ajax knew about director's behaviour before Overmars' reappointment), Dick Sintenie & Bas Soetenhorst, Het Parool, February 13, 2022.
12. Letter of Ajax to the VEB, February 25, 2022, www.veb.net/media/616787/20220225-brief-ajax.pdf
13. Report of the General Meeting of Shareholders of AFC Ajax NV, November 11, 2022.
14. VEB vraagt Ajax om opheldering in 'dickpic-gate', (VEB asks Ajax for clarification in 'dickpic-gate'), VEB, February 14, 2022, and Report of the General Meeting of Shareholders of AFC Ajax NV, November 11, 2022.
15. Sponsoren van Ajax willen meer uitleg van club: 'Grondig onderzoek nodig', NOS, February 9, 2022.
16. Het maakt Antwerp-eigenaar niet uit wat aan Overmars kleeft: 'Geen moreel kompas' (Antwerp owner doesn't care what sticks to Overmars: 'No moral compass'), NOS, March 21, 2022.
17. Royal Antwerp FC raakt sponsoren kwijt vanwege Overmars: 'Niet onze waarden en normen' ('Royal Antwerp FC loses sponsors due to Overmars: 'Not our values and standards'), NOS, 24 maart 2022.
18. Report of the General Meeting of Shareholders of AFC Ajax NV, November 11, 2022.

19. Je mag ook helemaal niets meer (You can't do anything anymore), December 22, 2022, Available for replay on NPO Start.
20. Van Basten criticises Ajax's purchase policy after Napoli debacle: ' Geld moet op het veld staan, niet op de bank' ('Money should be on the field, not in the bank'), Algemeen Dagblad, October 5, 2022.
21. Interview on ESPN, January 27, 2023.
22. Interview with Aad de Mos, April 4, 2023, Het Laatste Nieuws.
23. Ajax gaat werk maken van interne cultuurverandering (Ajax is going to work on internal culture change), Ajax statement on website, May 3, 2022.
24. Oud-speelsters: ook Ajax-vrouwen slachtoffer van Marc Overmars. 'Hij zag ons als flirtmateriaal' (Former players: Ajax women also victim of Marc Overmars. 'He saw us as flirt material'), Bas Soetenhorst & Anna Herter, Het Parool, September 15, 2022.
25. Onderzoek naar Overmars komt niet van de grond: 'Ajax werkt niet mee' (Investigation into Overmars does not get off the ground: 'Ajax does not cooperate'), NOS, May 13, 2022.
26. Tuchtkwestie Overmars niet van tafel: voetbaldirecteur werkt mee aan onderzoek ISR (Disciplinary issue Overmars not off the table: football director cooperates with ISR investigation), NOS, February 3, 2023.
27. KNVB meldt schorsing oud-Ajax-directeur Overmars bij FIFA, December 1, 2023.
28. FIFA Disciplinary Code 2023 edition, FIFA Website.
29. FIFA: schorsing Marc Overmars wordt wereldwijd doorgevoerd ('FIFA: Marc Overmars' suspension to be implemented worldwide'), Danielle Pinedo en Steven Verseput, January 9, 2024.
30. Reappointment COO withdrawn from AGM agenda, press release Just Eat Takeaway, May 4, 2022.
31. Minutes AGM Just Eat Takeaway, May 4, 2022.
32. Aandeelhouders Just Eat Takeaway steunen herbenoeming directeur Gerbig, die geschorst was vanwege grensoverschrijdend gedrag (Just Eat Takeaway shareholders support reappointment of director Gerbig, who was suspended for crossing boundaries), Robbèrt Misset, de Volkskrant, November 18, 2022.
33. De groeipijnen van 'puber' Just Eat Takeaway (The growing pains of 'teenager' Just Eat Takeaway), Jan Braaksma & Julia Cornelissen, het FD, November 16, 2022.
34. A Kiss After Spain's World Cup Win Prompts Many to Cry Foul, Constant Méheut, August 20, 2023, The New York Times.

35. Spanish football president's kiss sparks outrage after Women's World Cup final, Jack Snape and Ashifa Kassam, August 21, 2023, The Guardian.
36. FIFA Disciplinary Code 2023 edition, FIFA Website.
37. Former Spanish Football Association president Luis Rubiales is banned from all football-related activities for three years, October 30, 2023, FIFA website.
38. Luis Rubiales: Fifa uphold three-year ban against ex-Spanish football federation chief, January 26, 2024, BBC Sport.
39. Spanish Soccer Star Testifies About Unwanted Kiss, Rachel Chaundler, January 2, 2024, The New York Times.

20

The Case of ING and the Uproar over Executive Compensation

20.1 The Case[1]

20.1.1 ING

ING Group is a global financial institution of Dutch origin that offers banking, investments, life insurance, and retirement services. It provides a broad array of financial products and services to customers spanning individuals, small and medium-sized enterprises, large corporations, institutions, and governments. The group operates in over 40 countries across Europe, North America, Latin America, Asia, and Australia, focusing on retail and commercial banking as its core business. ING Group is listed on the Euronext Amsterdam as well as in Brussels and on the New York Stock Exchange. ING is well-known for its innovative approach to banking, especially its early adoption of digital and online banking services. This has allowed it to develop a strong presence in established and emerging markets.

Ralph Hamers has worked at ING since 1991 and joined the Board of Directors in May 2013. He became CEO in October of that year.

20.1.2 Remuneration Policy

The remuneration policy of ING, adopted by its General Meeting of Shareholders (AGM) in 2010, was designed to align with existing laws, regulations, and the Dutch Banking Code, setting the CEO's compensation slightly below the median for similar roles within the Euro Stoxx 50 index. Despite its establishment, the policy remained unimplemented for several years due to various factors. Notably, the global financial crisis led to ING receiving state aid in 2009, which was fully repaid by 2014. The initial steps towards enacting this remuneration strategy were taken in 2015.

In 2017, the Supervisory Board engaged an external consultancy to assess the total compensation of CEOs across different 'peer groups', including the Euro Stoxx 50, a selection of 20 banks, and 24 companies listed on the Amsterdam Exchange Index (AEX). This analysis revealed that the CEO's compensation at the time, €1.9 million, fell significantly below the group median, which stood at €3.2 million for the Euro Stoxx 50.

Between the end of 2017 and the start of 2018, the ING remuneration committee convened on four occasions to deliberate on CEO Hamers' compensation. During this period, the remaining non-executive directors were kept abreast of the findings and discussions.

By December 2017, the committee considered four potential adjustments to the CEO's salary: increases of 0%, 3%, 10%, and 40%. The HR department warned that a 10% hike could incite 'public and political unrest', while a 40% raise might trigger discontent not only publicly and politically but also within the bank's own management and workforce.[2] The committee's records from these meetings indicate a belief that CEO Hamers would stay with the bank regardless of whether his pay was increased, emphasising, however, the importance of offering a competitive compensation package.

On March 5, 2018, the Supervisory Board resolved to elevate the CEO's total remuneration to approximately €3.0 million, marking a near 50% increment from the previous year. This adjustment positioned Hamers' compensation below the peer group median of the Euro Stoxx 50, at about 93% of the median value. Further analysis by the Financial Times Dutch edition (FD) later verified that such a salary would place Hamers comfortably in the median range among the CEOs of the 25 AEX-listed companies.

On March 8, 2018, the Supervisory Board of ING made a public announcement regarding a significant adjustment to the CEO's remuneration, proposing an increase of 50 per cent from €1.9 million to €3.0 million, pending approval at the forthcoming Annual General Meeting (AGM) scheduled for April 23, 2018. Jeroen van der Veer, the non-executive chairman and former CEO of Shell, acknowledged in a statement to the Dutch Financial Times his anticipation of potential controversy following this announcement. Despite expecting a mixed response, he expressed hope for understanding from various stakeholders, including the employees under the collective labour agreement, who received a 1.7 per cent salary increase, emphasising the bank's need to maintain its competitive edge in the industry. Van der Veer remarked, 'We have delayed this action repeatedly but have now chosen to make a significant adjustment. Ralph Hamers is of premier league calibre but was receiving Jupiler League-level pay', adding, 'I completely get the emotional response. However, to emerge as champions of Europe, such steps are necessary'. He extended his hope that this perspective would resonate with the bank's employees, encouraging their understanding and support.[3]

Furthermore, in the 2017 annual report (page 96), the Supervisory Board reiterated its commitment to adhering to the remuneration policy ratified by the General Meeting of Shareholders in 2010, aiming to fulfil the policy's requirements 'both in letter and spirit': 'This statement underscores the board's dedication to ensuring that the compensation framework aligns with the agreed principles and standards, reflecting a balance between competitive compensation and adherence to corporate governance and policy expectations'.

20.1.3 Societal Outrage

On the very day the pay rise was announced, a wave of indignant responses surfaced. Critics drew parallels between the modest pay hike of just 1.7% for other bank employees and the starkly contrasting proposal for the CEO's salary. This was especially poignant given the bank's 2009 bailout, where it received €10 billion in capital support from the Dutch government; a sum that was fully repaid by 2014. The proposed remuneration meant the CEO would receive a salary thirty times that of the average bank employee and sixty times more than the lowest-paid worker. At this juncture, the largest trade union federation in the Netherlands (FNV) highlighted a remuneration guideline suggesting that top executives should not earn more than twenty times the salary of the company's lowest-paid employee. FNV criticised the decision, remarking, 'ING has now escalated that multiplier to sixty. Hamers is being paid threefold what he ought to'. Similarly, another major trade union (CNV) denounced the proposed salary increase as 'outrageous' and a throwback to 'old-school greed'.[4]

> In what universe does the top of ING live?
> —@JesseKlaver on Twitter

The proposed salary—increase for the CEO of ING elicited intense backlash, not just from the general public but also from political leaders. Jesse Klaver, the chairman of the Green Party in the House of Commons, criticised the decision on Twitter: 'In what universe does the top of ING live', highlighting the disparity between the CEO's substantial pay rise to over 3 million euros annually and the modest 1.7% salary increase for the bank's staff. Finance Minister Wopke Hoekstra denounced the pay hike as 'excessive' and detrimental to rebuilding trust in the financial sector.[5] During a finance committee session in the House of Representatives, Bart Snels from Groen-Links condemned the move as 'undesirable and socially insensitive', urging actions to halt it.[6]

In response to the widespread anger from customers, employees, and other stakeholders, ING's Supervisory Board convened on March 12 to revoke the planned salary increase, aiming to avoid further harm to the bank's reputation and employees. The decision to retract the raise was made public on March 13. The Chairman of the Supervisory Board, Van der Veer, admitted to underestimating the negative public sentiment in the Netherlands: 'We realise that we underestimated the public reaction in the Netherlands to this clearly sensitive issue', says Chairman of the Supervisory Board Van der Veer. 'We, as non-executives, are responsible for this proposal and regret the commotion it has caused'.[7]

20.1.4 Stubborn?

The issue of executive remuneration at ING has sparked controversy on multiple occasions before the 2018 backlash. In 2004, the bank's decision to hike top executive pay by 50% drew personal criticism towards Wim Kok, a former (left-wing) prime minister but now a non-executive director at ING. Previously, as a politician, he regularly condemned 'exhibitionist self-enrichment'. At the Annual General Meeting (AGM), Kok described his predicament as 'a devil's dilemma', torn between societal demands for wage restraint and the necessity for a company's pay structure to remain competitive. He acknowledged the challenging balance between these two perspectives.

> It's a devil's dilemma.
> —Wim Kok in 2004

The debate over executive bonuses resurfaced in 2011 when ING intended to award CEO Jan Hommen and other directors variable remuneration totalling 1.25 million euros. The plan was eventually scrapped amid widespread criticism, even though Hommen had pre-emptively declined the bonus, anticipating public disapproval. Nonetheless, the Supervisory Board had initially supported the bonuses as 'legitimate and earned'.[8] Reflecting on the controversy, Hommen expressed his regret that the proposed bonuses could undermine the restored trust between ING, its customers, and society.[9]

A similar outcry occurred in 2015, following the repayment of state aid, when CEO Hamers' salary was increased by 30%, which was 20% below what had been previously indicated in the remuneration policy and upon his appointment. Addressing the sensitive topic of pay increases in the Netherlands, Hamers remarked on the emotional nature of the discussion but emphasised ING's need for international competitiveness to attract global talent. He highlighted his acceptance of a 20% pay cut as a demonstration of 'courage' (NOS, May 2015), underscoring the complex dynamics between public sentiment and the bank's global operational requirements.[10]

20.1.5 Money Laundering Affair

What the outside world did not know at the beginning of 2018, but the directors of course did, was that ING had been the subject of a criminal investigation led by the public prosecutor since February 18, 2016. Money laundering is a criminal offence according to the law. Banks, insurers, and other financial institutions are legally obliged to prevent money laundering. They must comply with the rules set out in the Anti-Money Laundering and Anti-Terrorist Financing Act. If a bank has made it possible to launder illicit money, because the bank does not have its procedures in order the Dutch Central Bank can take measures or may submit a case to public prosecutor, which may launch a criminal investigation.

On February 27, 2017, a conversation had taken place between the chief prosecutor and the Board of Directors, after which, in May 2017, it was reported that a summons would follow if there was no progress in the bank's measures to prevent money laundering.[11] At the time of the remuneration proposal, directors had no estimate of the seriousness and extent of the money laundering affair and the very high settlement proposal that was later made by the public prosecutor. It was also unknown when the DA would come up with the results of the investigation. On September 3, 2018, half a year after the remuneration proposal, the bank and the OM reached a settlement agreement of 775 million euros.

20.1.6 Banker's Oath: Oath or Promise Regulation Financial Sector 2015

In response to the financial sector's challenges, particularly after the 2008 financial crisis marked by widespread scandals and abuses, the Banker's Oath was introduced in the Netherlands in 2013.[12] This initiative aimed to rebuild trust in the banking industry by instilling a stronger sense of moral duty among its professionals. The crisis had eroded public confidence significantly, leading an advisory committee to suggest in their report, 'Towards Restoration of Trust', that bank directors, both executive and non-executive, should commit to a moral-ethical pledge. The purpose of the Banker's Oath was to heighten their awareness of their obligations to both customers and society at large. By 2015, this oath was extended to include all banking staff, requiring them to vow to conduct their duties with integrity and care, adhering to relevant laws and regulations. The overarching goal of the oath is to foster a culture of ethical conduct and integrity across the banking sector.

> **Banker's Oath: Oath or Promise Regulation Financial Sector 2015[13]**
>
> I swear / promise that, within the boundaries of my function in the banking sector, I will:
>
> - Execute my function ethically and with care.
> - Draw a careful balance between the interests of all parties associated with the business, being the customers, shareholders, employees, and the society in which the business operates.
> - When drawing that balance, making the customer's interests central.
> - Will comply with the laws, regulations and codes that apply to me.
> - Will keep confidential that which has been entrusted to me.
> - Will not abuse my knowledge.
> - Will act openly and accountably, knowing my responsibility to society.
> - Will make every effort to improve and retain trust in the financial sector.
>
> So help me God! / This I pledge and promise!

Since 2015, over 90,000 individuals in the financial sector, encompassing executive and non-executive directors, have pledged adherence to the banker's oath. This commitment introduces bank employees to a unique framework of disciplinary law, overseen by the Foundation for Banking Ethics Enforcement. This Foundation lodges complaints with the independent Enforcement Committee, essentially serving as a judicial body composed of legal professionals and specialists. The committee evaluates each case against the established code of conduct to determine if the banker's oath has been breached and decides on the appropriate penalty. Sanctions can vary, including warnings, fines, compulsory educational courses, and even professional suspensions lasting up to three years.

20.2 Considerations

Was the substantial salary increase for the CEO morally appropriate?

See Table 20.1 for the Moral Consideration Matrix for INGs' Board of Directors. The non-executive directors felt ethically compelled to increase the CEO's compensation, acknowledging their responsibility towards the CEO and their goal to keep the company competitively attractive as an employer in the finance sector. Although the compensation plan was established earlier and commitments were made, its implementation was pending. Reflecting on a similar discussion about pay at ABN AMRO in 2015, non-executive director Peter Wakkie argued that the idea of not proceeding with a planned salary increase was unthinkable: 'I find it unacceptable to say: we hired you at this salary, but we are now going to cut it by a third. Because that's what you're essentially doing'.[14]

Moreover, Hamers' remuneration was also not in line with his peers and the 'premier league in which he played' and the exceptional performances

Table 20.1 The moral consideration matrix for INGs' Board of Directors

	Utilitarian, consequences	Deontological, moral norms
For +	- Retaining CEO is crucial due to strategic vision and leadership capabilities - A competitive compensation package is essential for attracting (international) talent - Risk of a dissatisfied CEO stemming from unfulfilled compensation promises	- Honouring commitments and promises in compensation plan - Ensuring remuneration policy is in full compliance with legal and regulatory standards (citizenship) - CEO's salary is lower than peers raise concerns about fairness and justice
Against −	- Negative publicity causing harm and reputational damage to company, its individuals, and the broader banking sector - The CEO's salary is 30 times the average employee's salary raises concerns fairness and equity - Trust in the financial sector has not yet been restored	- A salary increase amidst an ongoing investigation, with risks of legal actions and fines, reflects poorly on organisation's societal duties and ethical stance

he had delivered. Despite the low risk of him leaving due to dissatisfaction, anticipating his loyalty to remain steadfast even without a salary increase, his role in ING's strategy was pivotal for the bank's ambition to 'become the champion of Europe', as stated by the Chairman on March 8, 2018. This ambition was later validated by international analysts in 2020 'ING is now considered one of the best examples of digital innovation in the banking sector' (FT, February 2020). The Financial Times called Hamers 'a digital champion running Dutch lender ING' and Reuters spoke of 'a tech-savvy CEO'.

Conversely, public backlash concentrated on the rationale and concerns of other stakeholders, including the modest 1.7 per cent salary increase for employees, the significant pay disparity within the company, and the ongoing delicate trust in the financial sector. While non-executive members acknowledged these concerns, stating 'we understand the emotions', their considerations may not have been fully adequate. Van der Veer commented, 'It's a very Dutch debate. We paid off the state aid years ago with a lot of interest. Should we then continue to reward below the norm because it would otherwise cause uproar?'.[15]

At heart, the issue revolves around whether the Supervisory Board performed its due diligence and successfully weighed various perspectives. The situation's complexity is further highlighted by differing decisions from the Foundation for Banking Ethics Enforcement and its Appeals Committee, leaving the question of the Board's balance of considerations open-ended.

20.3 Epilogue

20.3.1 Non-Executives Responding in Public

In October 2018, Henk Breukink, one of the non-executive directors and chairman of the remuneration committee, engaged in the public discourse through an opinion piece in the Dutch Financial Times (FD), addressing the way the corporate sector is perceived and treated by politicians. He conceded that 'ING has shown negligence, at times maybe significant', in relation to the money laundering scandal, yet he highlighted the inherent challenges in detecting illicit funds through bank accounts. Breukink expressed frustration over the severe backlash from a coalition of media, Dutch Parliament, and the government. He critiqued the harsh treatment faced by individuals in organisations embroiled in controversies, especially when political forces intervene aggressively, leaving those implicated without a viable means of defence, for fear of further spotlighting the issue.[16]

Despite Breukink's candidness and the display of accountability and bravery in presenting a counter-narrative, his stance attracted criticism, epitomised by reactions like 'ING, stop pointing fingers and take a good look in the mirror'[17] and garnered scant public backing, thereby underscoring his concluding remarks. However, the FD's editorial commentary lauded Breukink for his frankness, stating, 'The critique of Breukink is valid. He may be fanning the flames, but his transparency is commendable as he alone voices what many observe in silence behind the scenes'.[18] Six months later, in April 2019, Breukink concluded his 12-year tenure on the board, stepping down not due to the controversy but as he reached the end of his appointed term.

Another director, Peter Wakkie, who was serving as a non-executive director at ABN AMRO, experienced a rather abrupt departure from the board. In a 2015 interview with NRC, he openly criticised Finance Minister Jeroen Dijsselbloem, who publicly distanced himself from a salary increase, for not upholding the remuneration policy that was put in place by his predecessor. Wakkie expressed his disappointment, stating that he expected the minister to react differently, for example, by saying that 'the decision was made under my predecessor. What I think of it is not relevant'. On the very day the interview was published, Wakkie's six-year tenure at ABN AMRO came to an end. ABN AMRO later clarified in NRC that 'the interview reflected Wakkie's personal decision', as noted by a spokesperson for the bank.[19]

20.3.2 Verdict Banking Ethics Enforcement (August 2022)

The Banker's oath opened the door for complaints to be addressed by the independent Enforcement Committee, a body of legal and expert members that acts in a judicial capacity. In 2018, a complaint was filed against Hamers and two non-executive directors with this Committee.

On August 3, 2022, the Committee delivered its judgment regarding the controversy over the compensation decision. Although expressing regret over the public discontent sparked by the compensation proposal, it found the complaint to be without basis, acknowledging that the non-executives had considered all pertinent interests. The Committee noted that the possibility of public opposition to the compensation plan was undervalued and overlooked by the non-executives. Additionally, while the potential repercussions of a criminal investigation were factored into the decision on remuneration increase and its public perception, the then-available details of the money laundering penalty were deemed insufficient to deter the proposal. Nonetheless, the Committee concluded that these misjudgments did not equate to a breach of integrity or recklessness. The verdict was contested by the prosecutor of the Foundation for Banking Ethics Enforcement, leading to an appeal.

20.3.3 Appeal Banking Ethics Enforcement (April 2023)

On April 13, 2023, the Appeal Committee reviewed and overturned the initial verdict, citing a failure to adequately care for and consider various interests, which harmed public trust in the bank. This failure was attributed to the CEO and non-executives, which substantiated the complaint regarding violations of conduct rules 1, 2, and 7 (but not rule 4) and issued a reprimand to the CEO, the non-executive chair, and the chair of the remuneration committee. The conduct rules to which the Committee referred: the bank employee works with integrity and care (1), makes a careful consideration of interests (2), complies with the law and other rules that apply to work at the bank (4) and contributes to the trust of society in the bank (7).

The Appeal Committee pointed out four main issues in its decision: the abrupt escalation to the maximum level allowed by the remuneration policy, disregard for internal cautions about the likely public uproar, the potential for the ongoing criminal investigation (alongside the significant salary hike) to severely tarnish the bank's reputation, and the omission of an assessment of public backing for the remuneration plan.

20.3.4 The CEO

In February 2020, Ralph Hamers transitioned to Swiss bank UBS, where he earned 12.7 million euros in 2022, approximately six times his salary at ING, positioning him among Europe's highest-paid bankers. Under his leadership, UBS's share value soared by 76 per cent.[20] He was succeeded at ING by Steven van Rijswijk, whose initial salary was set at 2.1 million euros, with his total compensation in 2022 reported as 2 million euros, according to the Annual Report.

Following UBS's acquisition of Credit Suisse on March 19, 2023, Hamers took the helm of what became the third-largest bank in Europe, placing him at 'the top of the Champions League'.[21] However, a week later, he resigned for the benefit of the stakeholders, citing unforeseen changes, and prioritising the welfare of the newly merged entity and its stakeholders, including Switzerland's financial landscape.[22] Sergio P. Ermotti, Hamers' predecessor at UBS, succeeded him.

Well after his move to UBS, in December 2020, the Hague Court decided that Hamers, as the actual leader, had to be criminally prosecuted in the money laundering case. The Court considered it important that the standard that even bank directors do not go unpunished if they have led prohibited actions, is confirmed in a public criminal process.[23] As of 2024, the case is ongoing. Meanwhile, other directors of financial institutions have also been identified as suspects in the money laundering case, including former directors of ABN AMRO Gerrit Zalm, Chris Vogelenzang and Joop Wijn.

Notes

1. The description of this case is largely based on information from the ruling of the Banking Sector Disciplinary Regulations, Report 3935, August 3, 2022.
2. Ruling of the Appeals Committee as referred to in the Disciplinary Regulations Banking Sector, April 13, 2023.
3. ING verhoogt beloning topman Hamers met 50% ('ING increases CEO Hamers' salary by 50%'), Ivo Bökkerink, Het Financieele Dagblad, March 8, 2018.
4. Vakbonden boos over 'absurde' salarisverhoging ING-topman ('Unions angry about 'absurd' salary increase for ING CEO'), Het Financieele Dagblad, March 8, 2018.
5. 'Buitensporig', noemt minister Hoekstra de salarisverhoging van de ING-topman ('Minister Hoekstra calls ING CEO's salary increase 'excessive'), NOS, March 8, 2018.
6. Report of the standing committee for Finance and the standing committee for European Affairs, March 8, 2018, 21 501–07, Council for Economic and Financial Affairs, No. 1503.
7. ING trekt omstreden salarisverhoging topman Hamers in: 'We hebben de publieke reactie onderschat' ('ING withdraws controversial salary increase for CEO Hamers: 'We underestimated the public reaction'), Wilco Dekker, de Volkskrant, March 12, 2018.
8. ING-top ziet af van bonus en salarisverhoging ('ING executives forego bonus and salary increase'), Het Parool, March 22, 2011.

9. Commissarissen ING drukten bonus van Hommen door ('ING non-executives pushed through Hommen's bonus'), Hans van der Lugt, NRC, April 1, 2011.
10. Interview NOS.nl: nos.nl/artikel/2034424-ing-topman-loonsverhoging-getuigt-van-moed.
11. Ruling of the Professional Conduct Regulation Banking Sector, Report 3935, August 3, 2022.
12. Regulation oath or promise financial sector 2015.
13. About the Banker's Oath, www.tuchtrechtbanken.nl/en/about-the-bankers-oath/
14. Uitleggen dat het deugt, lukte niet ('Explaining that it's right didn't work'), Chris Hensen & Teri van der Heijden, NRC, March 31, 2015.
15. ING verhoogt beloning topman Hamers met 50%, Ivo Bökkerink, Het Financieele Dagblad, March 8, 2018.
16. Het is de Tweede Kamer die het wantrouwen in de samenleving voedt ('The Lower House is feeding distrust in society'), Henk Breukink, het FD, October 2, 2018.
17. ING, stop met vingerwijzen en kijk eens goed in de spiegel ('ING, stop pointing fingers and take a good look in the mirror'), Roald van der Linde, 3 oktober 2018, and Wantrouwen ('Distrust'), Frédérique Six, Het Financieele Dagblad, October 12, 2018.
18. Vertrouwen bouwen ('Building trust',), From the editor, Het Financieele Dagblad, October 7, 2018.
19. Uitleggen dat het deugt, lukte niet ('Explaining that it's right didn't work'), Chris Hensen & Teri van der Heijden, NRC, March 31, 2015, and, Was interview wel of geen soloactie van commissaris Wakkie? ('Was the interview a solo action by non-executive Wakkie?'), Chris Hensen & Teri van der Heijden, NRC, April 1, 2015.
20. UBS-topman Hamers verdiende 12,7 miljoen, andere bestuurders juist gekort ('UBS CEO Hamers earned 12.7 million, other executives cut'), NRC, March 7, 2023.
21. Van de eerste divisie in Nederland naar de Europese bankierstop ('From the first division in the Netherlands to the top of European banking'), de Volkskrant, March 22, 2023.
22. The Board of Directors of UBS Group AG (UBS) announces today that it has named Sergio P. Ermotti as its new Group Chief Executive Officer, effective 5 April 2023, persbericht UBS, March 29, 2023.
23. Ruling The Hague District Court, ECLI:NL: GHDHA:2020:2347, case K18/220377, December 9, 2020.

21

Conclusion

> Science is organized knowledge.
> Wisdom is organized life
> —Immanual Kant (1724–1804)

21.1 Moral Identity and Moral Judgment

In this book, we explored the challenges that directors face when confronted with a moral dilemma and provide a structured framework to help them navigate these dilemmas. By unpacking the theoretical and practical aspects of moral decision-making in corporate governance, the book empowers directors to understand the nuances of moral identity and moral judgment, and how the complex interplay of stakeholder interests shapes moral decision-making.

Throughout the book, the exploration of moral identity and moral judgment emerges as foundational to ethical decision-making. We learn that moral identity isn't simply a theoretical concept but a living framework that influences all choices directors make. The public and private facets of moral identity shape how directors may perceive and balance the ethical priorities of their personal beliefs and organisational values. This duality becomes crucial when navigating difficult boardroom decisions where contradictory interests and conflicting moral norms are at play.

The book highlights that moral judgment is not a linear process, nor black or white, or right or wrong, but rather a complex evaluation involving different ethical, i.e. deontological and utilitarian, perspectives. Whereas the deontological perspective prioritises moral principles, the utilitarian perspective focuses on maximising positive outcomes for all stakeholders. Balancing these two views enables a more comprehensive approach to moral dilemmas, as neither can fully address every scenario on its own. By understanding these two ethical approaches, directors can identify and recognise where their tendencies lie and how this affects their decision-making regarding moral dilemmas.

21.1.1 Right-Right Dilemmas and Stakeholderism

Directors frequently encounter dilemmas where no clear-cut solution is available due to conflicting values. This book emphasises that these right-right dilemmas need a deep understanding of the organisation's values and its stakeholders, and sometimes require moral courage to make a decisive decision. Directors must then weigh the potential benefits and harms. Decisions made in these scenarios can have far-reaching implications that may not be immediately visible, be misunderstood and be criticised by stakeholders who have a different opinion on what would be the right thing to do.

Stakeholderism complicates matters further, as directors must consider a range of interests, including employees, shareholders, customers, and society at large. This multifaceted approach means that decisions made in the boardroom can have ripple effects across various groups. Understanding and prioritising these different perspectives while maintaining organisational integrity requires a well-structured decision-making process.

21.1.2 Moral Consideration Matrix

The book introduced the Moral Consideration Matrix. This Matrix guides directors in evaluating moral dilemmas and becomes part of an ethical decision-making model. In this book we used the comprehensive five-step framework of the Australian Institute of Directors, but the matrix can be included in any ethical decision-making model. The five-step framework of the AICD begins by framing the ethical issue, then shaping potential options, evaluating them (in our book through the Moral Consideration Matrix), refining the choice, and finally acting and communicating on the decision. The Moral Consideration Matrix serves here as a crucial tool to weigh conflicting principles and ensure that each option is thoroughly vetted against universal moral principles and corporate values, and stakeholder interests.

21.2 Lessons Learned by Moresprudence

In Part II, the practical application of the Moral Consideration Matrix I, the case studies illuminate how directors have navigated challenging moral dilemmas across various industries. Applying this matrix to the ten real-life case studies reveals how it provides practical insights into real-world scenarios, helping directors clarify their values and priorities. Also, by following this structured process, directors can identify potential biases and ensure that the decisions they make align with their moral principles, the consequences of their decisions for multiple stakeholders, and the long-term health of the organisation.

The exploration of moresprudence highlights an important facet of corporate governance: different directors can, and often do, make different decisions in identical situations. This variability is invaluable, as it vividly demonstrates that moral dilemmas in the boardroom are seldom black and white. These differences underscore the subjective nature of moral judgment and the impact of individual directors' values, experiences, and perceptions on their decision-making processes, and on the context in which the dilemma appears.

The case studies presented in the book provide rich insights into this diversity of decision-making. This diversity is especially significant because it reveals that there is no one-size-fits-all solution to moral dilemmas in the corporate world, and the often-used metaphor of a moral compass might be inappropriate. The Moral Consideration Matrix used for each of the cases reflects a complex interplay of moral judgment, corporate culture, and the specific circumstances at hand. The metaphor of a moral scale could be more appropriate.

Moreover, the fact that directors take different paths in similar situations provides a valuable learning opportunity. It shows that ethical decision-making is a dynamic process, influenced by changing variables and evolving stakeholder expectations. This realisation can help directors feel more confident in their ability to navigate the grey areas of governance, knowing that ethical complexity is a common and natural aspect of boardroom dynamics. Learning from the varied responses to similar situations allows current and future directors to appreciate the depth and breadth of moral decision-making. It opens up a dialogue about the rationale behind each choice.

21.3 Practical Application for Directors

This book aimed to offer a comprehensive guide for directors, providing both the theoretical understanding and practical tools necessary to make sound ethical decisions. The book emphasises that directors must:

1. Develop a strong moral identity that aligns with their organisation's values. Understand that moral values are subjective and biases in the boardroom are a danger towards resolving moral dilemmas.
2. Cultivate a balanced approach to moral judgment, considering both the impact to different stakeholders (utilitarian ethics) and the universal moral principles that are at stake (deontological ethics).
3. Recognise and navigate through moral dilemmas, especially right-right dilemmas, with courage and a focus on the greater good.
4. Use the Moral Consideration Matrix as a structured framework for moral decision-making and stick to it when acting and communicating. Sometimes, the decision-making process is more important than the decision itself because criticism will remain but explaining that the decision was the outcome of a careful decision-making process is essential for the organisation's reputation.
5. Learn from real-world case studies to anticipate challenges and refine moral strategies. Although the next moral dilemma in the boardroom will most likely be completely different, going through the same procedure and exercising with moral dilemmas, again and again, will lead to a significantly better way of dealing with them.

By doing so, directors can fulfil their duties while maintaining the trust of stakeholders and upholding the principles of corporate governance. Ultimately, the book challenges directors to elevate their ethical reasoning, ensuring that they lead with integrity in an increasingly complex business environment.

21.4 Practical Application for Outsiders

This book also provides invaluable insights for outsiders such as the broader society, journalists, and politicians. These outsiders often judge directors harshly, claiming they lack a moral compass. However, by immersing themselves in the case studies provided, outsiders can better understand the complexities directors face, fostering a more empathetic perspective when evaluating decisions made in the boardroom.

Please note that despite this nuanced understanding, it's essential to recognise that society, politicians, and journalists should continue to play their crucial roles in holding powerful individuals and companies accountable for the decisions they make and the subsequent consequences. This accountability remains fundamental in democracies to address and impact unethical and unsustainable behaviours by directors and companies that, for example, focus solely on financial results. Nevertheless, it's vital to balance criticism with nuance to fully understand, describe, and respond to the dilemmas at hand.

1. Engage with case studies to gain insights into the decision-making processes and challenges directors face, which can lead to more balanced and informed critiques.
2. Understand the complexity of moral dilemmas in corporate environments, recognising that ethical decisions are not always black and white and often involve conflicting values.
3. Appreciate the subjective nature of moral judgment, which varies significantly among directors and outsiders based on their personal values and experiences. Outsiders might be biased, too.
4. Reflect on the importance of a structured decision-making process, acknowledging that the process itself can be as critical as the decision, especially when explaining outcomes to stakeholders. The Moral Consideration Matrix might be equally relevant for outsiders to structure pros and cons.
5. Consider the broader implications of corporate decisions, recognising how they impact various stakeholder groups, including employees, shareholders, customers, and society at large. Balance critique with nuance to ensure a comprehensive understanding of moral dilemmas and their impact on stakeholders.

By focusing on these specific lessons outsiders can responsibly critique and understand the challenges inherent in corporate governance, improving the overall dialogue around ethics in the business world.

GPSR Compliance

The European Union's (EU) General Product Safety Regulation (GPSR) is a set of rules that requires consumer products to be safe and our obligations to ensure this.

If you have any concerns about our products, you can contact us on

ProductSafety@springernature.com

In case Publisher is established outside the EU, the EU authorized representative is:

Springer Nature Customer Service Center GmbH
Europaplatz 3
69115 Heidelberg, Germany

www.ingramcontent.com/pod-product-compliance
Lightning Source LLC
LaVergne TN
LVHW011008250326
834688LV00004B/144